Just War and the Ethic

"This book brings a just war perspective to bear on the ethics of spying, a topic of major importance in warfare but one that has usually been neglected in military ethics."—*James Turner Johnson, Rutgers University, USA*

"In this pioneering book, Dr. Cole applies the just war tradition to the ethics of espionage. He brilliantly uncovers hidden truths that are so obvious after reading them as to be virtually unassailable. A must-read for anyone interested in political ethics or intelligence studies."—*Davis Brown, Maryville University of St. Louis, USA*

The War on Terror has raised many new, thorny issues of how we can determine acceptable action in defense of our liberties. Western leaders have increasingly used spies to execute missions unsuitable to the military. These operations, which often result in the contravening of international law and previously held norms of acceptable moral behavior, raise critical ethical questions—is spying limited by moral considerations? If so, what are they and how are they determined? Cole argues that spying is an act of force that may be a justifiable means to secure order and justice among political communities. He explores how the just war moral tradition, with its roots in Christian moral theology and Western moral philosophy, history, custom, and law might help us come to grips with the moral problems of spying. This book will appeal to anyone interested in applied religious ethics, moral theology and philosophy, political philosophy, international law, international relations, military intellectual history, the War on Terror, and Christian theological politics.

Darrell Cole is Associate Professor of Religion and Chair of the Department of Comparative Religion at Drew University, USA.

Routledge Studies in Religion

For a full list of titles in this series, please visit www.routledge.com

Just War and the Ethics of Espionage

By Darrell Cole

 Routledge
Taylor & Francis Group

LONDON AND NEW YORK

First published 2015
by Routledge

2 Park Square, Milton Park, Abingdon, Oxon OX14 4RN
711 Third Avenue, New York, NY 10017

*Routledge is an imprint of the Taylor & Francis Group,
an informa business*

First issued in paperback 2018

Library of Congress Cataloging-in-Publication Data

Just war and the ethics of espionage / by Darrell Cole.
    pages cm. — (Routledge studies in religion ; 41)
    Includes bibliographical references and index.
    1. Espionage—Moral and ethical aspects. 2. Intelligence service—
Moral and ethical aspects. 3. War—Religious aspects—Christianity.
4. Just war doctrine. I. Title.
    JF1525.I6C65   2014
    172'.4—dc23
    2014014011

ISBN: 978-1-138-80215-5 (hbk)
ISBN: 978-1-138-54610-3 (pbk)

Typeset in Sabon
by Apex CoVantage, LLC

Contents

Introduction

Spies are an indispensable part of state security. They can play an important role in establishing a new state. George Washington, for example, was known as a master spy who ran a network of agents during the American Revolution that enabled the "founding Father" of the United States to compensate for Britain's superior military strength and mobility. Spies facilitated Allied victory in the Second World War. We insist upon explanations when the information spies provide is not acted upon by those in charge of our safety. The political hearings concerning the terrorist attacks on the United States on September 11, 2001, were convened in order to find out why the United States, with all the spies it employs, could not stop the terrorist attacks on New York and Washington. It was intelligence reports that touched off a new war in Iraq by providing the US administration with evidence (of a somewhat controversial nature) that Saddam Hussein was harboring terrorist groups and still working on a weapons-of-mass-destruction program. The history of the American Office of Strategic Services (OSS), Central Intelligence Agency (CIA), and British MI5 and MI6 (Secret Intelligence Service, SOS) is stuff of legend, literally. Ian Fleming, who had worked briefly with MI6 during World War II, went on to create perhaps the greatest legendary figure of popular literature and film in the twentieth century: James Bond.

Spying is important to a nation, but for every George Washington who is praised for his spying triumphs, there is a Benedict Arnold, the outcast spy shunned even in the country he aided. For every Ian Fleming with his glamorous James Bond, there is a John Le Carré with his Alec Leamas who declares in the film *The Spy Who Came In From the Cold* that spies definitely are not "moral philosophers measuring everything they do by the word of God," but "just a bunch of seedy squalid bastards like me—little men, drunkards, queers, hen-pecked husbands, civil servants playing cowboys and Indians to brighten their rotten little lives." When we think of all the things accomplished by fictional spies such as James Bond and Alec Leamas, we may wonder exactly what real spies do, for spies are what spies do and the morally troublesome nature of the world of spies is the subject of this book. The main job of a spy is to gain information that is not normally made public. The gathering of information serves to increase the knowledge of the one who employs the spy, which is why this sort of work is often referred to as "intelligence." Thus, the main job of spying is to gain information and, in order to gain information, spies typically tell and live lies. Also, spies have been employed as assassins for centuries. The skills it takes to get information seem similar to the skills it takes to be in a position to kill with stealth. The profession is, after all, known as "cloak *and* dagger." At times, the job of spying has been expanded by governments to include leading partisan groups in enemy-occupied territory in acts of sabotage and assassination, and leading covert operations in friendly or neutral nations. We have witnessed in recent times a clearer division between spies who merely gather intelligence, and other members of clandestine forces who participate in acts of sabotage, covert operations, and assassination. However, the division is not nearly as neat as it seems. Take, for instance, the kill-or-capture mission instigated against Osama Bin Laden. Spies as intelligence gatherers provided the needed information about Bin Laden's whereabouts and members of the CIA accompanied the military units on the mission. For our purposes, all members of the clandestine services are treated under one professional umbrella, so that—whether one collects data, interprets that data, or acts on that data with acts of sabotage—one is considered to be a member of one of the professional spying services. Thus, fiction aside, the profession of spying will seem questionable to people of honor and virtue. On the face of it, all morally serious people are going to have a hard time justifying their participation in "the great game."

The great Protestant reformer Martin Luther (1483–1546) once wrote a treatise with the title *Whether Soldiers Too May Be Saved*, in which he attempted to show that Christians could be good soldiers without making moral compromises that would endanger their relationship with God. Luther gave himself a task that many before and after him have taken up: to show how one could do the job of a military leader or simple soldier and still be a morally good person, not despite the fighting and the killing but because that fighting and killing was chosen for the right reasons, for the right motives, and then done well. In other words, can one be a good user of force and a good person at the same time? The just war tradition itself is one way to answer that question and Luther's treatise is an important contribution to that tradition which began with ancient Jewish and Greco-Roman thought, was adopted and worked out by Christian philosophers and theologians in conjunction with jurists and military theorists, and then ushered into the modern world with the help of theologian, philosopher, and father of international law, Hugo Grotius (1583–1645).

Ambrose of Milan (c. 340–397) is the first Christian philosopher we find in positive dialogue with the ancient just war tradition. But it is his pupil Augustine (354–430) who was the first Christian theologian to play a major role in shaping the tradition. Augustine thought that the peace, order, and justice of the earthly city, though a far cry from the true peace, order, and justice of the heavenly city, was worth preserving from the barbarians who came to pillage, rape, kill, and destroy. True, just war tradition contributor Paul Ramsey may have gone beyond the text in interpreting Augustine's approach to just war as one that justifies it purely on the basis of love (Ramsey 1961),[1] but it is a legitimate move for Ramsey to make, given Augustine's emphasis on the virtue of charity in the Christian life. In any event, by the time we come to Aquinas (1225–1274), another major shaper of the tradition, we find the just war being treated within a larger discussion on charity. For Aquinas, charity means desiring and seeking the other's good, even the enemy's. This is not a far cry from what Grotius would do with virtue, identifying it with good wishes toward the neighbor, including the enemy. The difference between Aquinas and Grotius is that charity for Grotius is no special, grace-given virtue from God, but is a natural virtue that can be acquired by all (a position that does not deny that all such virtues are a possible reality only because of a preserving grace from God in order to make life tolerable for all). Thus, we find Grotius using a Christian idea in such a way that it can reach back to the pagans and explain and find morally praiseworthy their acts of charity toward enemies and reach forward to an ever-more-secularized modern world to describe and prescribe appropriate attitudes and behaviors concerning the use of force. This book is an attempt to follow in Grotius's footsteps in a very small way. It is an attempt to appropriate the rich tradition of the past in a way to make it useful for contemporary moral problems with the use of force, particularly the kind of force employed in the world of spies.

James Turner Johnson has rightly argued that the just war tradition is an ongoing tradition and, as such, it pays attention to history. Moral philosophy can make good use of history when we think of history as "referring to the past as effective or alive in the present through both institutions and human consciousness" (Johnson 2011, 7). There is much to be gained by working within a historical tradition. By doing so, we are able to orient our thinking about a certain set of problems (here, those pertaining to the use of force) and move forward in helping to solve those problems. It is important to keep in mind that being a participant in a tradition does not mean that we are imprisoned by that tradition in the sense that we many never find a past contributor wrong or resort to mere proof-texting an important past contributor, but we keep the conversation alive with the worthy builders, for we may learn from them even while we depart from them as we continue to shape the tradition.

Philosophers, theologians, historians, military and political theorists, and international lawyers have all played major roles in shaping the just war tradition. There can be fruitful "cross pollination" between the various major players. A notable example is the 2007 *US Army/Marine Corps Counterinsurgency Field Manual*, which employs just war principles in a specific way that was pioneered and popularized by the theologian Paul Ramsey in 1968. This isn't to say that the authors of the field manual read Ramsey (although they certainly could have), but it is to say that a theologian first articulated a specific approach to dealing with counterinsurgents in 1968 and that his contribution to the tradition meant that when the field manual authors came to do their work at the turn of the next century, the tradition offered them the tools to get the job done. This present work leans heavily on philosophy and theology but strives to dialogue fruitfully with the other major players in the tradition, particularly history and law, with the goal of achieving a fruitful "cross pollination" concerning the use of spies.

The aim of this book is to explore how the just war tradition might come to grips with the moral problems of spying. The subject will be broached with reference to certain formative figures in the tradition—the Early Church Fathers, Aquinas, Luther, Calvin, and Grotius—whose work has proved to be normative sources for Christian ethics, especially Christian moral thinking on war, and enormously influential in shaping the tradition into what it has become: a Western moral tradition that crosses religious and secular boundaries. I will also make use of more contemporary inheritors of the early tradition, particularly Dietrich Bonhoeffer, a Lutheran pastor who volunteered for the German counter-intelligence corps during World War II and participated in a plot to assassinate Hitler. Bonhoeffer is not normally considered a resource for the just war tradition because some of his arguments suggest that all moral norms can be overridden in some circumstances. This places him in distinction to most just war approaches that hold that the just war criteria are unbreakable norms. However, Bonhoeffer's thought is fruitful for just war approaches that are open to a more flexible vision of proper tactics where cultural norms and circumstances play a considerable role in setting boundaries around who is a proper target for the use of force and what counts as a proportionate use of force. A common thread running through each of these figures is that the usefulness of their contributions stretches far beyond the boundaries of Christianity. They have helped to shape the just war tradition into a Western moral tradition. The goal is to explore how that tradition might handle the more obvious moral problems of spying.

The just war tradition perspective found here is dependent especially on the Christian philosophers and theologians who helped to build it, but it is not the sort of narrow moral tradition useless to those outside of the boundaries of Christianity. Just war morality has always been within Christianity that part of ethical reasoning that speaks to human beings qua human beings rather than simply to Christians. Philosophers and theologians as diverse as Augustine, Chrysostom, Aquinas, Luther, Calvin, Grotius, Jeremy Taylor, Karl Barth, and Bonhoeffer recognized—to borrow Aquinas's specific language—a kind of two-fold happiness for human beings: natural and supernatural. Even arguably the most pessimistic of the group—Calvin—recognized a kind of natural law in which God provides all human beings with enough moral sense so that they can achieve a relatively just sort of political order. The just war tradition is part of that baseline moral knowledge, which is why it is so amenable to "cross-pollination" between contributors from many different fields. Put differently, the just war tradition is ethics for everyone. Christians may have a special impetus from charity to participate in jobs that secure the common good and charity may give them a special impetus to carry out their jobs with a high regard for justice, but all human beings desire justice. In other words, all human beings can benefit from the kind of moral wisdom exemplified in the just war tradition. All human beings can benefit from moral knowledge that helps us to identify when circumstances occur that call for the use of force and that place useful strictures on what can count as a just use of force. Circumstances occur when the jobs spies do are necessary for our protection and to achieve justice. The just war tradition helps us to recognize those circumstances and to place limits on what may be done to protect us and achieve justice within those circumstances. As I will argue, the just war criteria will certainly hamper members of the clandestine services in their various jobs, but this is all to the good, for spies, like soldiers, do jobs that require that we hold them morally accountable for what they do.

The reason why force is justifiable in our world is that evil exists, and sometimes that evil takes the shape of violence being used on those who do not deserve it. Whether a contributor approaches the tradition from a Christian perspective like Paul Ramsey, a Kantian perspective like Brian Orend (2000), or a human rights perspective like Michael Walzer (1977) and David Rodin (2002) (to name just a few), the assumption shared between them is that evil exists and ought to be thwarted, sometimes with the use of force. True, Christianity provides a theological explanation of the existence of that evil, but whether one accepts the Christian explanation or not, all upholders of the tradition begin with a similar anthropology: human beings are capable of great evil and they may turn upon one another with terrible violence. When this happens, there is a need to respond to evil violence with a just use of force to repel such attacks. Just war thinking is all about figuring out when a use of force is an appropriate response to evil-doing and what sorts of acts of force are appropriate.

Upholders of the just war tradition are in general agreement about the morality of the use of force: it is good or bad depending on who uses it, the reasons they do so, and how they do so. These concerns are usually spelled out in the just war criteria known as the *jus ad bellum* (justice in going to war) and the *jus in bello* (justice in the tactics used in war). There are four widely accepted *ad bellum* criteria: right authority, just cause, right intention, and reasonable hope for success. There are two widely accepted *in bello* criteria: discrimination and proportion. The criterion of right authority enables us to determine if the person(s) ordering or using force have the moral authority to do so. The criteria of just cause, right intention, and reasonable hope for success enable us to determine if reasons behind the acts of force are morally good reasons. A just cause is one of self-defense or defense of others one has pledged to defend. Right intention means that we fight for the sake of the common good and not merely for personal gain or revenge. Reasonable hope for success means that we are reasonably sure that the goals we hope to achieve are obtainable. The criteria of discrimination (those targeted by our acts of force deserve to be targeted) and proportion (balancing the good and bad effects) enable us to determine if the acts of force are carried out in morally acceptable ways. The criteria that comprise the *jus ad bellum* are absolute, or deontological if you like, for they can never be overridden without sacrificing the very justice one wants to achieve in the first place. The criteria that comprise the *jus in bello* are flexible to some degree, and, so, more controversial in their application. That is why I have devoted a chapter (Chapter 2) to exploring the elasticity of these criteria in the spying profession.

The classic just war tradition holds that war is a rule-governed human activity and a justifiable part of statecraft. The just war tradition itself is conceived from within a broader view of just statecraft as a means toward the order and justice within the political community itself and among other political communities. The just war tradition attempts to describe under what conditions acts of force may be justifiable and what sorts of acts of force are not compatible with justice. Thus, just war thinking is that part of just statecraft that attempts to justify the use of force to secure political order and justice for political communities. The overall argument of the book is that spying, like soldiering, is an act of force even when there is mere intelligence gathering through simple observation, for that gathering of intelligence is done on behalf of a state that may use it for political purposes. Put differently, even the most non-coercive sort of job that a spy may do—and that is to simply observe and report—is done, ultimately, for potentially coercive purposes. As acts of force, the jobs that spies do may be a justifiable means to securing order and justice in and among political communities, and, thus, following the logic of classical just war thinking, something that may command moral allegiance from citizens.

In the first chapter, I put the formative philosophical and theological figures in conversation with contemporary literature that attempts to describe and defend the profession of spying as one that is necessary for the survival of the common good. In doing so, I clarify what has not always been clear in the literature: namely, how the moral problems of spying are more helpfully treated as moral problems in war and, therefore, how our understanding of the morality of spying is enhanced by thinking of it as part of the just war moral tradition. In other words, we begin to have a firmer grasp of the very moral nature of spying when we begin to consider that the authorization for using spies, as is the case in all uses of force sponsored by the state, is located in the authority of the one who authorizes said use, the intention of the one who authorizes it, and in the tactics employed by those who use force. A common defense of the necessity of spying is that nations cannot fully trust one another and that even allies may hide information vital the wellbeing of each other. Thus, civil authorities are compelled to gather information about their neighbors, at least in so far are that information has a bearing on their own security. The major figures who formulated the just war tradition, particularly in ancient Judaism and Christianity, shared philosophical assumptions about human nature that make them amenable to the underlying assumptions about human nature and politics found in the traditional defenders of the spying profession. In fact, Christian theologians were readily able to appropriate and add to the just war tradition because they held a theological anthropology that viewed human beings as the sort of creatures who now require the use of force to obtain justice and peace. The just war tradition attempts to describe under what conditions acts of force may be justifiable and what sorts of acts of force are not compatible with justice. I also argue for the primary importance of character for spies, if their use is to be just and their jobs justly carried out, for their jobs are secret and subject to little oversight while carrying out their duties.

The second chapter tests the limits of discrimination and proportion in the spying profession. The goal of the chapter is not so much to offer a full treatment of the various morally questionable jobs that spies do (such treatments will be offered in the remaining chapters), but to explore how the clandestine services test the traditional limits of the just war criteria of discrimination and proportion, limits that have been traditionally set by considering the combat behavior of soldiers in battle rather than spies in the field. I argue that spying can be justified when the tactics used are morally acceptable. Moral acceptability can be determined by testing to see if the acts of force meet the criteria of discrimination and proportion but the criteria cannot be applied to spying in the exact same fashion as they are applied to soldiering. The jobs that spies do are acts of force but they are not the same acts as those carried out by soldiers. Spying, like soldiering, has often been viewed as a game played without any rules. But, just as the logic of just war limits the type and degree of force soldiers may use on an enemy, so too does that same logic limit the tactics of the spy. The clandestine services do engage in activities that may call on us to reconsider what could be considered as right conduct in battle, but the rejection of older norms should not leave us norm-less. Who counts as a proper target in a clandestine operation, for example, may differ from what we find in ordinary soldiering but there are still limits on who may be targeted. I also explore the limits of proportion by looking at some moral problems peculiar to the clandestine services, such as the killing of one's own or oneself in the line of duty, making deals with the unjust, sabotage, and those problems engendered by the recent explosion of cyber warfare capabilities. Again, the goal here is not to offer a full discussion of these moral problems but to suggest how the moral criteria of discrimination and proportion must be rethought when applied to the spying profession.

The third chapter deals with the moral problem of lying and deception within the professional life of the spy. Every job that a spy does may require an extensive use of lies and deception in order to get the job done. Thus, any discussion of the morality of spying must include an exploration of the

moral problem of lying and deceit. Some forms of deception have traditionally been accepted in war, but spying pushes the boundaries of what has
been typically deemed morally acceptable. However, the compatibility of
lying with virtue is a major source of division within moral philosophy and
theology, and this division is explored with the goal of clarifying how lying
and deceit may not only be morally acceptable but actually morally praiseworthy in some cases, particularly in those instances where the spy may lie
or deceive in the line of duty. I also discuss the problem cases of lying to
one's own citizens, lying to allies, the use of propaganda, lying to eliminate
enemy agents, lying to possible recruits into the spying profession, and lying
to superiors.

The fourth chapter deals with the special problems engendered by covert
operations that may violate the autonomy of another nation state. I show
how covert operations are very difficult to justify, because one must be
able to square the threat to autonomy with the principle of proportion (the
expected good must outweigh the expected evil). Nevertheless, I hope to
make clear how a covert operation is justifiable if the targeted nation state's
autonomy is already lost or threatened by another intervening state, and the
operation is intended to restore the threatened or lost autonomy. I clarify
how virtue and moral good may be at odds with positive law, which prohibits covert operations, and how, in such cases, the right thing to do may be
to override the law. These topics will be explored by concentrating on four
well-known covert operations: the operation in Italy to keep communists
out of power, the operation in Iraq to remove Mossadeq, the operations
in Chile to keep communists out of power, and the operation in Poland to
weaken the Soviet Union's hold on the Eastern Bloc. No attempt is made to
justify these operations, but rather merely to analyze and critique them in
order to clarify how a covert operation may be justifiable and how hard it is
to justify one in actual practice.

The fifth chapter covers the moral problems of coercive interrogation.
Intelligence agents and others in the clandestine services have a history of
using coercive methods of interrogation and this history has not come to
an end, in spite of legal prohibitions. I examine the popular moral prohibitions on coercive interrogation and show why most of them fail to persuade
anyone committed to the possibility of the just use of force. They fail to
persuade because the logic behind them would compel us to forgo the use of
force against anyone to their harm. Put more clearly, most moral arguments
against coercive interrogation could serve equally as well as moral arguments against the use of force of any kind. Because it is so difficult to argue
that coercive interrogation is an absolute evil, we may be tempted to employ
it. Interrogation, whether it is soft or hard, is a tactic of warfare; that is to
say, it is a form of force used against the enemy for the common good. The
goal of the chapter is to formulate a moral position on coercive interrogation within a larger moral position that accepts the limited use of force for
the sake of justice. I show that, for practical purposes, coercive interrogation

is nearly always prohibited, because it fails to meet the basic just war moral criteria of proportion and noncombatant immunity. Nevertheless, there may circumstances in which the use of coercive interrogation could be conceived as a moral good. I argue that, if we consider coercive interrogation, as we consider all acts of the clandestine services, as acts of war that must comply with just war criteria, we will gain four advantages. First, our efforts to abide by the criteria will force us to place strictures on coercive interrogation so severe that the act will be very difficult to justify. Second, compliance with the criteria discourages the legalization of any form of coercive interrogation. Third, knowing that any act of coercive interrogation will have to comply with proportion and noncombatant immunity helps us clarify when circumstances have occurred that might make coercive interrogation justifiable. Fourth, we will see how only a person of exceptional character will be able to know when the criteria have been met.

The sixth chapter covers the special problems of resorting to assassination to achieve political goals. I show that assassination may be a justifiable tactic if the criteria of discrimination and proportion can be satisfied. However, like covert operations and coercive interrogation, the justification may be very hard to achieve in practice. I include a brief overview of how morality and law have related to one another on the topic throughout history and will show that, like covert operations and coercive interrogation, assassination may be a moral good that in some cases contravenes law. I argue that assassination would have to pass the same tests as any act of force against agents of a sovereign state: they must have right authority, just cause, right intention, and show reasonable hope for success. I also clarify who may be targeted for assassination. The clandestine services are typically used to target those who may not have counted as proper targets for the military and, so, special care is needed to ensure that the circle of proper targets does not become so widened that anyone may be included. This is especially true when choosing targets in the "War on Terror," where combatants are not always state-sponsored agents but may be civilians joined to criminal gangs. I include an extensive discussion of the problems of squaring any act of assassination with the moral principle of proportion. The consequences of assassination are hard to predict, and this is especially true when the target is a political leader. The consequences of precipitating a change of regime must be considered, including the effects on the populace that must live through the regime change and a new regime. I attempt to establish criteria for when we may determine that such acts are warranted.[2]

NOTES

1. James Turner Johnson (2011, 5) has argued this point against Paul Ramsey's interpretation of Augustine (Ramsey 1961).
2. Many of the ideas found in this book were first broached in Cole 2008.

BIBLIOGRAPHY

Cole, Darrell. (2008). "Whether Spies Too Can Be Saved." *Journal of Religious Ethics*, 36(1): 125–156.

Johnson, James Turner. (2011). *Ethics and the Use of Force: Just Wars in Historical Perspective*. Surrey, UK: Ashgate Publishing.

Orend, Brian. (2000). *War and International Justice: A Kantian Perspective*. Waterloo, Ontario: Wilfred Lauier University Press.

Ramsey, Paul. (1961). *War and the Christian Conscience*. Durham, NC: Duke University Press.

——. (1968). *The Just War: Force and Political Responsibility*. New York: Charles Scribner's Sons.

Rodin, David. (2002). *War and Self Defense*. Oxford: Oxford University Press.

Walzer, Michael. (1977). *Just and Unjust Wars*. New York: Basic Books.

1 Spying as a Morally Justifiable Part of Statecraft

One of the necessary functions of any government is to protect its people from harm. Governments traditionally see to the safety of their citizens by employing police and military forces to protect against threats from within and without. Governments also typically employ spies to protect their citizens. In this view, spying is like policing and soldiering: a form of state-sponsored force necessary for the protection of the common good. Thus, spying can be thought of as one of the forms of force used by the state to fulfill its function as a protector of its citizens. In this chapter, I first explore how spying may come to be so viewed. I then look at how Christianity has responded to the claim that force is a necessary part of a state's function. Although Christianity has responded to the state's use of force in a variety of ways, I concentrate on what is, by far, the most popular response: its appropriation of the just war tradition, which is Christianity's way of dealing with the facts of human nature as spelled out in sacred Scripture and how human government is to function, given the state of the world.

The moral concerns Christians have traditionally expressed about the use of force are similar in nature to the concerns of all thoughtful people who deplore violence. When early Christian philosophers and theologians began engaging these issues, as more and more soldiers and statesmen began converting to Christianity, they began doing moral work that would prove helpful to anyone interested in moral approaches to the use of force. The just war tradition as we know it today is one shaped in large part by Christian theologians. Looking briefly at how they appropriated and shaped that tradition will prove helpful to our task of showing the benefits of considering spying as an act of force that can be morally appraised within the just war tradition. I then turn to the profession of spying itself to see how the formative and normative figures in Christian philosophy and theology have dealt with the issue. I show that just war rationality speaks not merely to Christians, but to all people who desire order, justice, and peace. Having seen how spying is a justifiable profession for the common good, I then turn to the crucial issue of character; for spies, even more than soldiers, are given jobs of force that may require the professional to act at the very limits of what morality may allow and will certainly act in ways that may contravene accepted laws and conventions. Spies may have to break the laws of war, use morally unsavory people, lie, cheat, deceive, steal, betray, use covert methods in neutral or even friendly countries, employ coercive methods of interrogation, and assassinate. If such acts are ever justifiable, then the people who could be trusted to commit them would have to possess a high caliber of wisdom, justice, self-control, courage, and patience.

THE NECESSITY OF SPYING

Aristotle once pointed out that a state could not exist without an army to keep order and protect its citizens from outside invasion (*Politics* 7.1330a–1331a). Thus, it is no surprise to find that the earliest civilizations employed armies.[1] Similarly, the history of spying can be traced back to the beginnings of the first human organizations into political communities (Dvornick 1974, 3). As soon as we see the formation of what could be called political states, we see intelligence services. As a rule, the greater the political expansion, the more the intelligence services increase. Why the need for spies? Put simply, civil authorities employ spies to keep an eye on neighbors both friendly and otherwise. Augustus was the first Roman leader to understand the importance of rapid and regular intelligence, so he created the first intelligence service in Roman history. Christian rulers did not eschew the value of good spying. The first Christian Roman emperor, Constantine, created a new order of intelligence officers, with appropriate military ranks. Spies were a fixture of all political powers through the Middle Ages and into the modern world. The United States was able to win its independence only with the help of its superior use of spies. George Washington was known as the chief American master spy. He quickly learned the value of surprise against an enemy with superior strength. He was able to use the information gained from his spies to play an attrition game, hitting and running without ever letting the British make a substantial hit against his forces.

Wise and cautious civil authorities consider all neighbors as potential allies and enemies. To assume that a present friend or neutral will always remain so is a risky way of thinking. This is why writers such as G.J.A. O'Toole liken diplomacy to a kind of warfare (O'Toole 1991, 1). The truth of the claim resides in the fluid nature of the relationships between states. In diplomacy, all nations are potential adversaries as well as friends. In this sort of world, certain kinds of acts of force could be justified against allies. This is because friendly or neutral countries may initiate an act of aggression analogous to war that could be used to justify an appropriate act of force in response. So, for example, when one nation withholds information that is important to the security of another nation (when, say, Pakistan withholds information from the United States about the whereabouts of some terrorist leaders who pose a threat to US security), the threatened nation may be justified in finding out about that information.

But even when there is no overt analogous act of aggression, there is a concept of shared expectations in diplomacy among nations. Put simply, nations expect to be spied on, even by their friends. Such realities explain why Israel, for example, would feel the need to send one of its spies, Jonathan Pollard, to spy on the United States even though the United States has remained a staunch supporter of Israel. Those same realities explain why the United States (and Britain) returned the favor and spied on Israeli Prime Minister Ehud Olmert.

Neighbors can be potential threats both in the obvious way of becoming overt enemies and in less-obvious ways, such as possessing information crucial to the wellbeing of another nation but unable to share that information for reasons of its own. Thus, governments rely on intelligence services for information about all their neighbors. This state of affairs lead some, such as Miles Copeland, to argue that effective government actually requires treachery (Copeland 1969). The argument is that because we live in an amoral world, governments must on occasion act treacherously in order to fulfill their function as protectors of their citizens. Despite the title of Copeland's book, which gives the erroneous impression that his position is amoral, there are four moral points assumed. First, the world is so constituted that peoples and governments cannot always be honest and forthright with one another. Two, governments ought to protect their citizens, even if acts of perfidy are required. Three, acts of perfidy are not ordinarily good acts. Fourth, acts of perfidy are good kinds of acts—the right thing to do—when they are the only means governments have to shield their citizenry from harm. This is the basic moral position of all governments that employ spies.

Political policy and action can be guided by the information provided by spies. As Walter Laqueur has argued, "Government agencies concerned with national security and foreign affairs need to know the intentions and strategies of international rival, friends, and fence sitters, their capabilities and vulnerabilities" (Laqueur 1985, 40). Winston Churchill, for example, knew how much steel Japan could produce and sent a letter to Foreign Minister Yosuke Matsuoka pointing out how little steel Japan could turn out in comparison with the United States and Great Britain. He wanted to dissuade them from siding with Germany. Conduct in these circumstances is governed by rules of the game, and as Tony Pfaff points out, some games are rough, which means all players can expect rough treatment in some situations. What counts as reasonable conduct is found in the nature of the game itself (Pfaff 2006, 80). When one state holds secrets that would affect another nation's responsibilities to protect their citizens, such nations, as Pfaff aptly puts it, freely agree to "take the field." As stated before, all nations expect to be spied on to some degree, even by allies. However, friendly nations do not expect their allies to subvert, commit acts of sabotage, or assassinate within their territorial borders. In short, they do not expect to have their sovereignty challenged or compromised. Hence, not all the jobs spies typically do, and not all the political action taken as a result of the information spies supply, apply so readily to friendly countries.

Spies do more than collect information. They have traditionally played roles in acts of subversion, sabotage, fomenting insurrection, and assassination. While we have seen in recent times more of a practical distinction among the various branches of the clandestine services, so that we may rightly distinguish a clandestine professional who merely collects information from the clandestine professional who may act on that information, the distinction should not blind us to the fact that all of these jobs have always been seen as the traditional jobs of spies, and that lines are still crossed in may ways as members of the various clandestine forces work together. Those responsible for our safety must also find out what hostile intelligence services are seeking to do or find out, how they go about it, and what kind of people they use to do it and who they are. This is known as counterespionage, which is primarily a defensive job against hostile clandestine services. However, as Laqueur points out, the main function of an intelligence service is "to shield those it serves against surprise" (Laqueur 1985, 255). Britain's secret service, which quickly morphed into MI5 and MI6 (SIS), was founded just before the outbreak of the First World War in the wake of a perceived German threat. The goal of the CIA in its inception was to avoid another surprise attack like Pearl Harbor. This suggests why the US intelligence community bore the brunt of national criticism in the wake of the successful surprise attacks on "9-11." The US and British intelligence communities have been fighting the war on terror with an ever-increasing power and scope that has become controversial with citizens concerned about the lack of privacy. The United State's National Security Agency (NSA), which is similar to Britain's Government Communications Headquarters (GCHQ), has the power to collect data on Americans while pursuing terrorist suspects and people involved in nuclear proliferation, espionage, and cyber attacks. The legality of the program remains unclear, but the bone of contention between the legal opinions is whether or not the program is necessary to protect the nation.[2] In other words, the greatly increased scope and purpose of the intelligence services could be legally justifiable if that scope and purpose is necessary for the protection of the common good.

The gathering of information necessary to protect the common good is the main job of spies, but it is not the only one. Defenders of the intelligence profession argue that all of the traditional jobs of the spy are necessary for the protection of the state, just as all the traditional duties of the policeman and soldier are necessary. If we allow the argument to stand for the moment (for we will pry into the morally dubious nature of the various jobs in subsequent chapters), we must still ask if morally serious people should commit themselves to secular states that need to employ force in order to survive.

CHRISTIANITY, STATE-SPONSORED FORCE, AND THE JUST WAR TRADITION

The problem of justifying Christian participation in work that is necessary for the protection of the larger political order is not a new one. The founder of Christianity famously taught his disciples to refuse retaliation when struck and to help and pray for those who persecuted them. He also refused to use any force for self-protection. Nevertheless, this founder of a new religion claimed to be one with the God revealed in Jewish Scripture, and like that God, promised a day of wrath where force would be used to usher in a new world. The problem was how to think about the use of force in the "in between time." Soldiering (which is the mother of spying) has always been an ambiguous profession with its heroic and seedy sides, and thus a problem for Christians. Can a profession that is necessary to protect the commonwealth's very chance of survival and flourishing be proscribed for Christians? Christians have debated the issue for centuries, and the history is too lengthy to revisit here. Suffice it to say that the vast majority of orthodox Christians, both East and West, have agreed that Christians can engage in state-sponsored force for the sake of order, peace, and justice. Moreover, Christians have this sort of duty toward their neighbors even if the political authorities are not Christian. The body of thought known as the just war tradition, with its roots in ancient Judaism and Greco-Roman thought, was appropriated by Christian theologians and philosophers as a way of partnering with others for the common good by sanctioning Christian support and participation in the use of force, but in a way that would place limits on the force that could be used.

The major formative and normative figures in Christian theology who either helped shape the just war tradition itself, such as Augustine and Aquinas, or gave approval to it by extensive argument, such as Luther and Calvin, held definite ideas about human nature, culled especially from their appropriated Jewish heritage, and what that meant to the individual's relationship to earthly political communities. We see their thinking reflected in more contemporary theologians, such as Karl Barth and Dietrich Bonhoeffer. All refer to the New Testament document of Paul's letter to the Romans as the foundational teaching for the proper perspective on human nature, politics, and the use of force. Put simply and briefly as possible, these formative figures in Christianity held that Paul, reaching back to his Jewish scriptural teaching about the fall of humankind and the human rebellion against God fueled by self-love and resulting in an ever-increasing desire to dominate others, teaches that all are sinners in need of God's grace and that those who receive grace have a responsibility toward their neighbors whether they are Christian or not. Christians should support the governing authorities who punish the wicked and fight for the protection of the common good, and do so because God has ordained them for just this purpose

(Rom 1–8; 13:1–7, see also 2 Thess 2:6). In other words, the governing authorities are ordained by God to restrain evil and make civil life possible for everyone. Such is the theological lens that makes sense of what Scripture has to say about the use of force and this moves a certain important part of Christian political thinking away from narrow, sectarian concerns to wider concerns for order, justice, and peace.

The first thing we notice in this theological anthropology is that human nature is not currently what it was meant to be; it is now sick and in need of healing. Thus, whatever human politics may have looked like before human nature became sick, it now must take on the character of something that restrains evil. At least, the use of force to restrain evil is one of its essential purposes.[3] Augustine forcefully points this out when he argues that humanity is a mass of sin at odds with God (*City of God* 21.12) and that the earthly city is a human construct ordained by God to control this mass of sin, or as Barth puts it, "There exists in man a very deep-seated and almost original evil readiness and lust to kill. The common murderer or homicide is simply the one in whom the wolf slips the chain (Barth 1961, 413). For Augustine, the *raison d'etre* of the political state is to minimize disorder. So Christians should value the peace of Babylon, for they benefit from the peace and order provided by the state (*City of God* 19.26). Calvin would follow Augustine almost to the letter and emphasize that civil government is required to restrain wickedness in order to make a space for human beings to become truly human (Calvin 1960, 1487–88).

Luther's reading of Paul led him to expand on Augustine's argument concerning the dual citizenship of Christians. The result is his famous "Doctrine of the Two Kingdoms" wherein God provides two governments for human beings: heavenly government for spiritual matters and earthly government for worldly matters:

> If this were not so, men would devour one another, seeing that the whole world is evil . . . No one could support wife and child, feed himself, and serve God. The world would be reduced to chaos. For this reason God has ordained two governments: the spiritual by whom the Holy Spirit produces Christians and righteous people under Christ; and the temporal, which restrains the un-Christian and wicked so that—not thanks to them—they are obliged to keep still and to maintain an outward peace . . . Neither one is sufficient in the world without the other. (Luther 1962a, 91–92)

The Doctrine of the Two Kingdoms becomes the way Luther understands politics in the Bible. Luther follows Augustine in interpreting Paul to mean that the protection of the secular order is precisely the purpose of government. As Luther says elsewhere: "The wrath and severity of the sword is just as necessary to a people as eating and drinking, even as life itself (Luther 1962b, 73)." So, God ordained the governing authorities to be a terror to evildoers. Rulers ought to rule with justice and not permit injustice; that is their job.

Bonhoeffer is in essential agreement with the tradition, although he denies a conception of the state that reduces its purpose to the restraint of evil, thus giving the Two Kingdoms a closer relationship than envisioned by Luther (Bonhoeffer 1965, 95). However, unlike Barth, who held that the use of force was an *opus alienum* for the state, Bonhoeffer does not reject the idea that the restraint of evil is one of the primary functions of the state. Only the Church (by prayer and miracle) or divinely ordained government (by use of force) can save the world from plunging into the final abyss. Bonhoeffer's vision of the Two Kingdoms as complementary gives Christians more of an impetus to support the governing authorities in their efforts to restrain evil.

Our normative sources are one in holding the idea that a state willing to use force is necessary in a fallen world. All able-bodied citizens who feel so inclined, including Christians, ought to share in this particular job of using force. Thus, when the Roman general Boniface wrote to Augustine asking him whether or not he should remain a general now that he had become a Christian, Augustine urges him not to give up his profession but to maintain "a peaceful disposition" in war so that he may achieve the very aim of a just war: a just and lasting peace (*Letter* 189). Calvin points out that Jesus did not put an end to the office of temporal authority as an office compatible with being a follower of God. For Calvin, obeying God's moral law, which includes the duty to protect neighbors, is a duty of charity—it is "a work of spiritual power" (Calvin 1949, 42). Luther is adamant about the fittingness of Christians to participate in a governing regime that must use force to maintain order. In his lectures on the Sermon on the Mount, Luther comments on the passage where Christ teaches his disciples to love their enemies and to turn the other cheek (Matt 5:43–48). Luther answers that Christians should always do good to everyone except in their office as policeman, soldier, magistrate, or judge, where it is a "divine duty" to punish the wicked for the sake of the common good (Luther 1956, 123). Such people should be personally gentle—like all Christians—but still mete out punishment in their official work. For Calvin, whatever office God declares as divine is not forbidden to Christians and only a "brainless person" would claim that an office was both ordained by God and forbidden to followers of God (Calvin 1982, 77).

Bonhoeffer urges Christians not to withdraw from the world, but rather either to act as an agent for the state to help in its divinely appointed task or to fight against the secular sphere for a better political order. Thus, Christians are motivated by love to follow the example of Christ and act for the world, and this may mean taking part in the governing structures. Even Barth, who considers the use of force an *opus alienum* of the state, argues that force may be used for the sake of others. In such cases, the war is done in obedience to God and can be fought "with a good conscience" (Barth 1961, 463).

Theologians from Augustine to Bonhoeffer made strong arguments for Christian participation in the political community, but they also sought to control and limit the use of force that could be employed to protect peace and order. Governing and soldiering, like all offices, can be done well or ill. Morally upright soldiers should use force "dispassionately," that is, not out of personal revenge or gain but for the good of the well-ordered state.[4] This is helpful moral advice for all. For we hope that those charged with using force on our behalf will not behave like a gang of thugs.

We have seen that the kind of theological anthropology held by figures from Augustine to Bonhoeffer calls for human government to use force to restrain evil. The just war tradition is itself an attempt to formulate rules to govern that use of force. Thus, we should not be surprised by the Christian willingness to engage in just war rationality as a way to place moral limits on the use of force. When we turn to the rules governing the use of force, the just war tradition produces two sets of criteria: one that governs the justice of the decision to go to war—the *jus ad bellum*—and the other that governs behavior in war—the *jus in bello*. Aquinas helpfully enumerates three just war criteria that quickly became the foundation of the *ad bellum* in the Western just war tradition as we know it today: proper authority, just cause, and right intention (*Summa Theologica* II–II 40.1). Proper authority means that only those in authority have the right to decide when and how to use force. Just cause means that the objects of our force must deserve to have that force used against them. Aquinas quotes a list of just causes from Augustine, which include avenging wrongs, punishing a nation, or restoring what has been taken unjustly. Right intention means that we must intend to protect the good and avoid the evil. Again, Aquinas quotes a list of right intentions from Augustine, which include securing peace, punishing evildoers, and uplifting the good. These criteria comprise the foundation of the just war rules of *ad bellum*: criteria that must be observed when we are trying to decide if going to war is a morally good act. Aquinas's criterion of intention implies an additional criterion that he nowhere formulates but which later became a permanent part of the tradition, and that is reasonable hope for success. For, if we are going to be able to say truthfully that our intentions are upright, we must be able to calculate that we can achieve the good we wish to achieve by our acts of force. Any just use of force must conform to all four. We need only add that there are two additional criteria that govern how just force may be used: noncombatant immunity and proportion. The first places limits on who may be targeted in a just act of force, while the second places limits on how much force may be used. Thus, we see that just war rationality holds that the moral authorization for using force comes from the authority of the one who orders it, the intention of those who order it, and the tactics of those who actually carry out those orders.

We are now able to summarize our normative sources and see how they relate to what we have seen about the necessity of spying. The view of human nature that informs the politics of those we have taken as our normative sources is one that supports the idea that any state must employ a body of citizens to protect the common good with force. That is to say, each holds that human nature is so constituted that human politics without force is an impossibility. Even Aquinas, whose inundation in the work of Aristotle led him to a comparatively more positive view of human nature, shares with Aristotle the belief that a state is impossible without civil authorities to enforce law, and a body of people armed and with the very duty of using force on those who would disrupt order and threaten the common good. All communities, all nations, are comprised of human beings with potential for evil as well as good. One need not be a devoted follower of Thomas Hobbes to recognize that all neighbors are potential enemies as well as allies. Thus, the world conceived as a place where diplomacy may be likened to a kind of warfare, because one can never be absolutely sure about the perpetual good wishes of one's neighbors, is one that finds ready support in the anthropology underlying the sort of Christian thinking that appropriated the just war tradition. The message is simple: this is a world where the use of force is necessary, albeit tragically necessary, in order to protect the common good. Once Christian theologians began to appropriate the just war tradition, they began to shape it by specifying clear conditions for what can count as justifiable reasons for going to war and what can count as justifiable acts in war. Thus, in Christian hands, the just war tradition takes on a renewed urgency to limit what can count as a just war and to control the violence in war. The only question that remains is whether or not spying is a kind of use of force supportable by the just war tradition.

CHRISTIANITY AND SPYING

Soldiering as a profession was certainly approved of by our normative sources but what about spying? When Luther answered the questions about the profession of soldiering he, like Augustine, wished to encourage Christian soldiers that they can do their jobs without losing God's favor and eternal life (Luther 1962a and 1967). For Luther, soldiering is a profession beneficial for preserving the peace and order enjoyed by all citizens. Christians who become soldiers do so for reasons of charity: they soldier for love of neighbor. May the same be said for spying? One of the first things Luther does in defending the profession of soldiering is to follow the Early Church Fathers Ambrose and Augustine in discussing those portions of Scripture that seem highly favorable to soldiers and the fighting of just wars. Are there parallel portions concerning spies? The fact of spies is certainly recognized early enough in Scripture. Joshua sends two spies into Jericho (Jos. 2:6). Rahab helps them and is generously rewarded with her life, the life of her family, and a place in the community of Israel. Here, spying seems to be entirely consonant with God's will and with human flourishing. She is even heralded by the Christian writer of Hebrews as one of the heroes of faith whom Christians are supposed to emulate (Heb. 11:31). David sends out spies against Saul in the wilderness of Ziph (1 Sam. 26:4). Perhaps the most famous use of spies by David occurred when he fled from Absalom and placed Hushai the Archite as a double-agent/mole within Absalom's court. Hushai's assignment was to defeat the counsel of the traitorous Ahithophel and report to the priests-turned-spies Zadok and Abiathar, who, in turn, send messages to David (2 Sam. 15–17). Of course, there are bad spies in Scripture as well. Absalom, for example, sends out spies to help protect his false kingship (2 Sam. 16:10).

The lesson appears to be that there are good spies and bad spies; like soldiering, spying is an activity that is honorable or dishonorable, depending on whether it is just or not. The intention to achieve justice is the key for Luther. Christians do not fight as individuals for their own benefit, but do so as obedient servants of the authorities who have the responsibility to maintain a just order: "If worldly rulers call upon them to fight, then they ought to and must fight and be obedient, not as Christians, but as members of the state and obedient subjects" (Luther 1967, 99). Thus, the use of force takes its moral character from those who authorize it. Luther extends the idea of justified use of force to spying. Here is what Luther says about the nobles who joined the peasant rebellion in order to spy:

> Therefore, justice not only acquits those who were among the rebels with good intentions, but considers them worthy of double grace. They are just like the godly man, Hushai the Archite, who, acting under David's orders, joined and served the rebellious Absalom with the intention of helping David and restraining Absalom . . . Outwardly considered, Hushai, too, was a rebel with Absalom against David; but he earned great praise and everlasting honor before God and all the world. (Luther 1967, 102)

Luther attempts to justify the actions of the nobles by first locating acts of spying within Scripture that seem to have the clear moral approval of the author. He discerns what exactly makes such acts of spying praiseworthy (in this case, the intention of the spies for a just authority in a just cause), and then applies what he finds to the case at hand. The nobles are fighting for a just cause and their intent is to aid their cause by spying on the enemy. When one spies with just authority, good intention, and for a just cause—in short, when spies follows the just war criteria—one is doing something praiseworthy in the eyes of God. Thus, spying is a justifiable part of statecraft, and Luther justifies it in the same way he justifies soldiering: right authority, just cause, right intention. Nevertheless, spies who have the justification for spying do not have carte blanche on how they may achieve their goals. *Jus ad bellum* criteria may be on their side, but the *jus in bello* criteria—the rules governing how one may employ force—must be upheld if they are to be just, and this brings us to the crucial issue of character.

SPYING AND CHARACTER

The intelligence service is usually considered a profession similar to the military. The CIA's mission statement, for example, reads: "We are the nation's first line of defense,"[5] while the motto of MI5 is "Defend the Realm." The intelligence service, like that of the physician and lawyer, appears to meet all the criteria of a profession: (1) it serves an important human good that is necessary for flourishing, (2) it requires a high level of training which prepares the member for the autonomy they will exercise within the profession, (3) it has a monopoly on its services, (4) it is subject to internal checks and balances such as codes of conduct and regulative bodies, and (5) its members are expected to maintain a high moral character and exercise moral judgment in their duties.[6] The existence of an intelligence service is required for the security of the nation-state. Like the military, the intelligence service makes human flourishing possible. To become a member of the spying profession requires extensive training and prepares its members for acting autonomously in the field. In fact, much more judgmental leeway is given to low-level intelligence operatives in the field than to their military counterparts, who more often than not simply carry out the orders of their superiors. The spying profession is subject to internal checks and balances similar (and sometimes identical) to those faced by members of the military. That is to say, members of the intelligence profession are restricted by professional ideals and law, both national and international. However, only people of good character can be expected to abide by professional ideals and obey the law, particularly when we are talking about people who are regularly faced with extreme circumstances and who act in secret.

The issue of character is paramount in a profession whose members work largely in secret. The just war tradition was developed as a way to harmonize just statecraft with just acts of force and does so by placing limits on how much and what kinds of force may be used. Soldiers do their job in the open, at least most of the time, but not spies. One must have a real fear of being caught in order to be constrained by law and one is more likely to be caught when one works in the open. Spies are less likely to be so constrained and, hence, are more susceptible to temptations to get the job done regardless of the means. Too, the tactics used by spies may be more potentially damaging to character than the tactics used by soldiers. Soldiers may be forced to kill hand-to-hand, and this can certainly have a brutalizing effect on some characters, but spies are often called on to lie, deceive, play false roles for long periods of time, and act treacherously.

The spying profession requires its members to engage in activities that appear to be out of bounds for nonmembers. This may lead us to assume that the profession of the spy, like the profession of the physician or lawyer, appeals to professional status in order to justify acts that differ from what Jessica Wolfendale has called "everyday or broad-based morality" (Wolfendale 2007, 10). For Wolfendale, broad-based morality is simply those moral norms held by the majority of citizens outside of the profession. She argues that professional morality should be viewed as a subset of broad-based morality, thereby undercutting the notion that we could appeal to the profession as a way to justify acts considered immoral to most people. Nevertheless, she points out that professional acts that deviate from the norm could be justified if they contribute to the profession's "guiding ideals" and if those ideals serve important human needs (Wolfendale 2007, 26). In this view, the profession's ideals are inextricably linked to serving an important human need, for professional virtues are derived from what counts as excellence in professional functioning and that functioning must contribute to some need that is necessary for human flourishing. This connection between the profession and the good it serves gives us a regulative ideal that sets limits on what can count as a good professional act. Because the protection of human flourishing is what the profession is all about, and human flourishing always occurs within some community, the profession incorporates many of the moral standards of the community it serves. These everyday moral standards serve as checks on the sorts of duties the profession can carry out in the name of serving the community, which is made up of people who share a set of moral norms that they do not wish to see contravened. This does not mean that professional character traits never conflict with everyday morality. As Wolfendale points out, we want our lawyers, for example, to be ruthless in some professional contexts but not in all contexts (Wolfendale 2007, 40-1). A ruthless act by a lawyer in cross-examining a witness is good but it should not be the product of an unthinking habit, because our society does not value ruthlessness in nonprofessional contexts. Lawyers who lack the virtues that should guide them in their duties, and who lack the wisdom to know when to be ruthless and when to be kind, are a danger to the society they supposedly serve, and, so, are not good lawyers. We can extend the argument to soldiers: those who become ruthless killing machines may be good in the craft of killing other people but they are not good members of the military profession. In the same way, we expect professional spies to be able, for example, to lie and deceive in certain professional circumstances, but not outside of those circumstances. Spies who become congenital liars will not be very useful to anyone for very long. Lt. Col. Anthony Shaffer, a former operative in Afghanistan, reports that some in the clandestine service who learn to lie, cheat, and manipulate others in the line of duty use these same skills simply to advance their careers (Schaffer 2010, 8). Such people certainly cannot be considered good members of their profession.

The secret nature of their profession renders renegade spies a greater danger to the common good than are renegade soldiers. Thus, civil authorities typically go to some length to ensure the reliability of those recruited into the spying services by looking for candidates with good character. This has led scholars such as Chomeau and Rudolph to argue that intelligence agents should consider moral development "as important as physical, intellectual, tradecraft, and other criteria of professional competence" (Chomeau and

Rudoph 2006, 118). These concerns have always been a part of the creation of any professional intelligence service. Thus, we read as far back as in the code of Theodosius that admission into the intelligence ranks was hard. Candidates were examined with regard to their "ability, moral behavior, and the social status of their families" (Dvornik 1974, 140). A special intelligence corps was created, known as the Akritai, portrayed in the famous eleventh-century epic, *Digenes Akritas*. The Akritai were chosen from the best soldiers, much like the best are chosen for our contemporary special forces within the military, and their duties included spying on the enemy, harassing them, raiding enemy territory, and taking and interrogating prisoners. More recently, we find a recruiting office for MI6 establishing guidelines for the sort of talent the service should seek. The first and best type of agent is the "General Intelligence Officer," who should be a person of "character, integrity and intellect, combined with imagination and subtlety" (quoted in Jeffrey 2010, 640). The core values of the CIA are listed as Service, Integrity, and Excellence. Under the heading of Integrity, we read, "We uphold the highest standards of conduct," and under the heading of Excellence, we read, "We hold ourselves—and each other—to the highest standards."[7] The very nature of intelligence services demands such employees. Intelligence services expect their career employees to serve for a long time. Maintenance of security demands as little turn over as possible. Also, a great deal of time and effort goes into training an intelligence officer, and once trained officers quickly gain knowledge of projects and the identities of officers concerned with those projects. Consequently, intelligence services conduct thorough background checks on their recruits and put them through extensive psychological testing. But these methods only weed out a small fraction of candidates. They can only alert us to persons with suspicious backgrounds or those who are obviously psychologically unfit.

Intelligence services such as CIA and MI6 need people of the highest moral caliber, but they can employ others as well. The same MI6 recruitment guideline that calls for people with character and integrity also calls for "Unofficial Assistants" who work under natural cover and whose integrity and intellect are "important but less essential" (Jeffery 2010, 640). Presumably those with the higher moral caliber will be in charge of those with less integrity. This raises moral issues about using unsavory characters, issues that will be discussed in the next chapter. For now, we need to concentrate on the idea that all who work long enough in the spy profession can become unsavory characters because of the nature of the job. One of America's master-spies, Allen Dulles, tries to counter this concern when he argues, "The American intelligence officer is trained to work in intelligence as a profession, not as a way of life. The distinction is between his occupation and his private character" (Dulles 1977, 193). Dulles can mean one of two things here when he writes about the distinction between occupation and private character. He could mean that good intelligence officers are the kind of people who do bad things at work but not at home. Thus, while it is acceptable to do evil at work, good intelligence officers know how to stop doing evil when they go home. But this is a self-defeating conception of the profession, for it would mean that the very people the profession seeks will be rendered unqualified by acts required by the profession itself. Acts damaging of character are damaging whether or not they are done at home or in the line of duty. Put simply, people who damage their character at work will be people with damaged characters. Not only will that character show itself at home, but also in every area of their lives. A damaged character is like a broken arm. If I break my arm at work, it remains broken no matter whom I am with, where I am at, or what I am doing. People with severely damaged characters would be morally incapable of being trusted with secret work. Dulles, however, might simply be following a line of thought espoused by the likes of Augustine and Luther, that we must make a distinction between person and office in which acts appropriate to office are not appropriate to the private person. However, in making this distinction, Augustine and Luther wanted to maintain two important points: First, the acts appropriate to office but not to a private person could never be evil acts. Second, the distinction between private person and office, particularly an office that requires the use of force, should bring an element of dispassion to professional users of force in the sense that they will lack the disordered passions of those seeking personal revenge or acting out of malice.

Augustine and Luther are both concerned about the moral integrity of people who have jobs that require them to act in secular affairs of state. Augustine and Aquinas taught that professional users of force could act virtuously, but it is Luther and Calvin (and Bonhoeffer will follow them) who place a special emphasis on moral development as something that can be done by following a secular vocation.[8] So, all morally good secular vocations can serve as paths of moral formation. The value of this way of thinking is that it holds true for all people, in all places, and at all times. One cannot drive a wedge between work life and leisure to the point that bad behavior in one will not seep into the other. A person's character is the same on the job and at play. Thus, we can readily see the force of Chomeau and Rudolph's argument that intelligence agents should make moral development a normal part of their professional competence.

People who become policemen, soldiers, or spies must be sure that they do their duty with a good conscience. Because these offices of force can be paths of moral maturity, the person so called should do nothing morally blameworthy while performing the duties of the vocation. Thus, by viewing such professions as a divine vocation, a way of moral development, Luther has built into the very professions theological reasons for refraining from doing evil as a matter of course in the profession. Luther's insight (and it goes back to Aristotle) is that human character is shaped by human acts and, thus, human character is inevitably shaped by the work engaged in by human beings. Whatever you spend long hours doing cannot help but shape who you are. Thus, if one wishes to develop a morally good character, one must not work in a profession that demands immoral acts. Luther maintained that soldiering was a morally acceptable profession when its members followed the strictures of the just war tradition. For that tradition provided guidelines to help members of the military distinguish good from bad moral practice within the profession. Spying must maintain the same moral guidelines for it to be considered as a morally acceptable profession.

BREAKING THE LAW AND OVERRIDING ORDINARY MORAL NORMS

We have seen that our normative figures are one in holding that we may not do evil as a matter of professional course, but this does not necessarily mean that we may never break the law or override ordinary human norms in the course of doing our job. For breaking human law and overriding ordinary human norms are not necessarily evil and can sometimes be morally praiseworthy. Put more clearly, it is possible to break the law and retain a good character, even form our character for the better, in the very act of breaking the law or overriding a human norm of behavior. Bonhoeffer, for example, argues that moral maturity is achieved by living the responsible life, a life in which we are bound to God and free (Bonhoeffer 1965, 298–9). This is similar to Barth's argument, "Good human action is set free by the command of God, His claim and decision and judgment," and this sort of freedom means being aware of one's "particular condition and possibility and therefore himself, in the related sequence of events" (Barth 1961, 5). We are bound in the sense that we have an obligation toward our neighbors, and we are free in the sense that we can live self-examined lives and act in the concrete decision itself and not be bound by abstract rules. This suggests a key moral insight: that we may be required to break the law or override a moral norm in the process of becoming more morally mature, for moral maturity can be had only through right action and we may be involved in circumstances in which leaving behind ordinary moral norms is the right thing to do.

There is no principle to guide right action except reality, in the sense that we see the right thing to do in the given situation and the right thing to do may be to break the law. This leads us away from abstract, universal ethics to what is good here and now. Ethical theories with universals are wrong and irrelevant; wrong because no such criteria has ever existed, irrelevant because it detaches people from history.[9] Dogmatists who insist that we may never break a law or transgress ordinary norms think unhistorically and irresponsibly. Much like Luther, Bonhoeffer argues that success makes history and the ruler of history brings good out of evil.[10] This way of thinking implies an ethical component in successful action in history, which leads Bonhoeffer to argue that we "must take our share of responsibility for the molding of history in every situation and at every moment (Bonhoeffer

1972, 7). Those who take on this responsibility as something laid on them by God will "achieve a more fruitful relation to the events of history" than the dogmatists or the opportunists. In short, they will do their neighbors more good by making exceptions to otherwise accepted rules of behavior.

Bonhoeffer insists that the responsible person leaves behind the laws, the normal and regular, when confronted by the extreme situation that no law can control (Bonhoeffer 1965, 238). When this happens, human action becomes an *ultima ratio* bound by no law and one in which the morally right thing to do is something for which we incur real guilt, as opposed to simply feeling a kind of regret that is the product of false guilt. Our desire to be privately pure can lead us to become enamored of a kind of private virtuousness, disconnected from community, which can lead to self-deception and the refusal to engage in responsible action for the sake of maintaining private purity.

Bonhoeffer warns that the freedom to break the law or override an ordinary norm of behavior is a dangerous kind of freedom, because one could get used to contravening accepted norms and thus become the sort of person who can no longer recognize what is really bad or worse (Bonhoeffer 1972, 5). That is why he insists on the real nature of the guilt. We should be aware that something has gone seriously wrong in the world when we commit such acts. This awareness serves as a check on our tendency to justify ourselves as pure by making the exceptional act the normal act. Bonhoeffer's warning also alerts us to the problem of a profession that may overexpose its members to situations that call for exceptional acts.

Larry Rasmussen argues that Bonhoeffer fails to provide us with a way to test the when the time has come to make an exception to the rules we are supposed to obey (Rasmussen 1972, 112). Bonhoeffer, however, does argue for a kind of self-proving in which God grants perception of the "essential nature of things." I believe we can clarify Bonhoeffer's position, and show how it is compatible with traditional just war thinking that does not accept the necessity of evil position usually associated with Bonhoeffer, by looking at it, as does the Catholic natural law position, through the lens of the language of moral virtue. In so doing, I will not force on Bonhoeffer a way of thinking foreign to him in order to create an artificial likeness between his moral position and more secular moral rationality, for as Bonhoeffer admits, his scheme is similar to Aristotelian–Thomist ethics that make wisdom a cardinal virtue, and is thus obtainable by all (Bonhoeffer 1972, 10). Bonhoeffer is not usually considered as an heir to the Catholic natural law tradition, but he does make use of one of that tradition's main ideas: the moral facts of human nature that lead us to conclude that, only those with the virtue of prudence will be able to see into the "essential nature of things," and actions based on such knowledge would, in fact, demand a high level of prudence. How prudence works in such a situation is ably explained by John McDowell, who argues that "acting virtuously" in a situation where a certain sort of behavior is a "reason for behaving in that way, on each of the relevant occasions" (McDowell 1977, 331). This requires a certain kind of sensitivity or "perceptual capacity" (what Bonhoeffer refers to as the ability to see the "essential nature of a thing"). Since this kind of sensitivity is what accounts for the actions we call virtuous, sensitivity is what virtue is. This also entails that a general propensity to act in a certain way cannot be called a virtue, since in order for an act to be virtuous, there must be sensitivity to facts about reasons for acting in a certain way and when circumstances are right for such an action. This leads McDowell to conclude that you cannot have one virtue without all the virtues, since sensitivity—"the ability to recognize requirements which situations impose on one's behavior"—is virtue in general (McDowell 1977, 333). Thus, for our purposes, just acts in war— including spying acts—are actually "manifestations" of a single sensitivity.

The virtuous are not guided by a codified behavior, but rather by a certain conception of how to live—and will act in accordance with that conception. A person is confronted by a multitude of facts in a given situation, but the virtuous person is able to see a salient fact about the situation that elicits proper action. This salient fact is the kind of thing that silences reasons for acting other than virtuously. Virtuous persons, therefore, possesses the ability to see the salient fact in the injustice before them, and, hence, be in the best position to know when to resort to force and when not, and what sort of force is necessary to complete the job. As Bonhoeffer puts it, the wise person acts "in the fullness of the concrete situation and the possibilities it offers" while also recognizing the "impassible limits" set by the permanent laws of human social life. In this knowledge, "the wise man acts well and the good man wisely" (McDowell 1977, 333).

Bonhoeffer argues that "killing, lying, and expropriation" are wise acts, the right thing to do, when done "solely in order that the authority of life, truth, and property may be restored" (Bonhoeffer 1965, 261). In this way, the law is still hallowed. Historically important action oversteps the limits set by these laws but only if the law or limits are "re-established and respected soon as possible" (Bonhoeffer 1972, 11). Necessity cannot itself be made a principle, for this means establishing a new and worse standard. When we override a law with the realization of guilt, this realization is the product of a prior assumption that the law/limits are "the best means of self-preservation." In so arguing, Bonhoeffer has anticipated the argument by Michael Walzer about the importance of guilt in overriding ordinary moral norms in a time of supreme emergency. Walzer is particularly concerned with showing how Churchill's decision in the early days of World War II to use air power to attack at industrial sites in Germany (when Britain was in a supreme emergency) was the morally right thing to do, despite the massive civilian casualties (Walzer 1977, 323–25). Yet Churchill, in effect, dishonored the architect of the plan, Sir Arthur "Bomber" Harris, by refusing to honor him after the war. By acting in this way, Bonhoeffer and Walzer would agree that Churchill was admitting moral guilt for actions that were also morally correct; it was an declaration that such acts should never be carried out under normal circumstances, even the normal circumstances of war, but nevertheless ought to be carried out in extreme circumstances.

Bonhoeffer suggests how one may break the law and override common human norms of behavior for the common good and without becoming the sort of people who are morally damaged by doing their jobs. His position is very helpful in showing how it can be a morally praiseworthy act to break the law, lie, cheat, steal, or betray. However, Bonhoeffer, like Walzer, must be approached with caution, particularly where they differ with their forbearers in the just war tradition. The moral philosophy of the traditional normative sources clash with Bonhoeffer and Walzer not over the crucial issue of breaking human law and norms, but rather over contravening moral principles that set boundaries around what may qualify as good action. The difference may be said to come down to how one understands the action done as an *ultima ratio*. Bonhoeffer argues that such acts are irrational but this is mistaken. An act done as *ultima ratio* is done on the very edges of rationality, which is why it is called *ultima*, but it is nevertheless rational. Such acts are rational because they are the product of a wisdom that, as Bonhoeffer argues, can see into the reality of things and knows when the time has come to override what is normally considered the rational thing to do. However, overriding the just war criteria can never be rational—can never be the right thing to do—for the criteria establish boundaries around what may count as a right act of force. If human beings are the sort of creatures that Augustine, Luther, and Bonhoeffer envision them to be, then some principles may be needed as a check on what can count as "the wise thing to do," for human wisdom exists in finite human beings.

Julia Annas (2011) is surely right that the moral life is a kind of maturing process in which we gain wisdom in an increasing basis, which means that we become more skilled in the moral life as we live through various situations that call for the virtues to be exercised. Thus, becoming skilled in virtue is roughly like becoming skilled in a language. The more complex and risky the situation we find ourselves in, the more moral maturity, the more skilled we need to be in virtue, to meet that situation with some moral success. True, as Pelligrion and Thomasma have argued, the virtuous person internalizes moral rules so that they become part of the very character of the virtuous person, but virtues cannot serve as a substitute for moral principles because human beings are not equally morally skilled (Pelligrino & Thomasma 1993, 22). The point I wish to emphasize is that it is doubtful that anyone is so virtuous, so morally skilled, that they would never need moral rules or principles to help direct them toward right action in the kind of extreme circumstances faced by persons given the job to use force, especially the kinds of force employed by spies. In this view, principles such as the just war criteria serve as useful signposts of forbidden areas of moral action in the midst of highly pressurized circumstances. The temptation to expediency and safety will be severe in the jobs carried out by soldiers and spies. The just war criteria mark the boundaries around what can count as the right thing to do in any and all circumstances.

Bonhoeffer admits that his scheme does not imply lawlessness and that love is the ruling motive for wisdom (Bonhoeffer 1965, 261). Here is where Bonhoeffer can be usefully compared to Ramsey's Christian-love-of-neighbor approach to the just war tradition. For Ramsey, love (as charity) is the reason why war may be justifiable, and love provides the guidelines (particularly noncombatant immunity) for what can count as a good and loving act in war. Bonhoeffer agrees with Ramsey that love is the very reason why one must sometimes use force against enemies for the common good, but he differs from Ramsey in arguing that love may well lead one to do evil that good might come. So, for Bonhoeffer, an act can be both loving and evil at the same time. However, Bonhoeffer does not seem to realize that love can never be so detached from wisdom that it thinks it is operating "freely," for we do not shut off our thinking when we act, and our passions are as susceptible to weakness as our rationality. Bonhoeffer argues that the law is still hallowed in an instance of overriding the law when it is restored by the act. Love may be the motivating force, but it will take a good amount of rational calculation to know when such circumstances occur. The point is that there can be no such thing as a loving act, a morally praiseworthy act, that violates the just war criteria. Bonhoeffer's scheme, if not amended, is problematic in the same way as some forms of consequentialist ethics in which one could justify, for instance, boiling a baby in oil in order to return to a state of lawfulness and respect of persons.

CONCLUSION

Augustine and Luther wished to maintain that one's profession should never be a hindrance to one's moral maturity. One cannot do evil at work and fail to be tainted with that evil. When Augustine and Luther defended soldiering as a morally good profession they argued that there was nothing about the job of a soldier that required them to do evil as a matter of professional course. Professional duties cannot hinder moral formation. If spying can be defended as a morally good profession, it too must not obligate its members to do evil in the line of duty. In other words, spies cannot develop in a morally good way if their jobs require them to do evil. Moreover, a profession that requires its members to do evil will shape the character of its members in such a way that they will not be the sorts of people who can be trusted to inhabit a secret profession. Acts of force that contravene the just war criteria are always evil acts that shape agents for the worse. By looking at the jobs that spies do through the moral lens of the just war criteria, we may be able to identify with more clarity what can count as a morally acceptable job. The spying profession is not an inherently immoral profession, but like soldiering, it is a profession whose members' actions can, morally speaking, get out of hand in a hurry and to the great harm of many people.

NOTES

1. Lawrence H. Keeley argues that peaceful societies, even at the level of bands (20–50 people), are rare, and nonexistent at the level of states, which he defines as political organizations that incorporate thousands from numerous communities into a single territorial unit. One of the distinguishing marks of a state is its permanent police and military force (1996, especially 25–27).
2. The legality of the scope and power of the NSA has yet to be fully worked out in the courts. Federal Judge Richard J. Leon in Washington, DC, ruled that some of the NSA's phone data collections were unconstitutional. However, in a separate and later ruling, Federal Judge William H. Pauly III in New York ruled that the NSA program that collects phone data is legal.
3. Pacifists will, of course, disagree with this conception of human nature and the state, but they have a hard time reconciling the reality of the world around them with their theories. Stanley Hauerwas, for example, has remarked, "It would be fascinating to ask what forms of economic relations need to be fostered to make the resort to coercion and violence less necessary. The exclusion of Christians from such political involvement seems based on the assumption that all politics presuppose violence—an assumption I see no reason to accept in principle" (1994, 129). Thus, even a noteworthy pacifist such as Hauerwas has a hard time imagining economic relations between human beings that require no use of force, even if he denies the obvious in principle. For Augustine, Aquinas, Luther, and Calvin, any thought experiment concerning nonviolent politics must be a thought experiment about the sort of politics that may have existed before sin entered the world or after Armageddon.
4. See Augustine's *On Free Will* I.5 in Augustine 1953, 118–119 and Calvin 1972, 124–125.
5. Central Intelligence Agency official website at https://www.cia.gov/about-cia/cia-vision-mission-values/index.html. Accessed on January 20, 2014.
6. This list is derived from Oakley and Cocking, 2001, 5–78.
7. Central Intelligence Agency official website at https://www.cia.gov/about-cia/cia-vision-mission-values/index.html. Accessed on January 20, 2014.
8. Luther discusses this in terms of various "stations" in Luther 1958, 358; and 1967, 246; and Calvin's discussion of vocations can be found in Calvin 1960, 719–22; and 1964, 240–42. An excellent secondary source on Luther's idea of stations can be found in Elert 1953, 2:49–65.
9. In so arguing, Bonhoeffer anticipated some of the main arguments found in Alasdair MacIntyre 1981 and 1988.
10. Luther's similar arguments can be found in his exposition of Psalm 101 in Luther 1958, 147–207.

BIBLIOGRAPHY

Annas, Julia. (2011). *Intelligent Virtue*. New York: Oxford University Press.
Aquinas, Thomas. (1948). *Summa Theologica*. 1256–1272. Translated by the Fathers of the English Dominican Provence. New York: Benziger Brothers.
Augustine. (1953). *Letters*. Vol. 3. Translated by Sister Wilfred Parsons. New York: Fathers of the Church.
——. (1963). Ca. 388. "On Free Will." In *Augustine: Earlier Writings*, edited by J.H.S. Burleigh, 102–217. Philadelphia, PA: Westminster Press.
——. (1984). *The City of God*. 413–425. Translated by Henry Bettensen. London: Penguin Books.

Barth, Karl. (1961). *Church Dogmatics*, Volume III.4: *The Doctrine of Creation.* Edinburgh: T&T Clark.

Bonhoeffer, Dietrich. (1965). *Ethics.* New York: Macmillan Publishing Company.

——. (1972). *Letters and Papers from Prison.* Edited by Eberhard Bethge. New York: Macmillan Publishing Company.

Calvin, John. (1949). *Instruction in Faith.* 1537. Translated by Paul T. Fuhrmann. Philadelphia, PA: The Westminster Press.

——. (1960). *Institutes of the Christian Religion.* 1559. Translated by Ford Lewis Battles. Philadelphia, PA: The Westminster Press.

——. (1964). *Commentary on the Second Epistle of Paul to the Corinthians and to Timothy, Titus, and Philemon.* Translated by T. A. Smail. Grand Rapids, MI: Eerdmans.

——. (1972). *Harmony of the Gospels Matthew, Mark, and Luke.* 1553. Translated by A. W. Morrison. Grand Rapids, MI: Eerdmans.

——. (1982). *Brief Instruction for Arming All the Good Faithful Against the Errors of the Common Sect of the Anabaptists.* 1544. Translated by Benjamin Wirt Farley in John Calvin, *Treatises Against the Anabaptists and Against the Libertines.* Grand Rapids, MI: Baker Book House.

Chomeau, John B., and Rudolph, Anne C. (2006). "Intelligence Collection and Analysis: Dilemmas and Decision." In *The Ethics of Spying: A Reader for the Intelligence Professional*, edited by Jan Goldman, 114–125. Lanham, MD: Scarecrow Press.

Copeland, Miles. (1969). *The Game of Nations: The Amorality of Power Politics.* New York: Simon and Schuster.

Dulles, Allen. (1977). *The Craft of Intelligence.* Westport, CT: Greenwood Press.

Dvornik, Francis. (1974). *The Origins of Intelligence Services.* New Brunswick, NJ: Rutgers University Press.

Elert, Werner. (1953). *Morphologie des Luthertums.* 2nd ed. Munich: C. H. Beck.

Goldman, Jan, ed. (2006). *The Ethics of Spying: A Reader for the Intelligence Professional.* Lanham, MD: Scarecrow Press.

Hauerwas, Stanley. (1994). *Dispatches From the Front: Theological Engagements with the Secular.* Durham, NC: Duke University Press.

Jeffrey, Keith. (2010). *The Secret History of MI6 1909–1949.* New York: Penguin Press.

Johnson, James Turner Johnson. (1975). *Ideology, Reason, and the Limitation of War: Religious and Secular Conceptions: 1200–1740.* Princeton, NJ: Princeton University Press.

Keeley, Lawrence H. (1996). *War Before Civilization: The Myth of the Peaceful Savage.* New York: Oxford University Press.

Laqueur, Walter. (1985). *A World of Secrets: The Uses and Limits of Intelligence.* New York: Basic Books.

Luther, Martin. (1956). "The Sermon on the Mount." 1538. In *Luther's Works*, vol. 21, edited by Helmut Lehmann, 1–294. Philadelphia, PA: Fortress Press.

——. (1958). "Psalm 101." 1534. In *Luther's Works*, vol. 13, edited by Jaroslav Pelikan, 147–207. Philadelphia, PA: Fortress Press.

——. (1962a). "Temporal Authority: To What Extent It Should Be Obeyed." 1523. In *Luther's Works*, vol. 45, edited by Walther I. Brandt, 75–129. Philadelphia, PA: Fortress Press.

——. (1962b). "Admonition to Peace: A Reply to the Twelve Articles of the Peasants in Swabia." 1525. In *Luther's Works*, vol. 45, edited by Walther I. Brandt, 51–74. Philadelphia, PA: Fortress Press.

——. (1967). "Whether Soldiers, Too, Can Be Saved." 1526. In *Luther's Works*, vol. 46, edited by Helmut Lehmann, 87–137. Philadelphia, PA: Fortress Press.

MacIntyre, Alasdair. (1981). *After Virtue.* Notre Dame, IL: University of Notre Dame Press.

——. (1988). *Whose Justice? Which Rationality?* Notre Dame, IL: University of Notre Dame Press.

McDowell, John. (1977). "Virtue and Reason," *The Monist* 62(3): 331–50.

Oakley, Justine, and Cocking, Dean. (2001). *Virtue Ethics and Professional Roles.* Cambridge: Cambridge University Press.

O'Toole, G.J.A. (1991). *Honorable Treachery: A History of US Intelligence, Espionage, and Covert Action from the American Revolution to the C.I.A.* New York: The Atlantic Monthly Press.

Pelligrino, Edmund, and Thomasma, David. (1993). *The Virtues in Medical Practice.* New York: Oxford University Press.

Pfaff, Tony. (2006). "Bungee Jumping Off the Moral Highground: Ethics of Espionage in the Modern Age." In *The Ethics of Spying: A Reader for the Intelligence Professional,* edited by Jan Goldman, 66–103. Lanham, MD: Scarecrow Press.

Shaffer, Anthony. (2010). *Operation Dark Heart: Spycraft and Special Ops on the Frontlines of Afghanistan and the Path to Victory.* New York: St. Martin's Press.

Walzer, Michael. (1977). *Just and Unjust Wars.* New York: Basic Books.

Wolfendale, Jessica. (2007). *Torture and the Military Profession.* New York: Palgrave Macmillan.

2 Testing the Limits of Discrimination and Proportionality

Spying can be virtuous and just when it comes to spying on dangerous enemies. There seems to be nothing wrong—in fact, it is entirely admirable—to possess the skill it takes to find out about enemy strengths, positions, and plans. We also find it admirable when a comparatively small number of clandestine fighters can effectively harass unjust enemy forces and thwart their plans. Few would argue with this. The trouble is with the tactics. One usually thinks of "the great game" as one played with only one rule: expediency. Get the job done, regardless of how many rules you have to break: that is the way of spies. There is some truth to this notion. Wartime spying, for example, often includes aiding and even creating underground fighting cells within enemy-occupied territory. History tells us that these fighting cells sometimes disregarded the rules of war. Clandestine warriors during the World War II, for example, thought that the special nature of the sort of warfare they were fighting (small bands of patriots resisting Nazi tyranny) exempted them from the traditional rules of war. American and British operatives struggled to persuade native resistance fighters to fight according to the accepted laws of war. Resistance fighters had few qualms about wearing the uniform of the enemy in order to get into position for an act of espionage, even though the Hague Convention outlawed such acts.[1] They also did not always engage in a kind of combat that ensures at least a minimum of protection of civilians.[2] Resistance fighters often tortured prisoners of war or simply shot them out of hand.[3] Agents of clandestine groups sometimes killed one of their own or killed themselves in order to avoid capture and torture. In short, clandestine groups do not always behave as just soldiers, at least as justice is spelled out for the soldier in the just war tradition.

In this chapter, I examine how the just war criteria of discrimination and proportion must be re-imagined for the spying profession. I first examine the argument that our notions of fair play must change if we wish to win the sort of battles that clandestine services fight. I show that what counts as "playing fair" may change over time, but the moral criteria of discrimination and proportion can never be overridden; for these are the criteria that allow us to understand how such acts could be justifiable in the first place.

I touch upon some of the more troubling tactics used by clandestine groups as a way of examining the elastic nature of discrimination and proportion when applied to the jobs that spies do and a way of testing the very limits of what discrimination and proportion might allow. I argue that the just war criteria can never be overridden but they must be cast in a different light than what we see for soldiering. For spying, while surely an act of force, is not soldiering.

FAIR PLAY AND JUSTICE

Discriminate and proportionate acts of force may take forms that would be viewed, in other circumstances, as morally horrible acts. To return to Luther's essay on soldiering, he argues along with Augustine and Aquinas that soldiering is a work of neighbor-love insofar as soldiers serve and protect their communities, but he realizes that the acts of "stabbing and killing, robbing and burning" are hard to connect with acts of love (Luther 1967, 95). Luther employs an analogy with surgery to make his point. A surgeon cuts and sometimes amputates limbs. If we concentrate simply on the cutting and amputating, it looks as if the surgeon is a moral monster, but if we know why the surgeon cuts and amputates, it looks as if the surgeon is a moral hero. What distinguishes surgery from mere butchery is the intention of the surgeon and the precision of the cutting. Thus, intention and proportion are foremost in Luther's analogy. Just as a good surgeon cuts only where needed and amputates only that portion of the human body that is necessary to save life, so, too, do good soldiers and spies use minimum and precision force to get the job done. Good soldiering and spying, like good surgery, follows a set of rules that are constitutive of the practice. In other words, good surgery means, among other things, making incisions where they need to be made and not just any place on the body, and just war means following the just war criteria that make war just, and that includes the prohibition against indiscriminate use of force. The just war criteria can never be overridden if we wish to remain just. Spying in wartime—hot or cold—is never exempt from the very criteria that make the use of force justifiable. Some human norms are not prima facie, are not capable of being overridden by anyone who wishes to maintain a high moral caliber. Thus, if we follow the logic of Luther's analogy, which demands good procedure in spying as well as in surgery, then spying, like soldiering, takes its moral character not only from those who authorize it, its justification, and its intention, but also from the tactics employed in getting the job done.

European clandestine fighters in World War II reasoned that they did not have the numbers or means to fight the Nazi enemy by the accepted rules of war. Nazi massacres—especially of the Jews—were thought to legitimize the harsh actions of resistance fighters.[4] Similarly, when the Cold War set in, supporters of the CIA argued that any notions of "fair play" had to go out the door (Colby 1978, 77; and O'Toole 1991, 462). Thus, we may be led to believe that successful acts of subversion and espionage can admit to no strictures. Such thinking is unjust on the face of it—and dangerously close to the sort of language we hear from modern terrorist groups. In fact, it should come as no surprise that most modern terrorist organizations learned their craft by familiarizing themselves with the tactics used by clandestine agents in World War II.

The laws of war broken by underground fighters in World War II are not only still upheld in international law but, for the most part, have been strengthened. The 1907 Hague Convention IV, Annex, Section II, Article 23 (f) had forbidden the improper use of enemy uniforms, but this did not cover belligerents who wore no uniform or identifying insignia at all. Annex, Section I, Article 1.2 requires a "fixed distinctive emblem recognizable at a distance" (Roberts and Guelff 2005, 73). The 1949 Geneva Convention III Relative to the Treatment of Prisoners of War complements the relevant articles in the 1899 and 1907 Hague Conventions (Roberts and Guelff 2005, 243–98). The 1977 Geneva Protocol I: Additional to the Geneva Conventions of 12 August 1949, and Relating to the Protection of Victims of International Armed Conflicts, Part III, Section I, Article 37.1 prohibits the feigning of civilian, noncombatant status,[5] and Articles 38 and 39 elaborate the status of combatancy in an effort to widen the safety net and, thus, increase the numbers of those who must not be targeted (Roberts and Guelff 2005, 442–43).

The CIA argument about fair play nevertheless has an important point in its favor. As the cold war set in, there still existed in the Western mind, even after two brutal world wars, a notion of fighting as tournament. This carry-over from ancient, medieval, and Renaissance-style warfare looked upon war as a contest with rules to be observed.[6] In a tournament, each fighter must be given an equal chance at winning the prize, or it is not worth the bloodshed. In such cases, there was little to be had by defeating an opponent using "dirty tactics." Modern war is not like this and, truth be told, very few wars before modern times were like tournaments. Michel tells us that clandestine warfare is not "chivalrous" and sometimes uses "unfair" methods. Nevertheless, the notion of a "fair fight among equals" dwells deep in the Western psyche and the idea of "fighting fair" used to mean a lot to a young man trying to prove his manhood. Sneaking up on the enemy and shoving a knife in his back when he was not looking did not seem to be the sort of thing a hero would do.

The US government can be found countering this "fighting fair" mentality as early as 1946 in the government-supported Hollywood film, *13 Rue Madeleine*, which has its star James Cagney make an impassioned speech to spy recruits about the new way of fighting:

> Now, you're going to have a lot to remember and a couple of things to forget. The average American is a good sport, plays by the rules. But this

war is no game, and no secret agent is a good sport—no living agent. You're going to be taught to kill, to cheat, to rob, to lie, and everything you learn is moving you to one objective—just one, that's all—the success of your mission. Fair play? That's out. Years of decent and honest living? Forget all about them. The enemy can forget. And has.

The key phrases here are "plays by the rules," "good sport," and "fair play." These are phrases that capture the war-as-tournament ideal popular in the Western chivalric tradition. The Cagney character wants the audience to rethink what it means to play by the rules, to be a good sport, and to engage in fair play. What is necessary is a reconfiguring of the standards of behavior in war or at least the kind of battles fought by clandestine groups. Previously upheld norms of decency and honesty have to be set aside in fighting an enemy who has already set them aside. In other words, if we do not reconfigure our notions of fair play, we will lose to those who refuse to hold the same standards.

The supposedly inbred American notion of fair play is what the Cagney character is trying to dismiss, and it is what J. H. Doolittle tried to dismiss in his 1954 report to President Dwight D. Eisenhower on the covert activities of the CIA:

> It is now clear that we are facing an implacable enemy whose avowed objective is world domination by whatever means and at whatever cost. There are no rules in such a game. Hitherto acceptable norms of human conduct do not apply. If the United States is to survive, long-standing American concepts of "fair play" must be reconsidered. We must develop effective espionage and counterespionage services and must learn to subvert, sabotage and destroy our enemies by more clever, more sophisticated and more effective methods than those used against us. It may become necessary that the American people be made acquainted with, understand and support this fundamentally repugnant philosophy. (Leary 1984, 144)

Doolittle is at pains to gain support for a group of warriors who will not be fighting for tournament glory. Fair enough. There is nothing unjust about killing enemy soldiers, even if you have to employ distinctly sneaky ways to do it. Aquinas, for instance, argues that it is morally praiseworthy for soldiers to conceal their purposes to the enemy and lay ambushes (*Summa Theologica* II–II Q.40 A.4). If, however, we wish to fight just wars, we may never disobey the just war criteria that forbid us to target the innocent (principle of discrimination) or intend to wreak more damage than is necessary (principle of proportion). The danger of a "no rules" approach to war is that it eliminates all checks on our behavior in war.

Right conduct in battle is, nevertheless, largely culture dependent, which suggests that the content of discrimination and proportion are largely, if not absolutely, culture dependent. The flexibility of what can count as praise-worthy or blameworthy behavior in combat explains why Aquinas, for example, did not specify the content of discrimination and proportion as he had specified the content of the *jus ad bellum*. For the *jus ad bellum* criteria are constitutive of the very practice of just war, whereas the *jus in bello* criteria for Aquinas was, as Johnson has shown, the product of the chivalric code and the *jus gentium* (Johnson 1975, 8–21). This is why we find Aquinas arguing, "it is owing to the conditions of men, that certain acts are virtuous for some, as being proportionate and becoming to them, while they are vicious for others, as being out of proportion to them" (*Summa Theologica* I–II Q.94 A.3 obj.3). So, specific rules of behavior are not always absolutely fixed. Custom helps to determine what virtuous and vicious action looks like. Thus the content of the *jus in bello* criteria must be considered largely, if not absolutely, as rules of thumb that depend on circumstances. The wise person knows how to act appropriately in the given circumstances, knows when to disregard the rules of thumb. However, the *jus in bello* criteria are not absolutely flexible. If we wish to fight justly, we must always seek to achieve discrimination and proportion in our acts. What counts as discrimination and proportion may change but the underlying principles do not. Put differently, we may never target those who do not deserve to be targeted and we may never countenance recklessness in any acts that cause more harm than good.

The Select Committee to Study Governmental Operations with Respect to Intelligence Activities (Church Committee) that investigated alleged assassination plots by the CIA argued in its findings that, "We do not think that traditional American notions of fair play need to be abandoned when dealing with our adversaries" (U.S. Congress 1975, 259). This argument ignores the truth in the Cagney/Doolittle argument that previous norms must change because the enemy is no longer playing the chivalric game. The norms that were formulated from the chivalric way of fighting war are not absolute moral rules for fighting. They express ideals of a given culture at a given time in history. They had a very wide and long-lasting influence that is still felt today. Insofar as such notions have helped to limit the violence in war, they are all to the good. But they are not absolute norms. Nevertheless, there are still some rules that must be observed if we wish to fight justly. We may jettison some outdated norms but we do not become "norm-less" in the process. Even Bonhoeffer, who was willing to override any and every moral norm in certain circumstances, argues that every instance of overriding must be done in such a way as to restore the norm to its ordinary place in society. The goal is to change our norms without losing what underlies them, which are the virtues and principles that make us what we wish to be. Fair play must be reconsidered but not eliminated. What counts as fair play will change, but it must still be just. The goal of the rest of the chapter is not so much an attempt to provide a full analysis of the tactics covered here, but rather to consider how the content of the *jus in bello*—what counts as discrimination and what counts as proportion—must be reconfigured for the clandestine services, and to test the boundaries of this new configuration. For in testing the boundaries, we will show that, whereas the content has been re-imagined, the underlying moral principles have not: there are still categories of people who may not be targeted and we must still act in such a way that we expect more good than evil to issue from our acts.

PROPER TARGETS FOR CLANDESTINE GROUPS: RECONFIGURING DISCRIMINATION

Who counts as a proper target for agents of clandestine groups?[7] First, all members of the intelligence profession are proper targets, just as all soldiers and their commanders are proper targets in war. All members of the military are included as well. We may also include scientists who work on weapons systems and politicians involved in military or intelligence decisions. The key is that a proper target is not only those who constitute a direct physical threat but also those possessing vital information about projects that constitute a threat. We cannot determine people to be proper targets merely because they are the sorts of people who could become proper targets in the future. However, we may target individuals who would not normally be considered as proper targets in more traditional military operations. Scientists, for instance, who have engaged in military work but who are currently not so engaged may still be proper targets for intelligence collectors because they possess knowledge about something that threatens our security and they once participated in the very project that threatens our security. Let us suppose, for example, that a German scientist who worked on the atomic bomb for Nazi Germany decided to retire from the project. All scientists who work on such projects render themselves as combatants. In cases where those scientists quit working on such projects we might be led to think that they render themselves as noncombatants, and in some ways they do become noncombatants, at least in so far as they are no longer working in places that are legitimate targets for military attack. But scientists are not like ordinary soldiers who are discharged from the military. They do not become immune from all targeting. The scientist in question possesses knowledge that is crucial to the wellbeing of the Allies. The scientist gained that knowledge by direct participation in the project that constitutes the threat. We may also point out that agents may target recently discharged regular soldiers and question them about enemy strengths, positions, and so forth.

Here we notice that the widening of the circle of who may count as a proper target for spies—the reconfiguration—does not eliminate the circle. If, for example, Allied agents were reasonably certain that the scientist told his wife a great deal about the project, the principle of discrimination would by no means allow her to be targeted, for she at no time participated in a project that threatened Allied security. We might conceive of a way of questioning her in a strictly noncoercive fashion that does not make her an object of suspicion in the eyes of her government and, so, place her at risk, but that is the extent of what may be done with her.

Clandestine operations can justifiably target people traditionally considered off-limits in military operations. However, due care must be given to those who cannot be justifiably targeted but who may suffer as a result of a clandestine operation. The mere fact that the circle of possible targets has been widened in clandestine operations does not mean that there is no circle. Agents must minimize risks to innocent people even if it means taking further risks both to themselves and to the success of the mission. When we take such precautions, we meet Walzer's rightly formulated challenge that "what we look for in such cases is some sign of a positive commitment to save civilian lives" (Walzer 1977, 155–56). This reinforces the idea that our stated intentions have a public nature and we cannot excuse ourselves from the evil of our actions by appeals to private intention.[8] We tend to think that intention can only be discovered by asking what is in the agent's mind, or at least that is where the investigation should begin. But the investigation should begin by watching what the agent actually does. The description of an intentional act that is *the* description is determined by first asking the question, "Why are you doing this?" There may be more than one "why" but the last "Why you did that" in a series of "whys" is the answer and this answer can be checked by watching the agent's completed acts. Put differently, an act has many descriptions that are intentional but we cannot simply choose one of these and exclude the rest. We cannot simply direct our intention to this and not to that. Also, we must keep in mind Aquinas's restriction concerning carelessness. In answering the question of whether or not someone is guilty of murder through killing someone by chance, which would include killing someone as an unintended consequences of one's act, Aquinas argues, "if a man pursue a lawful occupation and take due care, the result being that the person loses his life, he is not guilty of that person's death: whereas if he be occupied with something unlawful, or even with something lawful, but without due care, he does not escape being guilty of murder, if the action results in someone's death" (*Summa Theologica* II.II. Q.65, Art.8). This does not mean that agents can never knowingly harm an innocent person; it only means that they cannot engage in activities that target innocent people, and neither can they engage in otherwise just acts in a fashion so reckless that innocent people are needlessly harmed. Again, no matter how broad the category of proper targets may be conceived for clandestine groups, there will be many people who do not fit into that category and we may demand that those boundaries be recognized in such a way that we can observe by the acts of the clandestine group that they have observed those boundaries.

Another "reconfiguring" of the discrimination circle concerns how clandestine groups treat captured enemies. Brown reports that experts in guerilla warfare advise their students to kill quickly any captured informer (Brown 1975, 329). Similarly, Michel argues that a clandestine group cannot "allow itself the luxury of keeping prisoners; it punishes traitors severely without trial, sometimes without verifying that treason has been committed" (Michel 1972, 9). Michel also reports that members of clandestine groups do not look on the killing of a collaborator as murder but as a just execution (Michel 1972, 219). The execution gains three things for the group: elimination of the collaborator and any further damage he or she might do, deterrence of others, and a favorable swing in public opinion. Nevertheless, killing collaborators, informers, and traitors is justifiable only if reasonable means are employed to insure the guilt of the person charged.

Brown and Michel are simply relating a common problem with agents working with underground groups in the field: the practical impossibility of taking prisoners. Traditionally, once enemies surrender or are captured, they become prisoners of war and must be treated as such. Prisoners of war become noncombatants. Clandestine warriors may not be able to take prisoners, because they cannot take care of them and they cannot trust the enemy to remain silent if set free. In such circumstances, captured enemies may have to be killed if the clandestine group is to survive and succeed. Thus, clandestine warfare denies the captured enemy a noncombatant status. This is a clear reconfiguring of who counts as being a noncombatant. However, this reconfiguring is not an elimination of the category of noncombatancy. There are still many people who cannot be captured and killed. Members of the military or clandestine groups are proper targets, as are all those who aid them in some direct way: informers and traitors. Nevertheless, as stated above, clandestine agents are unjust to execute people who have not been confirmed to be informers and traitors and it would be unjust to execute any enemy who could be reasonably dealt with in another way.

KILLING ONE'S OWN AND KILLING ONESELF

Agents who lead clandestine groups can be faced with circumstances in which they must kill one of their own. Richard Dunlop recounts that an underground fighter knows that if he is badly wounded and his group is "hard pressed by the enemy, he may have to be put to death by his own people so that he will not be captured and tortured" (Dunlop 1979, 370). Similarly, Richard Helms has described how OSS agents were given lethal tablets so they could of their "own volition commit suicide and avoid the possibility of betraying comrades under the pressure of vicious torture" (Helms 2003, 48). Can we suggest how discrimination may be reconfigured in order to include the tragic necessity of killing allies and even oneself? The concerns of the agents mentioned above are both humanitarian and practical. The captured agent or clandestine fighter will more than likely be tortured to death. The humanitarian goal is to spare the victim the suffering.

The practical concern is to make sure the captured fighter does not reveal crucial information under torture. Thus, the intention in this case could be twofold: first and always to make sure the enemy does not learn crucial information; second to spare the wounded fighter terrible suffering. Might the principle of *double effect* be invoked to justify such acts? Double effect is the principle by which we may be exculpated from the evil of such actions if certain conditions are met. First, the act must be a good or neutral sort of act. An act that is intrinsically bad cannot be justified through double effect. So, we need go no further in our double effect calculation once we have determined, for example, "He raped that woman." For rape names an action that is intrinsically bad—incompatible with virtue. Second, we must not intend the foreseen evil of the act. Third, the foreseen evil must not be a means to the intended good. Fourth, more good than evil is expected from the act. Roughly, the principle of double effect draws a distinction between intended and foreseen effects of a voluntary action, such that we are not held culpable for the foreseen effects but only for the intended effects.

The principles of proportion and double effect are often used to gauge the morality of acts of combat within war. An example would be when a belligerent uses air power on an important target within an enemy's population center. Bombing the target of an enemy is a good kind of act. The deaths of the innocent should play no role in answering the question, "Why did you bomb this target?" Hence, if the act is just, the intent is merely to destroy the legitimate target. However, you cannot simply describe acts out of existence. If the innocent people who live in the vicinity of the target are not a means to the objective, then we should be able to prove this with our acts and we do this by showing that due care is taken to harm as few innocent people as possible, even if we must lessen the effectiveness of the mission in so doing. We do this regardless of whether or not the enemy has deliberately placed its own citizens in harms way by using them as shields or by embedding its proper targets in the midst of civilian centers. By doing so, we meet the challenge by Walzer that we should see some evidence of positive commitment to sparing noncombatants and the challenge by Aquinas that we should show by our acts that we took precautions against carelessness in our otherwise good acts. Again, this reinforces the idea that intention is not simply some private mental act, but should issue in acts consonant with declared intentions. Thus, the failure to take due care in an act otherwise excusable under the principle of double effect renders the agent guilty of the unintended evil consequences of the act. Proportion demands that we calculate the expected good of destroying the target with the number of expected innocent lives lost. Thus, if the act is just, we may say in all honesty that the pilots may have foreseen but did not intend the deaths of innocent people only if the pilots and those who gave them their orders can demonstrate that due precautions were taken not to endanger the lives of innocent civilians.

To return to our example of killing one's own, we could argue that, if it is part of the intention of the actor to kill someone who does not deserve killing, then the act is unjust. The principle of double effect does not appear to exculpate in such cases since we cannot separate the act of killing from the goal desired. In such cases, we desire the death of the innocent—*that* is precisely how we achieve the goal of protecting the rest of the group. It makes no difference if the victim desires to die.

However, one could argue that we have not given the act its proper description. The argument here is that we need to focus on the description of the target as "innocent." Certain jobs that spies do could carry certain rules about the activity that make death at one's own hand—or by the hands of allies—a central part of what it means to play that sort of game. Spies could take on certain jobs knowing and accepting the fact that in this sort of job one may have to kill oneself or allow oneself to be killed by comrades. Put differently, certain jobs carry specific rules about the activity that make the possible death by one's own comrades a part of what it means to engage in that activity. In such cases, one could argue that the agent is deserving death by the rules of the game, even if tragically so. Justice would not be overridden in such cases, because the one killed would not be "innocent"— undeserving of being killed. The whole point of the principle of discrimination is to prohibit the intentional targeting of someone who does not deserve to be targeted. When we target undeserving persons, we are not giving such persons their due, we are not giving them justice. However, in cases where agents freely decide to engage in a kind of activity in which they might have to be killed by one of their own, then those agents are giving their due—they are given justice—when they are killed.

There is an additional worry, especially for the act of suicide: a bad decision could be made in a desperate situation. This is less likely to happen in a group decision but it must still be factored. James Olson points out that U2 spy plane pilots were given suicide needles, but they were not ordered to use them (Olson 2006, 135). This indicates that those distributing the needles felt moral qualms about ordering self-destruction and those qualms are probably the result of realizing that the pilots may make the wrong decision—they may not be able to make sound decisions like this one in desperate situations. They are alone. There is no group to help with the decision. All of this suggests that a group decision, even if the group has a leader to give the final order, is less likely to result in a needless killing of one's own and is, therefore, more likely to be just.

MAKING DEALS WITH THE UNJUST

As we consider how proportion may be reconfigured for the jobs that spies do, we should keep in mind that the reconfiguration should not mean undermining the moral principle involved, which is that more good than harm should issue from the act. Intelligence services often use criminals in their work. This means deliberately failing to target people who certainly deserve to be targeted for arrest and prosecution. Organizations such as MI5, MI6 (SIS), and the CIA contend that the criminals recruited by them are necessary in order to gather the information needed. Critics such as Robert White contend that such recruits are actually paid agents of influence who promote actions and policies favored by the intelligence services that recruit them (White 2000, 54). The moral goodness or badness of such actions may depend on the intentions of the recruiters. William Casey recounts a story of two Allied agents who made a deal with a Gestapo agent (Casey 1988, 210–213). In return for enough money to flee to South America with his family, the Gestapo agent provided vital information that aided military counterintelligence to round up many Nazis who had gone underground at the close of the war, quite a few of whom were famous and probably never would have been otherwise caught, namely General Schmidt Voygt, commanding officer of the Secret Police of all Germany, and Haupt-Sturmbannfuhrer Karl Wolf, chief of all German agents in Belgium and France. Such a case parallels those in other areas of law enforcement when "smaller" criminals are given favorable treatment for the sake of capturing more and "bigger" criminals. The intention is to bring as many to justice as possible, particularly those on the high end of command. There is no problem here with the target. Those targeted deserve to be targeted. We simply do not target one who deserves it so that we may target successfully more who deserve it, and probably deserve it much more than the one we fail to target. Proportion, too, is surely met in such cases when we have good reasons to believe that the operation will succeed in bringing to justice more people, or at least persons who deserve punishment more, or are more of a danger to society, than the ones allowed to go free.

A similar concern occurs when we have to give information to double agents in order to keep them in good graces with the enemy. Hyde recounts the case of double agent Dusko Popov, who was one of the most important double agents in service to the British in World War II (Hyde 1982, 204–210). He started working for the British in 1940 but began to worry his German employers (the Abwehr) by 1942 because he was not supplying them with very useful information. Both the Americans (with J. Edgar Hoover's blessings—head of the FBI) and the British (with the approval of the head of British Secret Service) supplied him with enough useful information to keep German Intelligence satisfied. The information had to be genuinely useful to the enemy. Again, in such cases, we choose to aid the enemy in such a way that we might do much greater harm to them in the long run. In such cases, we should give no more information than is necessary to keep the double agent in good graces with the enemy. To give more than is necessary is to violate proportion. For, presumably, the same amount of expected good could have been achieved with less harm; that is to say, less information could have been given to those who will use it for evil purposes.

Giving information to double agents can also cause concern for discrimination. The information given to the enemy may be harmful to state agents and others acting on their behalf. Do those others deserve to be put at risk by intelligence deals with double agents? We may answer in the affirmative if those put at risk are members of the military or intelligence services. We may so argue because members of the military and intelligence services come under the heading of proper targets, as specified above. Such people agree to "take the field" and know that they may be targeted by the enemy at any time. They are engaging in acts harmful to the enemy and can expect the enemy to target them. In other words, they play a game in which, in order to do harm to the enemy, they might be put at risk in various ways. One way they might be put at risk is when their government thinks that a greater victory will be attained in the long run by giving some information to the enemy that will put various members of the military and intelligence services at risk in the short term. This is what it means to play the game of state-sponsored force.

The proportionate stakes may be very high if a service decides to use those suspected of war crimes or crimes against humanity. MI6, for example, recruited Horst Kopkow who had been head of Gestapo Amt IV 2A dealing with war sabotage. He was the leading German expert on Soviet Intelligence. He was held on charges of war crimes but the charges could not be proven, so the war crimes commission provisionally released him to employment within MI6 (Jeffrey 2010, 654). The infamous Reinhard Gehlen is another example. Gehlen was the senior German intelligence officer on the Eastern Front during World War II. He amassed tons of microfilmed material on the Soviet Union and maintained an underground espionage unit that could operate everywhere in Eastern Europe. Gehlen gained a lot of information for his organization from the interrogation process of Russian prisoners of war, thousands of whom were tortured and executed. Gehlen and his team did not participate in the tortures and executions, but they were able to glean from the mass of information what would be most useful to enemies of the Soviet Union (USSR). Gehlen surrendered to the Allies and offered his services as an intelligence expert. He was accepted and later parlayed his initial successes into becoming head of intelligence for West Germany during the Cold War.[9] Let's assume for the sake of the argument that Gehlen was expected to be and proved to be a major ally in combating the USSR during the Cold War. Let's further assume that his role was crucial in building a foundation of good intelligence work on the USSR. If these assumptions are true, then it appears that we have a good prima facie case for the employment of Gehlen as being proportionate. Certainly more good (effective intelligence work on a very large and very powerful enemy) than evil (employing an ex-Nazi intelligence officer and shielding him from criminal prosecution) resulted.

The use of criminals may cause problems for the governments that employ them. Christopher Simpson has argued, for example, that major blowback problems occurred for the United States as a direct result of their employing ex-Nazis in their secret services. He lists six major blowbacks: (1) the rapid erosion of trust between the United States and the Soviet Union; (2) it made the Eastern European peoples more pro-Soviet; (3) the intelligence work provided by ex-Nazis was not effective, because it simply reinforced mistaken ideas held by the United States concerning the size of Soviet forces and Soviet intentions; (4) the long-term corrupting influence on US intelligence services from financing criminals; (5) large-scale intervention in domestic American politics during the 1950s, which includes manipulation of the US media, surveillance operations inside the United States, harassment of opponents, forming academic programs, political lobbying, and penetrating unions, corporations, religious groups and student organizations; and (6) obstructing justice by protecting Nazi immigrants (Simpson 1988, 277–85). A careful reading of Simpson exposes the weakness of the first, second, third, and sixth alleged blowbacks. There was very little trust between the United States and the Soviet Union during the last days of World War II and ideological conflict was inevitable. Besides, both sides used ex-Nazis in their intelligence services as well as in their scientific endeavors. Eastern Europe's leaning toward the Soviet Union, which was very short-lived indeed, probably owes more to the fact that the Soviet Union was heavily armed, on their borders, and clearly expressing intentions to make their neighbors "satellites" to the Soviet Union than to the United States employment of ex-Nazis. Also, as stated before, the Soviets were using ex-Nazis, as well. Simpson makes a highly contentious claim when he argues that the intelligence work by Gehlen and other ex-Nazis was not very good. The major histories of the period would seem to refute this claim (see note 9). The obstruction of justice blowback is hardly felt if the intelligence work provided by ex-Nazis was truly effective in combating the Soviets. The real trouble comes with the fourth and fifth blowbacks. However, Simpson is at pains to prove the fourth blowback; that is to say, he does not do a very good job of showing how the particular practice of employing someone like Gehlen led intelligence agencies to become more corrupt. Nevertheless, if such a case could be proved, then we would have a hard time calling the practice proportionate, and the concern is rightly reflected in the Church Committee report that warns against the use of underworld figures because it would give them the power to blackmail the government and avoid prosecution for past or future crimes (U.S. Congress 1975, 259). The large-scale interventions in domestic politics is also hard to trace to the employment of someone such as Gehlen. Simpson's basic argument is that the United States tried to influence public opinion on the threat of the Soviet Union and, thus, the need to employ any effective weapon against them. Simpson is, in other words, trying to argue that Donovan's argument about making the public aware of the dirty game that we must play to protect ourselves against the Soviets is in itself a morally bad idea. At least, he is arguing that the US government should not try to influence public opinion with such tactics. Simpson has a strong point here. The US intelligence services did employ underhanded tactics on American citizens in order to get them to "see the light," but it is very hard to connect those tactics with employing people such as Gehlen. In other words, the complaint really amounts to one leveled against the methods used by the US government to persuade its citizens that its intelligence services are doing the right thing for the common good, and not one leveled against the employment of people of questionable character.

The concerns expressed by White, namely that the CIA in particular employs criminals whose policies are then favored by the United States, are more clearly seen in the Cold War tactics of making deals with gangsters and warlords, most of them drug dealers, in order to fight communism. Alfred McCoy has shown how the CIA used warlords in places such as Burma, Laos, and Afghanistan, who trafficked in drugs, to mobilize mercenary armies against communist forces. The CIA knew about the drug trafficking but blocked all investigations (McCoy 2000, 119). Moreover, the CIA continued to block investigation even when it became known that, for example, the heroin produced in Laos was facilitating the addiction of roughly 80,000 US troops. CIA operations in Afghanistan led to a boom in heroin production in Pakistan, which serves as the primary source for heroin in the United States. McCoy reports that the former CIA director of the Afghanistan operation argued that the mission was to push the Soviets out of Afghanistan and that the mission was successful. The agency was not given the resources to consider the drug trade blowback problem (McCoy 2000, 132). A similar tale can be told about CIA operations in Nicaragua. One could argue that proportion could be met in such cases if the threat averted somehow outweighed the expected evil. However, while one could stretch a dubious point in the CIA's favor about the good consequences of successful operations in Afghanistan, insofar as the Soviets were kept from gaining a foothold in the region, one has a hard time even finding a point, dubious or not, in the operations in Nicaragua. A communist foothold in that region could hardly spell enough doom for anyone outside of it to warrant the dirty deals made to make a go of the operations. However, let us assume for the sake of argument that proportion could be met in all of the above cases. What about discrimination? Troops who took the field in Vietnam could reasonably be expected to face untraditional enemies— such as women, the elderly, and children—but they could not reasonably be expected to face their government's own awareness and complicity in providing them easy access to heroin. Even more troubling is the blowback to innocent civilians from the operations in Afghanistan and Nicaragua. Could we appeal to double effect in order to exculpate the CIA in these operations? Let us again assume for the sake of argument that fighting communist forces in these regions is both a good kind of act and one in which more good than evil is the expected result. Was the evil the means to the good? This looks like a promising argument for the operations, for, indeed, the evil effects—increased availability of illegal and harmful drugs to innocent civilians—were not the means to the good end, which is thwarting communist initiatives. Those same operations would have been carried out whether or not a thriving illegal drug resulted. So, again, whatever one thinks of the operations, one cannot reasonably hold that the CIA engaged in them in order to increase illegal drug trafficking. Nevertheless, we must hearken back to Aquinas's dictum that one is still morally culpable for the evil of an otherwise justifiable act if one has not taken due precautions to see that the innocent are not harmed. Here is where the moral culpability of the CIA, and the US administrations who gave them their orders, is easiest to see. In order to justify such operations, we must take into account the direct harm to innocents caused by these operations and deal with it in some appropriate way. Moreover, we would need to see how the CIA was actually willing to sacrifice efficacy for the sake of protecting the innocent. The very fact that the CIA was not given the necessary resources to consider the obvious drug-trade blowback problem suggests that those responsible for the operation cared little about the collateral damage to innocent people. Again, proportion and discrimination may be reconfigured for the jobs that spies do, but the underlying principles of the criteria cannot be dismissed. One may be justified in making deals with criminal warlords but not when those deals mean harm to those who do not deserve to be harmed.

We may also consider President Barack Obama's tactic of using the CIA to funnel funds to corrupt official Mohammed Zia Salehi, aide to Afghan president Hamid Karzai and chief of administration for the National Security Council. The goal of paying Salehi is to help in the effort to win the War on Terror. The Obama administration also rightly perceives that vast corruption within the Afghan government destabilizes the region and, thus, makes it a hotbed for terrorists. Here, we have the US administration carrying out a confused policy. On the one hand, it is fighting terrorism by, first, using the CIA to funnel money to a corrupt official in order that it may receive some practical, immediate, help in the effort to kill terrorists; and, second, by rooting out corruption in the government. On the other hand, by aiding a corrupt official, they are inevitably aiding in the corruption of the Afghan government, which, in turn, means fostering social conditions that breed terrorism. Thus, it is hard to see how proportion could be met in this instance. The reconfiguration of proportion certainly means that we must be open to the possibility that paying someone such as Salehi is the right thing to do, but it is not proportionate when it appears that more evil than good results from the act.

SPECIAL PROBLEMS IN SABOTAGE

Acts of sabotage may test the limits of the elasticity of proportion. Michel reports, for example, that the majority of Allied officers felt that subversive warfare methods such as sabotage of railways and destruction of depots did not really harm the German war machine as much as it harmed the French, by causing great inconvenience to the people, bringing heavy reprisals to the populace, and rousing public opinion against the cause (Michel 1972, 149). At first glance, then, the majority of sabotage missions against Germany were non-proportionate. However, the estimate is based on hindsight and one must remember that those planning those sabotage missions probably thought that more good than harm would result. Still, figuring out proportion in such acts is a tricky business. Let us take as a case study the operation against the heavy water plant in Norway during WorldWar II. The Germans were making progress with the atomic bomb early in the war. By 1942, they were obtaining enough heavy water to alarm Winston Churchill. The Germans operated a heavy water plant in Norway that quickly increased its production from 3,000 pounds a year to 10,000 pounds. The Allies sent in thirty-four commandoes to blow it up, but the mission was a disaster and none of the commandoes survived. In fact, the mission only served to alert the Germans that the Allies were concerned about their nuclear research. A British SOE (Special Operations Executive) team then parachuted into Normandy and managed to sabotage the plant, destroying all the plant's electrolysis tubes and half a tonne of heavy water. All the saboteurs escaped. However, the Germans wasted no time in beginning again and the Allies responded with heavy saturation bombing. Not one bomb hit the target, and many Norwegians were killed. The Germans continued shipping heavy water equipment into Norway. The Norwegian section of SOE had to decide among four alternatives: (1) blow up dynamite stacks next to the railway line, (2) blow up the ferry that would carry the railway cars with the cargo, (3) attack the railway cars as they were going by rail, or (4) sink the ship carrying the water to Germany. The first was rejected, because the risks to the workers was too great. There was no time to organize an attack on the railway cars. They doubted they could sink the ships carrying the water to Germany. Thus, they opted for the second alternative. We notice that the tactic most likely to succeed given the SOE's capabilities—blowing up the dynamite stacks next to the railway line—was rejected in favor of a plan less likely to succeed, precisely because blowing up the dynamite stacks posed too great a risk to innocent life. This meets Walzer and Aquinas's strictures on tactics in which we foresee the loss of innocent life and show the right intention of those planning the operation. Even more evidence of right intention can be seen in how they decided to sink the ferry: slowly enough that the passengers would have a chance to swim to shore, but fast enough that there was no time to move it to shallow water. Again, a concern for innocent life took precedent over an absolute determination to succeed at all costs; they could have used more explosives in order to ensure a quick sinking. They also placed people in a position to row out to the sinking ferry in order to save as many lives as possible. Twenty-seven passengers on deck were able to swim to shore, but another twenty-six were drowned. Was the operation worth it? Was proportion met? William Casey reports that Carl Wagner, a physicist driven out of Germany and a Nobel prize winner, told the American government in 1942 that Germany would be able to produce nuclear weapons in two years. Sabotaging the Norwegian plant played a large role in keeping that prediction unmet (Casey 1988, 54).

We learn from the above example that clandestine groups have to figure out if the price of their acts is too high for the good achieved. Agents can encourage some tactics that have a good chance of being proportionate, particularly in the area of administrative resistance that carry low risk factors. Such tactics include feigning ignorance of how to carry out tasks or exaggerating the difficulties of carrying out an order. Doctors can declare fit people unfit. Machines can be neglected and skilled technicians can fail to do their jobs well. The biggest problem here is that such people have to remain in place in order to carry out their acts of sabotage, and this means that they may have to play some role in doing evil in order to retain their place in the system they wish to undermine. Here is where we may strain the elasticity of discrimination as well as proportion. Doctors must declare some people fit. Machinists must still oversee the overall functioning of their machines. Even more troubling are those who, for example, aided the French resistance with acts of sabotage on the jobs that required them to do things like assist in manhunts for Jews (Michel 1972, 199). For example, administrators who aided Jews by failing to include many on lists for deportation still had to include some Jews on the list. Are these cases of doing evil so that one may continue in the job of undermining the very system that produces that evil? These acts probably meet the demands of proportion, but what about discrimination? We were able to suggest how one might be able to justify acts of killing one's own because those who play that game know the rules may require their death at the hands of their comrades, but the innocent victims here may not wish "to play the game" the way the agent does who enters the game willingly and cognizant of all the risks. Of course, we could argue that the Jews in question are quite likely to agree with the acts of the saboteur; that is to say, the likely victims would probably agree that it is better for the saboteur to condemn a few innocent people in order to remain in place so that many more might be saved who would not be otherwise saved. We say this *may* be true, but maybe not. In any case, it is extremely unlikely that the agent will be able to confer with the targeted victims, but not impossible. We can imagine a scenario in which agents could confer ahead of time with potential "targets" for future use in order to keep their jobs secure. In any event, we could argue that in such cases it is the Nazis targeting the Jews who are to blame, and the agent plays a cog in the wheel for the sole purpose of slowing down the turning process as much as possible.

A more-terrible dilemma may be faced by members of an unjust regime who decide to remain at their jobs as a way to undermine their own government. A good example here would be Arthur Nebe, Himmler's chief criminologist, who was already an expert criminologist when Hitler came to power. Nebe joined the Nazi party but soon turned against them when he found out about the murdering tactics of the Gestapo. He remained in Himmler's organization at the request of those plotting to overthrow Hitler.

After the attempt on Hitler's life, he was caught and executed. Many similar stories under the Nazi regime could be told, perhaps none more chilling than that of Kurt Gerstein, a deeply committed Christian who, for purposes of finding out about what was going on in the criminal Nazi machine and hoping to tell others and do something about it, first joined the Nazi party and later became a member of the Waffen SS.[10] Here was a man who in the apt words of Saul Friedlander, "penetrated hell with the sole intention of bearing witness before the world and aiding the victims" (Friedlander 1969, x). Gerstein had medical and technical knowledge valuable to the SS hygiene service, which oversaw the drinking water and disinfection systems in the military camps. He gained firsthand knowledge of the extent of the Nazi crimes when he was ordered to obtain 220 pounds of prussic acid. Gerstein had a rough idea what the acid was for and obeyed his orders in order to ascertain the extent of the SS operation. Learning the truth of the operations that had become the "final solution," Gerstein worked intently to sabotage as many missions as he could, usually by allowing the gas to decompose before it could be used. He also went personally to the plant in Kolin to pick up the gas and asked questions that left no doubt in the minds of those questioned as to what the acid was going to be used for. In this way, he was able to convey to outsiders what was going on in the camps and hopefully to start rumors among the citizenry. Gerstein dissuaded SS officer Hans Günther of the Central Security Office from trying to use gas on Jews in open trenches. He was also given the task of arranging for Zyklon B to be ordered from German Pest Control company, but managed to dispose of much of it by burying some shipments, diverting others, and using some for disinfection purposes. On a different note, if no less dangerous, he gave out many fake SS passes to people in need of protection. During all of this time, he lived in a state of permanent fear of being discovered.

We can think of similar examples that may occur in the War on Terror where agents may be asked to join terrorist gangs. As a character in John Le Carre's *Little Drummer Girl* remarks on being asked about training an agent for terrorist group penetration: "Terrorist organizations don't carry passengers" (Le Carre 1984, 242). Any agent who joins a terrorist group will likely have to commit acts of terrorism.

The people targeted by undercover agents, even if targeted with great regret, are very hard to conceive as deserving to be targeted. If people such as Gerstein and the double agent terrorist are just, then the justifiability of their acts must be grounded in the belief that someone else is responsible for the deaths of the innocents that occurred as a direct result of their actions. In other words, we have to conceive of circumstances in which moral agents are not morally responsible for some of their acts. Double effect is not necessary in these cases, because the evil acts cannot be imputed to the agent seeking the good in these tragic circumstances. Instead, the evil is imputed entirely to those creating the regime of evil and giving the orders. The evil regime exists and is bent on carrying out actions that will result in the deaths of many innocent people. Double-agents in these tragic circumstances agrees to stay at their posts, or even take up a post, for the sole purpose of reducing the evil consequences. Thus, we notice that the justification for such acts hinge entirely on proportion—more lives are saved by having a saboteur stay on the job even if it means some innocents will be harmed by that saboteur. We do well here to recall Bonhoeffer's arguments about being able to see into the essential nature of things in order to know how to act in the extreme situation. For we are now at the outermost edge of rational moral action. Agents may be faced with a circumstance in which their choices are two: they can quit their jobs and refuse to save anyone, or remain on the job and save as many as possible while playing a reluctant role in condemning others. If we follow Bonhoeffer's line of reasoning, we might condemn the former for irresponsibility, for saving their private virtue at the expense of others. If they can stay on the job and undermine the system and save many lives in the process—save many lives that would not have been saved if a willing state servant took their place on the job—then this is what they must do. Nevertheless, the psychological pressure could be tremendous. We may also consider the case of Edward Snowden, an US intelligence worker who, in June 2013, leaked a classified order from the FISA court, which authorized the collection of all phone-tracing data from Verizon business customers. Snowden quickly became a man without a country. The evil Snowden thought he was fighting against is surely less in scope and terror than the evil Gerstein knew he was fighting against, but the pressures are similar for both. When we think of the example of Kurt Gerstein, who remained a part of the SS in order to undermine their operations, we do well to remember that he was driven to such despair that he committed suicide. The pressures here are similar to all state agents who go "undercover" by joining criminal gangs and must participate in evil acts in order to bring an end to those same evil operations. The shelf life for such agents must surely be a short one.

Is it any wonder that John Le Carre would have his character of burned-out spy Alec Leamas make his embittered speech about the character of the typical spy? Le Carre portrays Leamas as a spy left out in the cold for too long. No human being can possess enough moral virtue—possess a strong enough character—to engage in such acts described above for very long. These are truly the exceptional acts that may indeed be just in a given circumstance, but the ability to see when such circumstances have occurred can be eroded by engaging in the acts themselves. Clandestine groups may face circumstances that force their members to make hard decisions about the possibility of using exceptional acts to get the job done, but it is not likely that individual members of those groups will be able to withstand the pressures upon them for very long. The more one engages in exceptional acts, the more one is likely to keep engaging in them if faced with similar circumstances, and even in circumstances in which the similarities are superficial. At the very least, this worry should lead us to hope that all agents are monitored with enough scrutiny to detect when they are succumbing to the pressures of the job. The moral principle underlying proportion is that more good than evil should issue from our acts of force. Agents and those who give them their orders need great deal of wisdom to be able to judge if their acts will do more good than harm. The moral principle underlying discrimination is that we never target those who do not deserve it. Discrimination and proportion may rightly be re-imagined for the jobs that spies do, but constant recourse to tactics that test the very limits of that reconfiguration will ultimately lead to the failure to abide by the underlying moral principles of the *jus in bello*. Given the pressures placed upon agents who are forced to commit criminal acts as part of criminal organizations, and the inevitable corrupting nature of such acts habitually engaged in, we must concern ourselves with the abiding innocence of the agents who do such jobs and see to it that we do not target them for jobs that no one can handle for very long.

CYBER WARFARE

The computer chip has offered a new way of doing the jobs of the spy and new challenges to our attempts to reconfigure discrimination and proportion. Agents can gain entry into an enemy's computer system, learn secrets, cause all sorts of havoc, and then cover their tracks so that the enemy may never know where the attack originated. One sort of trouble we may cause is to assault infrastructure by gaining entry into systems that regulate power, water, communications, and manufacturing processes. We can get an idea of what agents could do by remembering the large-scale electricity blackout of 2003 in parts of the United States and Canada. The blackout was the result of a SCADA (Supervisory Control and Data Acquisition) failure, the kind of failure that could be created by agents gaining access to the system.

The head of US cyber command, General Keith Alexander, has stated that any cyber combat would follow the "principles of military necessity, discrimination, and proportionality" (La Guardia 2011, 162). Thus, agents can send emails with viruses to infect a targeted individual or group without infecting others. For example, the computer virus STUXNET appears to have been designed for discriminate use against an enemy target, namely Iran's nuclear facilities. Other "logic bombs" have been designed that are capable of discriminate use. In such tactics, chips are tampered with so that a system malfunctions or an explosive device explodes off-time. Naturally, logic bombs can be used indiscriminately, as can any other offensive weapon, but such capabilities do not count against the morally good uses of such weapons. After all, AK 47 rifles as well as logic bombs can be used for good or ill. The only worry we have from the just war perspective is whether or not General Alexander's criteria are lexically ordered so that military necessity trumps discrimination, which would be unjust. Proportion is not a concern here. Even if military necessity was uppermost in the minds of mission planners, that kind of necessity fits well with proportion—the effort to do more good than harm by our actions in war. But when necessity and proportion are uppermost, the innocent may be targeted, which would violate the principle of discrimination.

We must always protect the innocent as much as possible in our acts of force. That is the way we meet the criterion of discrimination. To begin with, any method of obfuscation (covering our tracks) would have to be carried out in order not to throw unwarranted suspicion on innocent people who could then be targeted by our enemies. Second, we must consider that all attacks at infrastructure will inevitably include innocent people in our target range. Identifying targets with purely military functions are very difficult because military (and clandestine service) and civilian networks and systems are intermingled. If we shut down the power of a city, or a portion of a city, then we shut down the power of everyone in our target range, which could include hospitals and residential sections. Could we justify such an assault in the same way we might justify an air attack, by double effect? Whether we are talking about French underground fighters blowing up a power plant or talking about shutting down the power in, say, Tehran, in order to gain some military advantage, we must concern ourselves with the issues of discrimination and proportion. Are the innocent people intentionally targeted? Do we carry out the mission in order to gain some advantage from the ill effects upon the citizenry? Or are the ill effects to the citizenry simply a regrettable effect that we could well do without? If the latter, then have any precautions been taken to lessen the misfortune to innocent citizens? The exact outcome of cyber attacks may be hard to quantify. What results could we expect if, for instance, we caused Tehran's power supply systems to malfunction? How long would they malfunction? How many people would die? Even if we can answer these questions in such a way as to leave little doubt that the mission was not conceived or carried out in a way that would lead us to believe that harm to innocents was intended, we must ask ourselves is the harm to the innocent worth the goal we expect to reach in the assault. If so, then such acts could be justified.

A more discriminate and proportionate use of cyber assault is to infiltrate government communications networks and computer systems to learn secrets and destroy those systems if we wish. We have a creditable history of such use. The NSA used cyber attacks on Yugoslavia air defense systems during the conflict in Kosovo in March of 1999. In 2005, the Pentagon created the Joint Functional Component Command-Network Warfare group to engage in cyber attacks. The United States successfully employed cyber attacks in Iraq and managed to read enemy emails and text messages and knocked out all these communications around Baghdad in conjunction with General David Petracus's offensive surge in 2007. In May 2010, the US Cyber Command was set up to direct all of the United States's offensive and defensive cyber actions, thus creating a coordinated command and control center which is less susceptible to out of control operations that may contravene discrimination and proportion.

Another issue that tests the limits of proportion is privacy. Intelligence collection for security purposes has always posed concerns for proportion, for such tactics ask that we trade off a certain losses of privacy for certain gains in security. With the escalation of terrorist violence, increased camera surveillance has become the norm in many places. Special software has been developed that allows agents to identify likely terrorists. The software maps behavior patterns and relationships. In order for the tactic to work, it requires much more data on people than would be necessary if suspects were placed under observation. This means a loss of privacy for everyone, because everyone who "surfs the net" and sends emails and text messages would be mapped if they "surfed" to certain places and contacted certain people or organizations. We are now encountering a huge shift in how we collect intelligence on real and potential enemies. Previous methods of spying meant that we first had reasons to believe that certain individuals or groups needed to have more data collected about them, and then did so through observation or other means. This meant a suspect had already been identified, which then led to collecting further information about them. Cyber spying has shifted the ground so that we now collect data about people who get our attention because of what they are doing in the cyber world, and later decide whether or not they are worthy to be considered suspects and targeted for even more data collection. Thus, to be clear: cyber capabilities mean that we are now collecting information on a broader range of people in order to increase our pool of likely suspects. Such acts could indeed be proportionate if the goal in security is real and cannot be had otherwise. Here we are reminded of the differing court decisions on some of the NSA's activities where there appears to be a tacit agreement in the opposing court opinions that what the NSA does could be legally acceptable if it is necessary for the protection of the common good.

CONCLUSION

Spying is not soldiering. Both professions carry out jobs of state-sponsored force and both jobs may mean killing enemies, but the professions are distinct and cannot be equated to such a degree that we can usefully apply the just war *in bello* criteria to one in the exact same way as we apply them to the other. We have to re-imagine discrimination and proportion if they are to be usefully applied to spies. Nevertheless, that re-imagining cannot discard the underlying principles of the criteria while remaining faithful to the tradition. The tradition can and must be built on if it wishes to remain a living tradition, but the very moral foundations of the tradition cannot be changed. The range of those who may count as innocent may shrink but we must still be able to recognize those who may not be targeted in any way. The range of what may count as a proportionate act may be harder to calculate and, so, harder to achieve for some clandestine jobs, but we must still do our best to calculate as honestly as possible whether more good than harm will come from our acts.

Testing the Limits of Discrimination and Proportion 55

NOTES

1. 1907 Hague Convention IV: Respecting the Laws and Customs of War on Land, Annex, Section II, Article 23 (f) forbids the improper use of the uniform of the enemy. See Roberts and Guelff 2005, 78.
2. The principle of discrimination is reflected in 1907 Hague Convention IV, Annex, Section II, Articles 22–28. See Roberts and Guelff 2005, 77–78.
3. 1907 Hague Convention IV, Annex, Section I, Article 4, states that prisoners of war must be humanely treated. Also, Annex, Section II, Article 23 (c) forbids the killing and wounding of one who surrenders. See Roberts and Guelff 2005, 73 and 77.
4. For more on this see Michel 1972, 7–10.
5. 1977 Geneva Protocol I, Part III, Section I, Article 39.3 states that the prohibitions on using enemy uniforms does not affect existing rules of international law applicable to espionage. Presumably, this refers to the existing rule (in 1907 Hague Convention IV, Annex, Section II, Article 30) of not having to treat spies as prisoners of war, and thus, possible subjects for trial and execution. See Roberts and Guelff 2005, 79 and 443.
6. For more on this notion as just war as tournament and the chivalric tradition, see Johnson 1975, 64–75; and Russell 1975, 213–257.
7. How the criterion of discrimination relates to assassination is too large a topic to be covered in this section. The topic is treated in full in Chapter 6.
8. For a full discussion of this topic, see Cole 2011, 174–191.
9. Christopher Simpson is skeptical about Gehlen's achievements but Gehlen's biographers give him credit for a great deal of effective intelligence work against the USSR. See Simpson 1988; Cookridge 1971; and Hohne and Zolling 1972.
10. The Gerstein story is told by Friedlander 1969; and Joffroy 1969.

BIBLIOGRAPHY

Aquinas, Thomas. (1948). *Summa Theologica*. 1256–1272. Translated by the Fathers of the English Dominican Provence. New York: Benziger Brothers.
Brown, Anthony Cave. (1975). *Bodyguard of Lies*. New York: Harper & Row Publishers.
Casey, William. (1988). *The Secret War Against Hitler*. Washington, DC: Regnery Gateway.
Colby, William. (1978). *Honorable Men: My Life in the C.I.A.* New York: Simon and Schuster.
Cole, Darrell. (2011). "War and Intention," *The Journal of Military Ethics* 10(3): 174–91.
Cookridge, E. H. (1971). *Gehlen: Spy of the Century*. New York: Random House.
Dunlop, Richard. (1979). *Behind Japanese Lines: With The OSS in Burma*. Chicago, IL: Rand McNalley.
Eisendrath, Craig, ed. (2000). *National Insecurity: US Intelligence After the Cold War*. Philadelphia, PA: Temple University Press.
Friedlander, Saul. (1969). *Kurt Gerstein: The Ambiguity of Good*. New York: Alfred A. Knopf.
Helms, Richard. (2003). *A Look Over My Shoulder: A Life in the Central Intelligence Agency*. New York: Random House.
Hohne, Heinz, and Zolling, Hermann. (1972). *The General Was a Spy: The Truth About General Gehlen and His Spy Ring*. New York: Coward, McCann & Geohegan.

Hyde, H. Montgomery. (1982). *Secret Intelligence Agent.* London: Constable and Company.

Jeffrey, Keith. (2010). *The Secret History of MI6 1909–1949.* New York: Penguin Press.

Joffroy, Pierre. (1969). *A Spy For God: The Ordeal of Kurt Gerstein.* New York: Harcourt, Brace, Jovanovich.

Johnson, James Turner Johnson. (1975). *Ideology, Reason, and the Limitation of War: Religious and Secular Conceptions: 1200–1740.* Princeton, NJ: Princeton University Press.

La Guardia, Anton. (2011). "The New Realm of Cyberwar," in *Modern Warfare, Intelligence and Deterrence*, edited by Benjamin Sutherland. Hoboken, NJ: John Wiley & Sons.

Le Carre, John. (1984). *The Little Drummer Girl.* New York: Bantam Books.

Leary, William M. (1984). *The Central Intelligence Agency: History and Documents.* University, AL: University of Alabama Press.

Luther, Martin. (1967). "Whether Soldiers, Too, Can Be Saved." 1526. In *Luther's Works*, vol. 46, edited by Helmut Lehmann, 87–137. Philadelphia, PA: Fortress Press.

McCoy, Alfred W. (2000). "Mission Myopia: Narcotics as Fallout from the CIA's Covert Wars." In Eisendrath, Craig, ed. (2000). *National Insecurity: US Intelligence After the Cold War*, edited by Craig Eisendrath, 118–48. Philadelphia, PA: Temple University Press.

Michel, Henri. (1972). *The Shadow War: European Resistance 1939–1945.* Translated by Richard Barry. New York: Harper and Row.

Olson, James M. (2006). *Fair Play: The Moral Dilemmas of Spying.* Washington, DC: Potomac Books.

G.J.A. O'Toole. (1991). *Honorable Treachery: A History of US Intelligence, Espionage, and Covert Action from the American Revolution to the C.I.A.* New York: The Atlantic Monthly Press.

Roberts, Adam, and Guelff, Richard. (2005). *Documents on the Laws of War*, 3rd ed. New York: Oxford University Press.

Russell, Frederick. (1975). *The Just War in the Middle Ages.* London: Cambridge University Press.

Simpson, Christopher. (1988). *Blowback: American Recruitment of Nazis and Its Effect on the Cold War.* New York: Weidenfield & Nicolson.

U.S. Congress. Senate. Select Committee (Church Committee) to Study Governmental Operations with Respect to Intelligence Activities. Ninety-Fourth Congress. (1975). *Alleged Assassination Plots Involving Foreign Leaders: An Interim Report.* Washington. DC: Government Printing Office.

Walzer, Michael. (1977). *Just and Unjust Wars.* New York: Basic Books.

White, Robert E. (2000). "Too Many Spies, Too Little Intelligence." In *National Insecurity: US Intelligence After the Cold War.* edited by Craig Eisendrath, 45–60. Philadelphia, PA: Temple University Press.

3   Lying and Deception

Justice in war is in part about belligerents giving each other their due. If belligerents are to be just, they must give justice to the enemy in war by not violating the just war criteria. The just must not use unjust means in battling an unjust enemy. But spies must tell lies in the line of duty. They must tell lies to the enemy, to officials of neutral countries, and to officials and ordinary citizens of their own countries. The problem that must be addressed is one of claiming that, by lying to the enemy, the enemy is given what is owed to them. More troubling still is the claim that the citizenry intelligence services are supposed to be protecting deserve to be lied to, that citizens get what is owed to them when they are deceived by their intelligence services.

Another problem centers on the issue of lying and character. Can the virtuous person lie and remain virtuous, remain a reliable and trustworthy member of the profession? Lying is at the heart of spying, and moral philosophers and theologians, even if we limit our attention to those who contributed to the just war tradition, cannot be made to speak with one voice on the moral permissibility of lying. This may be the most important moral problem of all for us to consider, since spying is nearly synonymous with lying. In order to gain the information they are paid to get, spies may have to tell and act out all sorts of lies. Intelligence agents are often trained to maintain the fiction of another self. They may have to acquire the habit of being able to respond without hesitation to a new name. Some may be called on to have an entire fictitious case history memorized, to the point of being able to live the part as an actor. The spy may have to live the part for weeks, months, and in the case of a mole, even years. In short, spying and lying often go together. We should not be surprised to find that, therefore, many of the discussions in Christianity about the permissibility of lying take place in the midst of a larger discussion about those portions of the scriptural narrative that concern spies and those who aid them, especially the stories of the Israelite spies aided by the lies of Rahab (Josh. 2) and David's use of spies against Absalom (2 Sam. 15–17).

The goal of the chapter is to show how and when lying and deception may be morally justifiable acts. I look first at the Christian case against lying in all circumstances. The absolutist Christian case against lying is especially important for two reasons. First, it is constructed by many of those who helped to build the just war tradition. Second, the absolutist case, particularly as it is argued by Augustine, had a significant impact on later Western moral philosophy and theology. I then look at the Christian case for the permissibility of lying in some circumstances, for it, too, had a significant impact on the Western moral tradition. I show that the latter not only coheres with common sense attitudes about lying, but it also makes much better sense on its own terms as Christian theology. I explore how the permissive view also has a stronger common and moral sense claim to its credit as we turn to practical advice. Finally, I look at some problem cases in order to trace the contours of what can count as good and virtuous lying within the clandestine services.

LYING AS AN ABSOLUTE EVIL

The Greek rhetorician and satirist Lucian, writing in the second century, begins his dialogue, *The Lover of Lies*, with the following exchange:

> TYCHIADES: Can you tell me, Philocles, what in the world it is that makes many men so fond of lying that they delight in telling preposterous tales themselves and listen with especial attention to those who spin yarns of that sort?
>
> PHILOCLES: There are many reasons, Tychiades, which constrain men occasionally to tell falsehoods with an eye to the usefulness of it.
>
> TYCHIADES: That has nothing to do with the case, as the phrase is, for I did not ask about men who lie for advantage. They are pardonable— yes, even praiseworthy, some of them, who have deceived national enemies or for safety's sake have used this kind of expedient in extremities as Odysseus often did in seeking to win his own life and the return of his comrades. (Lucian 1921, 321)

Tychiades's claim that lies are sometimes not only pardonable but even praiseworthy, particularly when done in order to deceive enemies for the common good, is a popular one in the ancient world. The sentiment can be found in Homer (*Odyssey* I.296), Xenophon (*Boyhood of Cyrus* I.6 and *On the Art of Horsemanship* V.9), Thucydides (V.9), Virgil (*Aeneid* II.390), Plutarch (*Marcellus* 32 and *Sulla* 39), and Polybius (IX.12 and V.100).

Augustine, in sharp contrast to the ancient tradition, gave an unequivocal "no" to all forms of lying and had an enormous impact on the Western philosophical tradition, both religious and secular. According to Augustine, "That man lies who has one thing in his mind and utters another in words, or by signs of whatever kind" (*On Lying* 3). For Augustine, lying is a sin no matter the intentions of the liar, because the liar must, by definition, subvert the very reason God created human beings with the ability to use words: to convey truth (*Enchiridion* 22).

Augustine's most able defender in recent scholarship has been Paul Griffiths, who argues that the whole issue of lying in Augustine cannot be separated from the idea that beings are ordered hierarchically according to the extent of their participation with God. The more we express the image of God in us, the closer we are in communion with him. As Griffiths point out, for Augustine, "insofar as we are anything at all we are that image" (Griffiths 2004, 79). Because the image of God is discernible in us in every aspect of our being, the image must be discernible "in the means by which we form thoughts and bring them to utterance." Augustine is able to argue this way because he believes truth-telling as part of God's nature is reflected in the communication within the Trinity, and that when we say that human beings bear the image of God in them, we mean that they bear this Trinitarian image that always has truth-telling as a part of its nature. Whenever we lie, for whatever reason, we reject the gift of speech that reflects the Trinitarian image in us. Thus, even if one lied in order so save another's life or to deceive the enemy of one's nation, it is still a sin (though it is the least-serious form of the sin). So it is no surprise to find Augustine condemning Rahab for her lies (*Against Lying* 15.31–32). Augustine would have us believe that Rahab's lie, as well as those told by the Egyptian midwives in order to save the innocent Jewish newborn (Ex 1:15–22), and the lies told on David's behalf against the unjust regime of Absalom, are exhibitions of pride and a desire for autonomy in that they are examples of humans thinking they know better than God in what their good consists. Such acts are, in the words of Griffiths, "performatively incompatible with the love of God" (Griffiths 2004, 99). Thus, all lies damage what is essential to the dignity of the human person and undermine what is divine about the human being.

Aquinas follows Augustine in making all lying a sin (*Summa Theologica* II–II Q.110, A.3) and in distinguishing the severity of the sin that attaches to different kinds of lies, with the least blameworthy lie being one that saves another's life (*Summa Theologica* II–II Q.110, A.2). This would strike the ancients as strange, for it would seem obvious to them that prudence would dictate a lie for the sake of justice in some circumstances. But for Aquinas, it is "unnatural and undue for anyone to signify by words something that is not in his mind" (*Summa Theologica* II–II Q.110, A.3). In other words, because speech is a God-given skill for truthful communication, lying breaks the natural law, and the natural law is absolute, admitting of no exceptions.

Calvin has an extended discussion about lying in his commentary on the actions of Rahab and the Israelite spies. Tellingly, Calvin finds spying as intelligence gathering to be morally acceptable. He does not find it necessary to defend Joshua's act of sending out spies, as he did Joshua's acts of genocide. Calvin comments that Rahab demonstrates "singular courage and prudence" in hiding the spies and making a pact with Israel (Calvin 1854, 43).

He argues that her treachery is not criminal, because "she only acquiesced in the judgment of God" (Calvin 1854, 46). Calvin makes a similar and more-detailed argument of this sort when he comments on Joshua's genocidal practices and brutal treatment of foreign kings. Such acts can be justified only when commanded by God: "It would therefore have been contrary to the feeling of humanity to exult in their ignominy, had not God so ordered it. But as such was his pleasure, it behooves us to acquiesce in his decision, without presuming to inquire why he was so severe." (Calvin 1854, 158). Calvin goes on to argue that no excuse except the direct command of God could have exculpated Joshua "from the guilt of detestable cruelty, cruelty surpassing anything of which we read as having been perpetrated by savage tribes scarcely raised above the level of brutes" (Calvin 1854, 163).

Genocide and brutality, therefore, are morally justifiable, but not lying. Hence we find Calvin condemning Rahab not for her treachery and the resulting destruction of her fellow citizens but for lying to the king's officials sent to capture the spies, which, according to Calvin, can never be lawful, because "that cannot be right which is contrary to the nature of God. And God is truth" (Calvin 1854, 47). Her actions as a whole are still praiseworthy in Calvin's eyes, but not pure, for they are tainted by the lie. So, Rahab did wrong but "the principal action was agreeable to God, because the bad mixed up with the good was not imputed" (Calvin 1854, 47–48). Calvin does not make it clear why the bad—the lying—is not imputed to Rahab. He could mean that a bad act done with a good intention is not imputed to a person or he could mean that this particular bad act was not imputed to Rahab because it was an act within a series of acts that we can call "treachery" and this "treachery" was ordered by God. While it is probably true that Calvin meant the latter rather than the former (there is nothing else in Calvin to suggest that good intentions outweigh an evil act), the point that stands out is that lying, rather than wholesale butchery, causes Calvin the most concern. Such is the legacy of Augustine on lying.[1]

Augustine's influence went far beyond Christianity; we see it in the position taken by German philosopher Immanuel Kant, who followed the Western Christian tradition in making all lies a moral evil. Kant was not interested in the theological reasoning behind the Christian tradition, but he was concerned about the absoluteness of whatever is right and good and whatever is wrong and evil. For Kant, a lie is "an intentional and untruthful declaration to another person" (Kant 1949, 347). Every lie, whatever the motive, intention, or goal, and not matter who the lie is told to, is wrong because it is "against duty generally in a most essential point," namely the denial of the human dignity of the person lied to and of "mankind generally, for it vitiates the source of the law itself" (Kant 1949, 347). Kant is able to so argue because he held that truthfulness is the ground of all duties based on contract. Too, from Kant's foundational moral formula that we must always treat people as ends and never as a means, we conclude that lying is always wrong because it treats the person lied to as a means and therefore violates the dignity of both parties. The liar always undermines the basic duty human beings have toward one another. There can be no exceptions: "To be truthful (honest) in all declarations, therefore, is a sacred and absolutely commanding decree of reason, limited by no expediency" (Kant 1949, 348). One consequence of Kant's view is that we are guilty of no moral wrongdoing when, for example, we tell the truth to a murderer pursuing a victim and thus facilitate another murder, but we are guilty of moral wrongdoing if we lie to the murderer. As Kant argues, "he does no harm to him who suffers as a consequence" (Kant 1949, 348).

Kant's extreme view has two important points in common with Augustine. First, all lies harm what is essential to human dignity. The Augustinian school may put it in terms of the loss of the image of the Trinity, while the Kantian school may talk about the loss of "rational integrity (Bencivenga 2007, 54)," but they agree that every lie undermines what is essential to humanity. Second, those who tell the truth have no responsibility for the expected evil consequences of their truth-telling. On their view, telling a lie always has an evil consequence; namely, the undermining of human dignity. Telling the truth, however, does not always have an evil consequence, for you can never tell what is going to happen as a result of telling the truth. All you do know is that you have done no evil by telling the truth and you are not responsible for any evil consequences that may occur as a result of that truth-telling.

LYING AS A POSSIBLE GOOD

The other strand of Christian thinking about lying is found first in Eastern Christian Fathers, such as Clement of Alexandria (*Stromata* VII.9) and Chrysostom (*On the Priesthood* I.8 and *de Poenitentia* VII.5) and the Western Father Cassian (*Conferences* 17). These held with the ancients that lies told in public defense or in order save an innocent person's life were acceptable. Especially noteworthy for our purposes is Chrysostom's remark in *de Poenitentia* where he praises Rahab: "O beautiful falsehood, O beautiful deception, not of one who forsakes divine commands, but of one who is a guardian of piety" (author's translation).

Griffiths is right to point out that Chrysostom thinks of speech as a "morally neutral device to be deployed for good ends according to the demands of prudence" (Griffiths 2004, 141). But he is wrong to take issue with Chrysostom's comparative (with Augustine) inattention to the question of the purpose of speech. Chrysostom's assumption is that speech is for communication and that communication is a matter of justice and prudence, and this assumption, contra Griffiths, sits quite well with both Scripture and Tradition. This may be a comparatively thin theory of the purpose of speech, but thinness does not necessarily imply mistakenness, nor, it should be added, does thickness necessarily imply correctness. Griffiths is also wrong to argue that Chrysostom's view on speech could lead to the conclusion that sin could be praiseworthy and that it might be prudent in a given circumstance to break the second commandment of the Decalogue and blaspheme God. First, to argue that speech as a category of human action is neutral is not to argue that all actual spoken words are neutral. Speech, like most human acts, requires some description if we are to judge rightly its praiseworthiness or blameworthiness. Some acts can be judged very quickly, such as acts that contravene a clear commandment of God. One can hold Chrysostom's view on speech and also hold that blaspheming speech is inherently evil, as are all acts of blasphemy. Thus, blasphemy is a description of something that is inherently unjust. A similar example would be the relationship between sexual acts, which are neutral, and rape, which names an inherently unjust sex act. Thus, we can see why it is mistaken to suggest that the logic of Chrysostom's position would lead us to praise sin; for, in his view, lying is not always a sin.

We find Cassian agreeing with Chrysostom on Rahab and arguing further that, for her lies,

> whereby she chose to conceal the spies rather to betray them, she deserved to share an eternal blessing with the people of God. If she had chosen to speak the truth . . . there is no doubt that she and her whole household would not have escaped the approaching destruction and that she would not have deserved to be included among those responsible for the Lord's birth, to be numbered on the roll of the patriarchs. (*Conferences* 17.17.1–2)

For Cassian, then, Rahab is rewarded and given a place of honor precisely because she chose to lie. The truth is not something that should be spoken at all times to all people. Cassian, along with Basil the Great (*Homilies on the Psalms* 7.1), also approves of the false council given by Hushai (David's "mole" in Absalom's court) to Absalom (*Conferences* 17.19.5), and has this to say about the woman who hid David's spies in a well and lied to the men sent by Absalom to capture them:

> By this trick she saved them from the hands of their pursuers. Tell me, then, I ask you, what you would have done if a similar situation had arisen for you who now live under the Gospel. Would you have chosen to conceal them by a similar lie . . . thus fulfilling what is commanded, "Do not spare your help to save those who are being led to death and to redeem those who are being slain." Or by speaking the truth would you have given over those who were hidden to those who were going to kill them? What, then, of the apostle's words? "Let no one seek what is to his own benefit but rather to what is another's." And, "Love does not seek what is its own but rather what belongs to others." And what does he say about himself, "I do not seek what is beneficial to me but

what is beneficial to the many, so that they may be saved." For if we
seek what is ours and wish to hold on obstinately to what is beneficial
to us, we shall have to speak the truth even in difficulties of this sort,
and we shall become guilty of another's death. But if we fulfill the apos-
tolic command by placing what is helpful to others ahead of our own
wellbeing, without a doubt the necessity of lying will be imposed upon
us. (*Conferences* 17.19.6–7)

So, for Cassian, love may necessitate lying, just as, for Augustine, Aquinas,
Luther, Calvin, and so many others in the Christian tradition, love may
necessitate fighting and killing.

Arguing from the Augustinian perspective, Griffiths argues that Cassian's
position implies that the need to protect others from harm outweighs the
need to obey God's commands. However, Griffiths assumes that lying is
always disobedient to God's commands, which is precisely what Cassian
denies. Griffiths also objects to Cassian's position because Cassian argues
that the prima facie ban on lying can be overridden only with great serious-
ness, but he provides no way to check our fallen weakness to rely on the lie
as an easy solution to our problems. The weakness of the objection is that
Griffiths ignores the context of Cassian's work as a whole, which is clearly
and powerfully centered on the Holy Spirit-driven virtuous life of the Christian. The prudent person is the person who knows when to lie. Just and
charitable lying may well indeed be the sort of act that requires a great deal
of prudence, but that is no argument against the act, only a warning against
a too easy slide into a sort of lie that is the product of a lack of virtue.

Strangely enough, Luther, who followed Augustine (or at least believed he
was following Augustine) on most matters theological and moral, rejected
the Augustinian position on lying and sided with the Eastern Fathers and
Cassian. This was because Luther was always willing to part from Tradition, and even Augustine, when he found it clearly contrary to the teaching
of Scripture. Luther's discussion on lying occurs within his discussion of
Abraham's lies about the identity of his wife when he enters Egypt (Genesis
12:11–13) and Gerar (Genesis 20:2). Luther argues that lies told for the sake
of someone's good—and he refers explicitly to the lies of Hushai the Archite,
who was David's spy in Absalom's court (2 Sam. 15:34) and the woman by
the well who lied to protect David's spies (2 Sam 17:20)—are not really lies,
but rather "a virtue and outstanding prudence, by which both the fury of
Satan is hindered and the honor, life, and advantages of others are served"
(Luther 1960, 292). Luther follows the reasoning behind the Decalogue's
prohibition on lying, which suggests, as Luther maintains, that "strictly
defined, it is a lie when our neighbor is deceived by us to his ruin and own
advantage" (Luther 1960, 292). Luther expands this definition in a later
lecture when he argues, "there is only one kind of lie, namely, that which
harms one's neighbor in his soul, as the lie of Satan, in his body, or in his
possessions or reputation" (Luther 1961, 327). Hence, for Luther, the moral

goodness of lying—like the moral goodness of spying itself—takes its character from the rightness of those who authorize it (the rightful ruler of Israel
in this case), the justified cause, and the intention of the one who deceives
(to hinder the false kingship of Absalom, in this case, and to put the true
king back on the throne).

The influence of Augustine and Calvin on lying, rather than of Cassian
and Luther, was enormous in the Christian West until the time of Grotius
in the seventeenth century. Grotius is the one to recover in the Christian
West the ancient (and more Eastern) way of looking at these matters.[2] Grotius argues that the morality of pretense (deceit with actions) and falsehood
(deceit with words) is found in whether or not truth is owed to the person
to be deceived (*Laws of War and Peace* III.I.XI, hereafter cited as *Laws*). A
person, in short, may not be entitled to the truth in a given circumstance.
In other words, Grotius considers human speech a God-given skill to be
used for justice, which may or may not involve telling the truth to unjust
enemies. Justice, then, is the arbiter of who is entitled to the truth.[3] Thus,
for Grotius, one can speak a falsehood to one who knows it is a falsehood in order to deceive a third party who is eavesdropping (*Laws* III.I.XIII)
or lie to save innocent life (*Laws* III.I.XVI). Nevertheless, there are limits,
even for Grotius, who maintains that falsehoods cannot be justly extended
to promises and oaths. When we make a promise or oath, we establish a
relationship with God as well as other human parties. So, promises and
oaths must be kept, no matter how tempting it may be to break them (*Laws*
III.I.XVIII–XIX).[4]

Grotius's views did not die with him. Thus, we find the famous Anglican
divine Jeremy Taylor, a mere thirteen years after the publication of Grotius's
ground-breaking work, reminding his readers that lies to save the life "of
a useful and public person hath not only been done at all times, but commended by great and wise and good men" (Taylor 1828, 352). Taylor's
position deserves fuller attention, for it is one of the most thorough discussions on the subject since Augustine and is, in its own way, both a reply to
Augustine and Calvin's concern about lying and the nature of God, and
an anticipation of Bonhoeffer. Taylor wants to answer the question: can
truth be practiced at all times? Taylor is not convinced by the argument that
we ought always speak the truth because truth is the nature of God. God
always speaks the truth because it is his nature, he fears no one, and has
power to bring all his purposes to pass. Human beings are not God however
they may be conceived in the image of God. Their affairs are so ordered
that they have ends to serve, which are just, good, and necessary but cannot always be served by truth. For God, truth is always to the advantage of
charity and justice but this is not so for fallen human beings for whom truth
may be the enemy of charity and justice.

Taylor argues that any correct description of human speech must carry
connotations of justice. He follows Luther in culling his definition from the
Decalogue and argues that lying is "something said or written to the hurt of

our neighbor, which cannot be understood otherwise than to differ from the mind of him that speaks" (Taylor 1828, 351–52). So, Taylor argues, Holy Scripture includes our neighbor's rights and justice in the command to speak the truth. Speech reflects a universal contract in human intercourse that demands that we be just to those with whom we are speaking. Not everyone deserves truthful speech from us. Deceitful speech for the sake of charity in order to save the innocent is a good, and an act of justice toward those saved and toward those deceived if they did not deserve the truth. Telling the truth is not always an act of justice but only when it concerns something that is a real good to the person to whom we speak. When telling the truth is the cause of evil, then the person to whom we speak has no right to it. "Truth is justice when it does good, when it serves the end of wisdom, or advantage, or real pleasure, or something that ought to be desired" (Taylor 1828, 361). Truth-telling in the Trinity is always just because the Father, Son, and Spirit always deserve to have the truth told to them, but this is not the case with communication between all human beings in all circumstances.

Moreover, when we are in a state of war, deception is expected, and, so, it is lawful to deceive the enemy in war. Also, causing false rumors to be spread is an acceptable part of warcraft. Taylor uses Elisha's lie to the Syrian army as an example of a prophet of God intentionally deceiving the enemy of Israel in war (2 Kings 6:19). Thus, we can conjecture that Taylor would have no objection to tactics made possible by current cyber deception capabilities that allow us to falsify enemy communications such as email and voice over and IP server. However, Taylor does not argue that all lies and deception against enemies are morally acceptable. He follows Ambrose, Aquinas, and Grotius in making an exception in matters of treaties, contracts, promises, and agreements with the enemy.

Taylor argues that it makes no difference to his argument if one prefers the language of lesser evil or higher good. "Who," he asks, "would not save a good person from the rage of persecutors and tyrants?" Even if you look at this circumstance as one in which an evil is done to the person lied to, that evil is not as great an evil as betraying the innocent with the truth. To save a just person "is a higher justice than the obligation of telling the truth to the persecutor; to whom it is a great charity, if from him we take the power of doing evil, as it is justice to rescue the innocent" (Taylor 1828, 360–61). Thus, you even do good to those lied to in this circumstance because you prevent them from doing further evil.

Taylor, like Luther, sometimes appears to argue that, properly speaking, what he has been discussing as good lies are not really lies at all. Taylor defines a proper lie as words spoken with the intention to deceive someone to their harm and who does not deserve that harm. Thus, the lie, in the proper sense of the term, is always unjust and Taylor even cites Augustine as his authority. However, deceptive speech and practice aimed at those who do not deserve the truth are not lies proper, even though Taylor occasionally slips and uses the term in the looser sense. He argues that there is a prejudice against lying because of the meaning and evil sound of the word; we think that malice always accompanies a lie and, therefore, it appears hard to justify. However, malice in war is lawful. Taylor insists, "in war it is no lie, but an engine of war against when the enemy is to stand upon his guard" and that faking speech in combat is not morally different than faking a blow (Taylor 1828, 372).

We find Taylor's concerns taken up in more recent times by Sissela Bok, who argues that we can deceive in order to prevent a crisis from occurring (for example, Allied deceptions against the Axis in World War II). As Bok argues, "Whenever it is right to resist an assault or threat by force, it must be allowable to do so by guile" (Bok 1978, 144). Once hostilities commence, all sides expect deception, which means it is de facto public. Because such deceptions are public there is little chance of them disrupting the basic, everyday expectations of truthfulness that make life tolerable.

Dietrich Bonhoeffer, a Lutheran theologian who joined the German counter-intelligence corps (the Abwehr) during World War II and participated in a plot to assassinate Hitler, began writing a paper on truth-telling that he never finished but is nevertheless instructive. Bonhoeffer takes up this question broached by Luther and Taylor about what really counts as a lie and asks the question, "What is meant by telling the truth?" He thinks the Augustinian tradition on lying results in *reductio ad absurdam*, which issued most infamously in German philosophical circles in Kant's position that one ought to tell the truth even if to a killer seeking his victim. Thus, a lie cannot simply be "a deliberate deception of another man to his detriment," because that would mean that we would have to say that "lying" is what occurs when we deceive the murderer or the enemy in war (Bonhoeffer 1965, 368–69). If this is a lie, then lying acquires a potential moral justification that conflicts with the accepted meaning of the term. For Bonhoeffer, telling the truth means something different according to the situation in which we find ourselves. Similar to Grotius and Taylor, Bonhoeffer brings in justice as the arbiter of what sort of speech people deserve. We must ask, "whether and in what way a man is entitled to demand truthful speech of others" (Bonhoeffer 1965, 363). According to Bonhoeffer, when certain relationships ("orders of life") breakdown so that one no longer respects the other, "words become untrue." Bonhoeffer uses the example of a teacher questioning a child about a family secret. The teacher asks questions that should not be asked. The teacher has failed to respect the reality of the institution of the family. Should the child lie to protect the family secret, the child's lie would contain more truth (respect the reality of the institution of family and school, which has no right to family secrets), is in more accordance with reality, than if he betrays a family secret. Insofar as wrong is done in this communication, it is the teacher who is the wrongdoer. What the child has done is not "lying." Likewise, when we deceive murderers and our enemies in war, we have not "lied." Thus, Bonhoeffer follows Luther, in the sense that we should not describe what the agent does as "lying."

For Bonhoeffer, a lie is the deliberate destruction of the reality created by God. The purpose of our words is "to express the real, as it exists in God" (Bonhoeffer 1965, 370). For God's truth creates out of love while the so-called truth of Satan, which is revealing what ought not be revealed, is speaking words out of hatred and envy. True words "deny neither the Fall nor God's word of creation and reconciliation." How then do we speak the truth? By perceiving who causes me to speak and what entitles me to speak. By perceiving the place in which I stand. By relating this context to the object, which I am making some assertion. Thus, much like Chrysostom and Cassian, Bonhoeffer has situated his arguments about lying and truth-telling within a larger conception of the Christian as a Holy Spirit-formed character with the ability to see into the "essential nature of things" and know when the time has come to deceive.

Before moving on, I should point out the more permissive view of lying within Christianity makes much better sense of the Scriptural passages where lying is prominent than does the absolutist school. The Augustinian school certainly has on its side those portions of Scripture that make no bones about the evil of lying. However, the school founders on those portions of Scripture where noble lies, or praiseworthy deceptive speech, seem to be evident. The Augustinian school cannot avoid the criticism that it has assumed a definition of lying incompatible with that found in Scripture and that the view expressed by the Eastern Fathers, Luther and others better accords with Scripture where the prohibitions against lying are, as Luther and Taylor pointed out, fixed on those who would speak falsely against the innocent in order to injure them (see, for examples, Ex. 20:16; Lev. 19:11; Deut. 5:20). We might add that Augustine and Aquinas's interpretation of the passages in Scripture where lying seems commended as praiseworthy—in short, where they must try to deny the obvious—make for amusing and far-from-convincing reading.[5] We should also point out that Augustine's idea of speech as something governed by the Triune image of God has little scriptural warrant. In fact, speech as governed by justice seems a much easier scriptural fit. The scriptural narratives suggest that the more permissive side is right to argue that speech is simply a form of communication and may, therefore, be good or bad depending on what one is saying, to whom one is speaking, and in what kind of circumstance. Although exegetes may find some room to deny that certain biblical narratives obviously find lying praiseworthy, the narratives of the Egyptian midwives lying to the authorities, Rahab lying to the authorities, Hushai and others lying for the sake of David's regime, and Elisha lying to the Syrians are very hard to deal with for those who wish to deny that any narrative shows a praiseworthy lie. The examples of Rahab and Hushai are particularly telling. Although the narrative never explicitly says that Rahab's lies were good, the narrative is clearly one written to praise Rahab for saving the spies, helping Israel, and making a place for herself and family in the people of Israel, and she did this by lying. The narrative never hints at a blameworthiness of the act by which she is praised by the Christian writer of Hebrews (11:31). One cannot separate the means by which Rahab succeeded in doing her praiseworthy deed for Israel and the reasons she is held as a hero of faith. As the Puritan divine John Owen put it: what Rahab did was "in itself lawful, just, and good" (Owen 1960, 81). Hushai may even be a more formidable hurdle for the anti-lying exegetes. Hushai is presented as a hero in the narrative and his heroics are the products of lies and deception. He is, as Walter Bruegemann has written, a "master of double-talk" (Bruegemann 1990, 311). Hushai is presented as more than a mere agent of David's but an agent of God who uses Hushai as an answer to prayer to save David's kingdom from Absalom. In short, one is hard pressed to get around the obvious: praiseworthy lies are a part of the biblical narrative. The Augustinian school simply cannot handle the sacred text as convincingly as can the permissive school.

THE GOOD OF LYING OR WHY TRUTH TELLING IS NOT ALWAYS VIRTUOUS

We are now in a position to summarize why the more-permissive moral tradition on lying—that represented by Chrysostom, Cassian, Luther, Grotius, Taylor, and Bonhoeffer—is so morally compelling: love and justice, both to God and neighbor, are so well served by it. Thus, we find Chrysostom referring to Rahab as a guardian of piety, because justice to God in her circumstance meant deceiving an unjust person who sought to harm the just spies. In this view, lying to an unjust person may be what is owed to God. Thus, we find Cassian and Luther admiring the lies told by David's spies, because this is an expression of the highest possible good—charity—that can be sought in the circumstances. Cassian and Luther do not deny that telling the unjust the truth is a good, but in circumstances where the truth given to the unjust will harm the just, love motivates the desire to protect the just. On this view, one cannot practice charity toward the innocent neighbor when telling the truth is a vicious act that will harm the innocent. Thus, we find Grotius and Taylor reminding us that justice in truth-telling is telling the truth to those who are entitled to hear it. Thus, one cannot be just toward the innocent by giving information to the vicious that will prove harmful to the innocent; for the vicious are not owed such information and the innocent are owed the protection from harm. Thus, we find Bonhoeffer reminding us that God's truth judges created things out of love but Satan's out of hatred and envy, so that speaking betraying words—words of truth—to people like Nazis is not following the nature of God but of Satan. We follow the nature of God by speaking words that reflect the reality of the situation we face.

The normative sources that hold the more permissive view on lying do not reason from natural law, as do those who hold the more strict view. However, we can suggest how those on the more permissive side might answer those who hold the more strict view: they may deny that natural law demands truthful speech at all times. They could point out that in Aquinas's discussion of the natural law (*Summa Theologica* I–II Q.94), there is no mention made of lying. In fact, the prohibition on lying occurs in his discussion on justice (*Summa Theologica* II–II Q.110). In Aquinas's discussion of the natural law, he argues that the first principles of practical reasoning yield the formal principle to do good and avoid evil (*Summa Theologica* I–II Q.94, A.2). The content of that formal principle, at least in regards to acting justly, is specified in the Decalogue (*Summa Theologica* II–II Q.122). Aquinas interprets the prohibition on lying in the Decalogue as an absolute moral prohibition on using speech for deceitful purposes (*Summa Theologica* II–II Q.122, A.6), and, thus, is able to conclude that lying is forbidden by the natural law. Only then is Aquinas able to argue that speech is given to speak only the truth. In other words, there is nothing in what Aquinas argues about the natural law itself in *Summa Theologica* I.II. Q.94 that leads to the necessary conclusion that truthful speech is somehow a part of the natural law. That conclusion can only be drawn after Aquinas interprets the Decalogue as he does. But as Luther observed, this is not a persuasive interpretation of that portion of the Decalogue, which does not forbid all lying but the use of false speech to harm a neighbor. Hence, Aquinas's argument about truthful speech as part of the natural law is dependent on an interpretation of a command in the Decalogue that is far from convincing. For Chrysostom, Cassian, Luther, and their followers, speech is given for justice and love, neither of which can be achieved if our truth-telling to the vicious enables the vicious to harm the innocent. Thus, there is no necessary incompatibility between following the natural law and lying to the vicious for the sake of love and justice, when those lies are told by those whose duty it is to use such tactics when necessary, authorized by right authority and with right intention. When such tactics are necessary, then it is truth-telling and not lying that will require an explanation.

PRACTICAL MORAL ADVICE

We may find it useful at this point to consider an example of the sort of lie a spy might tell in order to show where all our moral advisors stand on this matter. Imagine yourself as an Allied spy posing as a shopkeeper in France during World War II. You have been called on to do many things: contact partisan groups, organize espionage activities, and even aid any Jewish refugees who may want to find friendlier places to live. Imagine further that, during a general roundup of suspects by the Gestapo, you are questioned about your activities. Telling the truth means death for partisans and Jews, and an end to useful operations against the German forces. Augustine says to tell the truth and leave injustice to the Gestapo. Deceiving the Gestapo would be a sinful assertion of your autonomy, an example of your sinful pride rearing its ugly head, an example of how you think you know better than God where your good lies. Aquinas says tell the truth, because not to do so would go against natural law. Aquinas, we must keep in mind, does not locate justice in the relationship between you and the innocent people you might save, but solely in the relationship you have with the one to whom you are speaking—the Gestapo agent. For Aquinas, the person you are speaking to, even a member of the Gestapo, is always entitled to the truth. Calvin would agree with Aquinas but would say more about not doing something contrary to the nature of God. Kant would point out that you demean the human dignity of the Gestapo agent specifically and undermine human dignity generally when you lie to him, and, besides, you are not guilty of wrongdoing when you tell the truth and you are not morally responsible for how the Gestapo agent acts on your information. We may lose many lives by telling the Gestapo agent the truth, but as one of Kant's more recent interpreters puts it, we would be giving up something more important than our lives if we lied, we would be giving up our "rational integrity" which is the basis of our dignity as human beings. Thus, we should never contradict rational standards even "in the face of Hitler" (Bencivenga 2007, 54).

You find such advice troubling because it seems to contradict virtue: for prudence, justice, and charity would seem to indicate that the relationship between you and the innocent people you might be able to save is more worthy of consideration than the relationship between you and a Gestapo agent. However, there are other moral advisors. The Greek and Roman ancients; the Eastern Fathers Clement, Basil the Great, and Chrysostom; the Western Father Cassian; Luther; Grotius; Taylor; and Bonhoeffer are of one opinion: lie. All would agree that virtue demands a lie in such cases. Cassian and Luther would emphasize that lying in this case is an act of love. Taylor would point that, while human beings are in the image of God, they are not God, and that the goals of the spy in this conflict against Nazis are just and good and these goals cannot be served by the truth in this circumstance. Human dignity is not undermined by such lies. On the contrary, it is affirmed whereas truth to the Gestapo agent does undermine human dignity, for it wrongly affirms an equal worthiness of the Gestapo agent in comparison with the innocent people he intends to harm. All would emphasize that justice is not achieved by betraying the innocent and aiding evildoers. Bonhoeffer, who actually had some hands-on experience with Nazis, would point out that Nazis are enemies of just and peaceful order and work to destroy the reality created by God.[6] True words (deceiving words) by the agent deny neither the Fall, in the sense that the agent perceives the reality of the situation created by the evil regime, nor God's word of creation and reconciliation, in the sense that the agent is working toward the good and protection of a just and peaceful order. The agent perceives who is causing him to speak and what entitles him to say these words in this circumstance. He perceives that he is a just combatant facing an evil regime. The object is saving the lives of innocent people. Love and justice, then, can be found in the spy who aids the innocent by tricking the guilty.

PROBLEM CASES

The more permissive position on lying is quite convincing and accords with contemporary concerns about how one might go about justifying lies. Sissela Bok, for instance, argues that lying has a negative impact on trust and social cooperation and, as such, needs justifying. Bok makes a persuasive argument that any society must maintain a basic principle of veracity, which holds that "truthful statements are preferable to lies in the absence of special considerations" (Bok 1978, 30). The principle places the burden of proof on lies to be justified. As Bok points out, the principle does not necessarily override all others but it does lead us to insist that all reasonable truthful alternatives have been considered. Bok argues that the justification for lying must be aimed at "reasonable persons" (Bok 1978, 91). Any moral statement must be capable of public statement and defense. She makes much of this concept of publicity, for it challenges private assumptions and hasty conclusions. The Golden Rule is a test of publicity, for we can ask if we would wish to be lied to in like circumstances. Publicity "would remove the self-righteous belief in the unquestionable necessity for their lies" (Bok 1978, 100). Her argument about the need for public justification squares well with the permissive school's idea that speech is a form of communication and a matter for justice to decide on how it ought to be employed. As an act of justice, then, deceitful speech must be capable of defense before others, as are all moral acts that bear on the common good. Convincing ourselves that our deceptions are just is not good enough, for we prefer ourselves and are not good judges when our success is at stake.

A word of caution is nevertheless necessary. Lying is the sort of practice that can get out of hand in a hurry. Thus, Bok is right to argue that in professions where crisis situations are frequent, such as the clandestine services, unjust deceptive practices are more likely to spread to the harm of "self, profession, clients, and society" (Bok 1978, 120). Self-serving motives have to be clearly addressed in order to set clear professional standards. Lying to enemies can be considered just because of retribution and defense. Too, enemies who act unjustly forfeit their ordinary right to be treated fairly. However, enemyhood can be bestowed too freely and paranoia can result.

Self-preservation is the main rationale for military secrecy. Nevertheless, there must be criticism or legitimacy will never be distinguishable from excess. Thus, Bok rightly argues that, "Every effort must be made to press public officials to justify their case for secrecy, to produce reasons, and to show why particular practices of concealment are necessary" (Bok 1982, 203). In this view, information about the origins and conduct of a war should never be kept secret. Bok is surely right about making public all relevant information about the origins of a war. However, we might be cautious about sharing all information about a war's conduct. For example, the misinformation and deceptions used to trick Nazi Germany before the D-Day invasion were so successful that it would have been foolish to share this information with the public. Once such information is made public, the tactics are rendered useless. Justifications ought to be forthcoming from the government, but such justifications cannot all be equally public. Appropriate committee review must suffice when the information would hinder justice.

Lying to One's Own Citizens

A popular argument against all forms of deception in a democracy is that, "In principle, deception and democracy are inimical" (Barnes 1990, 320). The basic idea is that, since all citizens have a say in the policies of a democratic government, they cannot exercise that privilege well if they are deceived about the facts of a given circumstance. Hence, a citizenry deceived is a citizenry manipulated and ruled. None of this is to say that citizens cannot see the advantage of and even agree to temporary deceptions. The argument is that a government's deception of the enemy, and even of its own public to a lesser extent, is legitimate in wartime, but only so long as the deception is temporary and subsequently explained. The moral excuse for such deceptions is basic survival. One could not win a war without some amount of deception of the enemy and even one's own citizens.

The problem in the Cold War was that the conflict between the democracies and communist states created a climate of war with no foreseeable end, barring the total collapse of one side, in which tactics justifiable only in time of war (always "hot" wars in the past), were applied. The same might be said about the War on Terrorism, which alternates between hot and cold, depending on chance and opportunity. What the Cold War and the War on Terrorism have in common is their resistance to a tangible conclusion. The problem is more acute in the War on Terror than it was in the Cold War. At least the collapse of the Soviet Union meant an ostensible end to the Cold War, but what will count as the end of the War on Terror? The elimination of a fanatical form of Islam? The elimination of all known terrorist gangs? Or simply a marked decline in their operational activities? The Soviet threat was treated as a "hot" enemy to be combated with tactics justifiable in the arena of fighting a hot war, and those tactics include lying and deception. We have treated the War on Terror in the same way. In order to justify "hot" operations in a "cold" war or in the War on Terror, one must show that the enemy is just as dangerous hot or cold, or at least nearly so. In other words, if some enemy nation state or terrorist gang poses a serious enough threat, then those countries would be justified in using "hot" tactics, such as lying and deception, in order to defend themselves. Nevertheless, deception in cold war and in the War on Terror must be treated as a kind of quasi-hot war operation that reflects the reality that the war is not actually "hot." This means that, while deception may be justified as a necessity in the War on Terror, it should not be employed indefinitely. Otherwise, the deception can become self-justifying, with no end in sight as long as the enemy still exists. Thus, in the apt words of Barnes, "To be an unqualified success, deception by a democracy in peace-time must be used like a medicinal but addictive drug: little and under continuous supervision" (Barnes 1990, 321).

Lying to Allies

We may also be tempted to lie to our allies. Christopher Felix describes an operation in which the United States supported a monarchist group in Eastern Europe (Felix 2001, 112–13). The CIA wanted information about Eastern Europe and, in order to get that information, led the monarchist group to believe that the United States was interested in helping the group to achieve its goals, when in fact the United States merely wanted information. In short, the United States deceived an ally in order to get information from that ally. Felix justifies the practice based on the notion that these sorts of deceptions are part of the game and that all players run the risk of being deceived in this way when they agree to play. In other words, the monarchist group knowingly entered into a game in which the rules stipulate that the players are not always entitled to the truth. Thus, the monarchist group is not treated unjustly when it is deceived. However, we need to remind ourselves of the negative weight of lying and deception, which is the breakdown of trust and social cohesion. Even among the various intelligence communities, there must be some level of trust if they are to engage in successful cooperative ventures. Deceiving allies cannot help but foster an air of mistrust among all those who would think about doing business with the United States. In this particular case, the United States could have been open about its goals in entering into a relationship with the monarchist group, and admit that it wanted information and was willing to help the group to some extent for that information. That help could have taken many forms (money, training, equipment, information, etc.) that would have been attractive to the group. Either the United States did not wish to risk a rebuff from a group that might have demanded more than it was willing to give, or the United States is so used to deceiving in such circumstances that it merely followed form in an unreflective manner. We can only hope it was the former, which, at worst, would merely show bad judgment about one case rather than a weakness in the very character of those calling the shots with other clandestine groups. In either case, there is a definite lack of right intention even if right authorization and just cause are present.

Propaganda

Breakdown in trust and social cohesion is an especially important worry when we engage in gray-and-black propaganda, for people can begin to cease to believe anything that is told to them. Citizens do not knowingly enter into a game with their government in which they expect to be deceived, at least not in peacetime. Citizens tend to think that they are always entitled to the absolute and full truth. Gray propaganda distorts facts that come from a secondary source. A good example of this sort of propaganda and the uses to which it can be put is the use of the notorious Protocol M document in Great Britain in 1948.[7] As the Cold War started to form in the late 1940s, Britain and the United States began to see that answering the false accusations and claims of the Soviet Union were not very effective, even when good and truthful answers were forthcoming, because the damage was already done by the public nature of the accusations. Once news has been put out that someone, or some country, is engaged in nefarious deeds, the thought has been planted and distrust sown in all but the closest of allies. Thus, Britain and the United States decided to retaliate with like weapons. British Foreign Minister Ernest Bevin created the Information Research Department in the Foreign Office to create propaganda. Protocol M was a document with the alleged Soviet plans to disrupt the Marshall Plan for German recovery. The British handlers knew the document was a fake, but Bevin used it for three reasons: (1) to counter an imminent Soviet threat to the British occupation zone in Germany; (2) to remind his own country, and particularly a government that might be too Soviet friendly, of the Soviet threat; and (3) to give a timely push to the Marshall Plan that was being debated in the US Congress. As Ollivant shows, the information was leaked in such a way that the mere news of the document, without any express confirmation on the truth of such by anyone in the government, had the desired effect on the three points.

Unlike gray propaganda, the black variety is a complete fabrication of message and source. One notorious form of black propaganda occurred during World War II when the OSS used what was known as "sibs" (from the Latin word for "whisper") to loose rumors among certain populations meant to confuse them and get them to lose confidence in their government. Some were outrageous, such as the rumors planted about Hitler and Mussolini being queer for each other. Others, less outrageous and therefore more effective, included the rumor aimed at causing friction within the Axis alliance in which it was widely spread that Mussolini was preparing to run to the Swiss for political asylum as soon as the Allies invaded Italy. Kermit Roosevelt, Jr. reports that the sib was so effective that the US minister in Bern requested that the State Department give the information "careful protection" (Roosevelt 1976, 215).

Any justifiable use of propaganda, gray or black, must weigh the negative effects and decide whether or not the goal is worth the harm. Probability of success should play a role in the decision-making process. Success in these cases is measured by expected effectiveness. Let's return to the above examples. When we look at the Protocol M case, we would want to know how likely the goals of the leak were to be achieved and was it leaked in such a way as to deflect concern from citizens that their government is lying to them. In this particular case, there is every reason to believe that the goals would be achieved. Also, the document was never used as a basis of policy. Bevin was able to use false claims about Soviet intentions in such a way that it was not very likely to create distrust and break down social cohesion. Thus, the

British government did not use Protocol M with any intention to harm its citizens, but rather used it to lessen the likelihood of any harm. When we turn to the Mussolini case, we would want to know whether or not there was enough existing mistrust between the Italian and German governments to make the propaganda likely to cause worry among the Germans. Was Mussolini considered to be the sort of person to make the propaganda believable? In this case, there was enough mistrust between the two governments, and Mussolini was a volatile enough character, to make the propaganda likely to achieve its desired effect of causing further friction between the two.

Lying to Eliminate Enemy Agents

Lies are sometimes used to eliminate enemy agents. One popular way to get rid of enemy agents is to fabricate evidence that will lead to them being eliminated by their own service or another. These are lies told in order to harm proper targets. Former CIA operative James Olsen argues that the tactic is justifiable if such agents cannot be caught by other means, and if the evidence is fabricated in such a way that it does not compromise non-agents, particularly friends and relatives who could become targeted if the evidence is not carefully created with their protection in mind (Olson 2006, 131). This satisfies Bok's principle of veracity in so far as the deception is not resorted to without considering other means. The operation also meets the criterion of discrimination in so far as it is planned with the express intent of bringing harm only to the target. We can judge intention in the operation by observing how the plan is worked out. If sufficient care is taken, no one other than the target should be harmed. The only problem occurs when we are dealing with troublesome enemy agents who work for a government that routinely eliminates the families of agents proven treacherous. In such cases, any sort of evidence fabricated with the intent to eliminate the enemy agent may also eliminate the agent's family. This is roughly like the dilemma faced by bombers who must strike targets that have been deliberately placed in population centers. The difference is that in the latter case, the enemy places innocents in harm's way for the express purpose of using them as shields, relying upon our moral queasiness at killing innocent people, whereas in the spy case, the government may establish such a brutal policy merely as a way to ensure that its agents behave themselves. In other words, in the spy case, the enemy government probably enforces such a brutal policy concerning the families of spies not only as a way to prevent us from achieving our goals against them but also as a way of controlling the behavior of their own agents. Such moves have indirect but intended consequence of making our goals against them harder to achieve. Nevertheless, the principle of double effect probably exculpates us from the moral guilt, in some cases. Eliminating a dangerous enemy agent who cannot be dealt with in any other way is a good kind of act. The unintended effect—the elimination of family—is not a means to the goal and we gain nothing by it. The real question in such cases is whether the elimination of a particular enemy agent is worth the collateral damage to the innocent. This would have to be decided on a case-by-case basis, but we can probably rule out such methods against low-level operatives when there are significant risks to the innocent.

Lying to Possible Recruits

Lying to possible recruits for intelligence services or operations poses different problems. George Bull tells how he was given the task of interviewing West German scientists in order to determine whether they were the sort of people who would be useful recruits for gathering intelligence in communist countries (Bull 1995, 63–69). Such tasks consist of three levels of deception. First, agents must devise a believable reason for initiating the interview process. Second, agents cannot allow potential recruits to realize that they are, in fact, being interviewed. Third, agents must preserve their own cover throughout the process. So, the people interviewed in this way are deceived about the reason for the conversation, what the conversation is really all about, and the identity of the person with whom they are talking. This is a case of eliciting your own citizens or allies through deception. We can see why it is desirable for the interviewer to deceive: the interviewee could go public and blow the agent's cover and technique. We may argue that the interviewer does not lie with any intent to harm the interviewee and that the level of deception does not cause any harm to the interviewee. The autonomy of the interviewee is overridden but it is hard to argue that it has been overridden to an intolerable degree, at least if the information elicited is used purely for the purpose stated (identification of possible recruits) and the information is not used against them for any other purpose. For, we can imagine a slip by the interviewee in which some secret is revealed (or suspected by the agent, who certainly will have the skills and wherewithal to look into the matter) that would put the agent in a position of power to blackmail the interviewee into doing some job.

We must also consider the deception that may be involved if the recruiter continues to deceive the recruit about the nature of the employer. Miles Copeland reports that it is not unusual for prospective agents to think they are working for government X, when they have really been recruited to work for government Y (Copeland 1978, 128–29). We can imagine a scenario in which, say, a Palestinian official is recruited by a US agent under the guise of working for France. The ruse is thought necessary because the Palestinian official, though ripe for use as an agent, is known to detest the US. Such "false flag" recruitments, as David Perry calls them, put the prospective agents at risk for reasons unacceptable to the recruit and serves as a form of coercion, presumably because the recruit's autonomy is not respected (Perry 2009, 139–47). One may counter that all citizens willing to reveal secret information about their country are proper targets in the spy game. Such citizens certainly put themselves in harm's way if they express a willingness to share information with foreign governments.

Lying to Superiors

Most intelligence officers are like employees in any other profession: They wish to keep their jobs and they know that they must please their masters if they are to remain employed. This poses an acute and perennial problem for intelligence personnel; namely the temptation to tell their masters what they want to hear whether it is accurate or not. Giving information you know to be inaccurate is lying, but it is, within the intelligence profession, the worst kind of lie because it undermines the profession's *raison d'etre*. Intelligence-gathering professionals exist in order to give accurate information, whether it is pleasing to those who receive it or not. Intelligence personnel who knowingly report inaccurate information to political leaders responsible for acting on their reports are similar to soldiers who turn on their own citizens. In both cases, a profession that is justifiable only because it protects its citizens does work harmful to that citizenry. When soldiers are given blatantly unjust orders to fire on their own innocent citizens, they must disobey, even if it means a court martial. Intelligence personnel must report to their superiors what they consider to be the truth, even if it means getting fired by unjust and ignorant supervisors or political leaders. Such a move may take considerable wisdom and courage, but we hope such virtues are sought and possessed by our intelligence-reporting personnel.

CONCLUSION

Lying may be a moral good in some circumstances, but we should remind ourselves of the context of Cassian's defense of the noble lie: only the virtuous can be trusted to know when and how to lie (and when to tell the truth regardless of the consequences). Ideally, spies should possess the sort of character than enables them to know when to lie in the line of duty and to resist the temptations to lie in the line of duty when not necessary or to lie when not acting as a spy, or to lie to superiors in order to save their jobs. Put differently, spies need to be shaped by the virtues of wisdom, justice, courage, and self-control. Only those spies shaped by the necessary virtues will be able to know when not telling the truth is what is owed to neighbors, both good and bad.

NOTES

1. The Augustinian argument, though held by Calvin, was not always accepted by the Reformed followers of Calvin. Thus one finds the nineteenth-century Puritan theologian Thomas Boston treating the Decalogue commandment against lying in a distinctly Lutheran manner that concentrates on the element of lying in order to harm an innocent neighbor (Boston 1853, 434–35).

2. The Christian East had no need to recover because they never followed Augustine. Contemporary Eastern Orthodox philosophers and theologians treat Western notions of lying as evidence of the West's overly legalistic and pietistic development. See, for example, Engelhardt 2000, 289.
3. We may be tempted to use what Aquinas argues about private property in order to construct an argument about lying similar to what we find in Grotius. For Aquinas, human ownership of property is not a part of the natural law but rather is specified by human, positive law. There is no sin—no theft— in taking another's private property when necessary, for "need has made it common" (*Summa Theologica* II.II Q.66, A.7). Thus, our private property is not something we are entitled to in an absolute sense. When others are in need, they may take from our surplus what they need, because necessity makes them entitled to what is necessary. In other words, what is owed to the person in need specifies what is just in the circumstance. Similarly, one could argue from the same principle that the truth is not something we are entitled to in an absolute sense. Necessity may demand a lack of truth, and, thus, what is just in speech would depend upon circumstances. Aquinas, however, does not make this argument because private property, unlike speech, is not part of the natural law. The entitlement argument for lying is incompatible with the belief that human truthful speech is part of the natural law.
4. On this point, Grotius is in agreement with Aquinas's argument, which is actually derived from Ambrose (*On Duties* II.7.33) that all agreements with the enemy must be kept (*Summa Theologica* II–II Q.40, A.3).
5. Aquinas argues that the those portions of Scripture that seem to praise those who lie should not be understood in a literal sense but in a mystical sense; thus, the lying words of people such as Rahab should be understood as containing "mystical truth" (*Summa Theologica* II–II Q.110, A.3). We find the same reasoning in Augustine's *On Lying* 33.
6. In a similar vein, Bok argues that when society is in collapse, one lie will not "add to the chaos or the degradation" (Bok 1978, 112). Public debate in these circumstances is pointless.
7. I have taken the facts of the case from Ollivant 1990, 275–96.

BIBLIOGRAPHY

Ambrose of Milan. (1926). *On Duties*. Ca. 391. In *Nicene and Post-Nicene Fathers of the Christian Church*. First Series, vol. 10, edited by Philip Schaff. Buffalo, NY: The Christian Literature Company.

Aquinas, Thomas. (1948). *Summa Theologica*. 1256–1272. Translated by the Fathers of the English Dominican Provence. New York: Benziger Brothers.

Augustine. (1947). *Enchiridion*. Ca. 420. In *Fathers of the Church*, vol. 2. New York: Fathers of the Church.

——. (1983a). *On Lying*. Ca. 394. In *Nicene and Post-Nicene Fathers of the Christian Church*. First Series, vol. 3. Edited by Philip Schaff. Grand Rapids, MI: Wm. B. Eerdmann's Publishing Company.

——. (1983b). *Against Lying*. Ca. 420. In *Nicene and Post-Nicene Fathers of the Christian Church*. First Series, vol. 3. Edited by Philip Schaff. Grand Rapids, MI: Wm. B. Eerdmann's Publishing Company.

Barnes, Trevor. (1990). "Democratic Deception: American Covert Operations in Post-War Europe," in *Deception Operations: Studies in the East-West Context*, edited by David A. Charters and Maurice A. J. Tugwell, 297–324. London: Brassey's.

Basil the Great. (1963). *Homilies on the Psalms.* Ca. 320. In *The Fathers of the Church.* Vol. 46. Washington, DC: Catholic University of America Press.

Bencivenga, Ermanno. (2007). *Ethics Vindicated: Kant's Transcendental Legitimation of Moral Discourse.* Oxford: Oxford University Press.

Bok, Sissela. (1978). *Lying: Moral Choice in Public and Private Life.* New York: Pantheon Books.

——. (1982). *Secrets: On the Ethics of Concealment and Revelation.* New York: Pantheon Books.

Bonhoeffer, Dietrich. (1965). *Ethics.* New York: Macmillan.

Boston, Thomas. (1853). *The Complete Works of the Late Rev. Thomas Boston,* Vol. 7, edited by The Rev. Samuel M'Millan. London: William Tegg & Co.

Brueggemann, Walter. (1990). *First and Second Samuel.* Louisville, KY: John Knox Press.

Bull, George G. (1995). "The Elicitation Interview," in *Inside the CIA's Private World: Declassified Articles from the Agency's Internal Journal 1955–1992,* edited by H. Bradford Westerfield, 63–69. New Haven, CT: Yale University Press.

Calvin, John. (1854). *Commentary on the Book of Joshua.* 1560. Translated by Henry Beveridge. Edinburgh: Calvin Translation Society.

Cassian, John. (1997). *Conferences.* Ca. 429. In *Ancient Christian Writers.* Vol. 57. New York: Paulist Press.

Charters, David A., and Tugwell, Maurice, A. J. (eds) (1990). *Deception Operations: Studies in the East-West Context.* London: Brassey's.

Chrysostom, John. (1802). *Homiliae IX de Poenitentia.* Ca. 385. In *Patrologia Cursus Completus Series Graeca,* vol. IXL. Paris: J. P. Migne.

——. (1926). *On the Priesthood.* Ca. 387. In *Nicene and Post-Nicene Fathers of the Christian Church.* First Series, vol. 9, edited by Philip Schaff. Buffalo, NY: The Christian Literature Company.

Clement of Alexandria. (1956). *Stromata.* 212. In *Ante-Nicene Fathers of the Christian Church.* First Series, vol. 2, edited by Philip Schaff. Grand Rapids, MI: Wm. B. Eerdman's Publishing Company.

Copeland, Miles. (1978). *The Real Spy World.* Sphere Books. Sussex: Sphere Publishing.

Engelhardt, H. Tristam, Jr. (2000). *The Foundations of Christian Bioethics.* Netherlands: Swets & Zeitlinger Publishers.

Felix, Christopher. (2001). *A Short Course in the Secret War,* 4th ed. 1963. New York: Madison Books.

Griffiths, Paul J. (2004). *Lying: An Augustinian Theology of Duplicity.* Grand Rapids, MI: Brazos Press.

Grotius, Hugo. (1925). *The Laws of War and Peace.* 1646. Translated by Francis W. Kelsey. Oxford: Clarendon Press.

Homer. (1996). *The Odyssey.* Translated by Robert Fagles. New York: Penguin Books.

Kant, Immanuel. (1949). *Critique of Practical Reason and Other Writings in Moral Philosophy.* Translated and edited by Lewis White Beck. Chicago, IL: University of Chicago Press.

Lucian. (1921). *Lover of Lies.* In volume III of *Lucian,* Loeb Classical Library. New York: G. P. Putnam's Sons.

Luther, Martin. (1960). "Lectures on Genesis: Chapters 6–14." 1536. In *Luther's Works.* Vol. 2. Edited by Jaroslav Pelikan. Saint Louis, MO: Concordia Publishing House.

——. (1961). "Lectures on Genesis: Chapters 15–20." 1536. In *Luther's Works.* Vol. 3. Edited by Jaroslav Pelikan. Saint Louis, MO: Concordia Publishing House.

Ollivant, Simon. (1990). "Protocol 'M'," in *Deception Operations: Studies in the East-West Context*, edited by David A. Charters and Maurice A. J. Tugwell, 275–96. London: Brassey's.

Olson, James M. (2006). *Fair Play: The Moral Dilemmas of Spying*. Washington, DC: Potomac Books.

Origen. (1897). *Homilies on Judges*. Ca. 244. In *Die griechischen Christlichen Schriftseller der ersten Jahrhunderte*. Vol. 30. Berlin: Akademie-Verlag.

Owen, John. (1960). *An Exposition of Hebrews*. 1671. Evansville, IN: Sovereign Grace Books.

Perry, David L. (2009). *Partly Cloudy: Ethics in War, Espionage, Covert Action, and Interrogation*. Lanham: Scarecrow Press.

Plutarch. (1876a). *Marcellus*, in *Lives of Illustrious Men*, 216–229. Translated by Dryden. Boston: Little, Brown and Company.

——. (1876b). *Sulla*, in *Lives of Illustrious Men*, 321–338. Translated by Dryden. Boston: Little, Brown and Company.

Polybius. (1927). *The Histories*. Translated by W.R. Paton. New York: G.P. Putnam's Sons.

Roosevelt, Kermit, Jr. (1976). *War Report of the OSS*. New York: Walker.

Taylor, Jeremy. (1828). *Rules of Conscience*. 1659. In *The Whole Works of the Right Rev. Jeremy Taylor*. Vol. 13. London: Thomas Davison, Whitefriars.

Virgil. (1990). *The Aeneid*. Translated by Robert Fitzgerald. New York: Vintage Books.

Xenophon. (1946a). *Boyhood of Cyrus* in *Cyropaedia*, 1–132. Translated by E.C. Marchant. Cambridge, MA: Harvard University Press.

——. (1946b). *Art of Horsemanship*, in *Scripta Minora*, 295–364. Translated by E.C. Marchant. Cambridge, MA: Harvard University Press.

4 The Justifiability of Covert Operations
Four Case Studies

A nation may wish foreign powers to do something or refrain from doing something that bears on the security of that nation. When overt uses of influence are deemed unwise in such situations, covert methods become attractive. The President of the United States, for example, possesses constitutional leeway to ensure for the security of the United States by planning and executing "activities conducted in support of national foreign policy objectives abroad" in such a way that "the role of the United States government is not apparent or acknowledged publicly" (Daugherty 2004, xv). Put as simply as possible, covert action is "influence" in which the initiator of the operation is veiled. The rationale is that the foreign entities we wish to help would suffer in some way if knowledge of that help were made public. The US constitution gives the President latitude to support the national interest in foreign affairs by various means, including military operations, without the declaration of war. Similarly, the Prime Minister in Great Britain had recourse to SOE (Special Operations Executive) throughout World War II for behind-the-lines activities. After the war, SOE was absorbed into MI6 with paramilitary functions given to the elite SAS group, which works closely with MI6. Covert operations offer the opportunity to nations such as the United States and Great Britain to influence foreign entities with a broad range of activities that fall between, on the one side, more overt measures such as diplomacy and economic incentives, and on the other side, military intervention. The founding US presidents all resorted to covert operations when they felt the need, so the tactic can hardly be thought of as new. Nevertheless, worries about the nature of various covert operations beginning in the 1950s led US lawmakers to formulate the Hughes-Ryan Amendment of 1974, which requires the President to justify proposed covert operations as important for national security.

Constitutional questions aside, there are good moral arguments against carrying out any covert operation. Covert operations usually involve interfering with the autonomy of another nation. Thus, all such operations carried out in peacetime are illegal. Also, the foreign entities we wish to aid may not be entities with present sovereignty and every covert operations carried out without the express consent of the sovereign leaders of the nation is a violation of that nation's autonomy. Thus, covert operations in neutral or friendly countries can be morally troubling. In this chapter, I analyze four covert operations in order to explore the contours of what may count as a justifiable covert operation. I first look at the operation in Italy in 1958, instigated to prevent communists from taking over the country. This case serves as a means of introducing the main analytical elements that help us examine the moral issues crucial for deciding the justice of covert operations. I then turn to the operations in Iran in the early 1950s and Chile in the 1960s–1970s, also instigated with the primary goal of preventing communist rule. Finally, I turn to the operations in Poland in the early 1980s, initiated to bolster the Solidarity movement, in order to topple communist rule in Poland and, ultimately, throughout Eastern Europe.

OPPOSING COMMUNISM IN ITALY

A good example of early Cold War covert operations is described by ex-CIA head William Colby, who was involved in an effort to prevent Italy from being taken over by communists in the 1958 elections (Colby 1978, 109–35). The Soviet Union was covertly aiding the Italian Communist Party with funds that amounted to more than $40 million a year. The United States decided to back opposition parties through the CIA. Strictly speaking, as Colby admits, the operation was illegal, but illegal means were thought necessary to counter the illegal tactics used by Moscow. The CIA sought to defeat the Communist Party by providing aid to the center parties and allowing these parties to govern in any way they saw fit. According to Colby, there were never any strings attached to CIA help that pulled the center parties to follow American directions. The goal was simply to keep the communists out of power.

One of the morally troubling aspects of this operation is that it interferes with the autonomy of Italy. The tactic poses an additional problem if we wish to subject it to the logic of the just war criteria, for the "battlefield" here is in a neutral or friendly sovereign state.[1] This puts the United States in the position of justifying its intervention in such a way that it can claim that Italy is given its due by that interference. Autonomy is such an important moral and political principle that interventions must be justified and, as Michael Walzer has argued in more recent times, the burden of proof is on political leaders who intervene (Walzer 1977, 86). Walzer helpfully explores the limits of the moral and political principle of autonomy through John Mill's argument against intervention in *On Liberty*, where Mill argues that nonintervention is the principle that guarantees that a self-determining community remains self-determining. The problem, as Walzer points out, is that "it isn't always clear when a community is self-determining" (Walzer 1977, 89). In the present case, the Soviet Union had already intervened so extensively in Italy that it is at least doubtful that Italy was a self-determining community at the time of the United States' intervention. Intervention may be justifiable when another foreign power has already intervened. Counter-intervention is justifiable, Walzer argues, if we "always act so as to recognize and uphold communal autonomy" and we consider the risks to the people. In short, just counter-intervention requires respect for autonomy and proportion.[2]

Another pertinent question is whether or not it is ever just to do something that is illegal. Of course, we may question the law itself. Aquinas, for instance, argues that any law that is not a just law may be broken without harm to justice, for in such cases there is no true law to be broken, but only a perversion of law (*Summa Theologica* I–II Q.95, A.2). This is a good argument for breaking unjust laws, but it is hard to make the case that the law against interference in a sovereign government's affairs is an unjust law. Not all just laws, however, can be kept with absolute fidelity if we wish to achieve justice. This is what Luther is concerned about when he argues, "There are so many cases and so many exceptions to any rule that it is difficult or even impossible to decide everything accurately and equitably. This is true of all laws; they can never be formulated so certainly and so justly that cases do not arise which deserve to be made exceptions" (Luther 1967, 100). For Luther, an absolute fidelity to the written rule or law may defeat justice. So, not every act of breaking a just law is a form of injustice. Wisdom and justice must work together if we wish to know when and how to bend or break a law. Thus, Luther argues,

> In Greek this virtue, or wisdom, which can and must guide and moderate the severity of law according to cases, and which judges the same deed to be good or evil according to the difference of the motive and intentions of the heart, is called *epieikeia*; in the Latin it is *aequitas*, and *Billichkeit* in German. Now because the law must be framed simply and briefly, it cannot possibly embrace all the cases and problems. This is why judges and lords must be wise and pious in this matter and mete out reasonable justice, and let the law take its course, or set it aside, accordingly. (Luther 1967, 100)

Are the virtues of wisdom and justice on display in this operation? On his side, Colby has the fact that an enemy nation—the Soviet Union—was using illegal means to subvert the law of noninterference, and those means had to be countered by like means if the United States wished to do anything about it. This seems to make moral sense to us, for we tend to agree with Luther and Bonhoeffer that prudence sometimes dictates that breaking the law for the overall good is just, especially when breaking the law achieves what the broken law is trying to achieve but could not achieve unless it is broken, under the given circumstances. Put differently, legality does not exhaust morality. Here we have a case where the law was insufficiently applied to an enemy nation and, thus, necessitated interference in order to restore the status quo, which is the very thing the law is trying to protect. In this case, by breaking a law, the CIA actually restores the order of non-interference that the broken law is trying to protect.

The sort of moral reasoning displayed here is compatible with that found in W. D. Ross's position that some moral principles produce prima facie obligations rather than absolute obligations (Ross 1930). The argument in our case is that the law of noninterference produces a prima facie obligation not to interfere with the government of another nation, but the obligation can be overridden when good reasons can be offered. However, we must be careful whenever we think we have good reasons to override a prima facie obligation. Here we can see how the logic of prima facie obligations as a part of practical reasoning is compatible with an ethic of virtue. The virtues of justice and love work in a complimentary fashion such that the just act is, ideally, always the loving act. The ideal, unfortunately, is not easy to achieve. Aquinas, for example, argues that unruly passions can lead to bad action in the imperfectly virtuous (an accurate description of most human beings); thus, a person of virtue (imperfect virtue) may still have trouble figuring out what is the right thing to do in a given circumstance.[3] In order to see how this is so, we need to understand how the virtues and passions work together in the virtuous person. For Aquinas, practical wisdom or prudence is the exercise of reason applied to right action (*Summa Theologica* II–II Q.47, A.4), but prudence is dependent on the other moral virtues, especially self-control and courage, for right operation. Self-control is the virtue that restrains the passions of the concupiscible appetite that incline us to pursue the suitable and avoid the harmful (*Summa Theologica* II–II Q.141, A.1). Courage is the virtue that restrains the passions of the irascible appetite that incline us to resist whatever prevents us from obtaining what is suitable or promotes the harmful (*Summa Theologica* I–II Q.61, A.2, II–II Q.123, A.1). The passions can be calmed by reason applying cognized principles to a particular occasion (*Summa Theologica* I Q.81, A.3). Thus, we may need a set of intellectually cognized checks in place to prevent an easy slide into simply justifying whatever expediency recommends, which is exactly the sort of danger we may encounter when we are tempted to intervene in a situation where some good is likely to accrue to us or where some harm to us is likely to be avoided. The sort of checks that would be useful in our case are those offered by Beauchamp and Childress (1994, 34), for they are precisely the sort of checks that may enable us to justify counter-intervention. They are:

1. Better reasons can be offered to act on the overriding norm than on the infringed norm.
2. The moral objective justifying the infringement has a realistic prospect of achievement.
3. No morally preferable alternative actions can be substituted.
4. The form of infringement selected is the least possible, commensurate with achieving the primary goal of the action.
5. The agent seeks to minimize the negative effects of the infringement.

In this case, the defense is that Italy is already being interfered with by one foreign power and that further interference by another foreign power is meant to restore Italy to the desired state of noninterference. If the CIA does not intervene, then Italy will continue to be manipulated by the Soviet Union and will not govern in a state of noninterference. The CIA did have a realistic prospect of achieving their goal of restoring Italy to a state of non-interference. There were no realistic alternatives short of open and armed hostilities. The decision to use covert action rather than open action suggests that the infringement was the least possible in the given situation and was commensurate with achieving a free Italy. Finally, in this case, the CIA minimized the negative effects of the infringement in two ways: first, by backing the center parties rather than right-wing parties that may have been more malleable in US hands, and second, by using action in which there were no strings attached, which means that autonomy is returned to Italy as soon as the Soviet-backed party is defeated.[4] In this way, the United States could make the plausible argument that justice was done to Italy by interfering with Italy's elections.

The positive stance exhibited here toward the covert operation in Italy and, later, in Poland and (to a lesser degree) in Iran, should not be read as blanket approval for all such actions. The goal of the chapter, in fact, is not to justify any particular covert operation but simply to make the case that covert operations are possibly justifiable. In exploring the contours of what may or may not count as justifiable covert operations, one must assume a certain set of facts about the case to be true. In every case of a covert operation, the facts can be hotly contested. Naturally, as the facts change, so do our moral judgments. In order to show how covert operations might be justifiable, I have assumed certain facts to be true that show the interventions in the best light possible. For example, I have assumed that Colby has told the truth about the lack of strings attached to the backed political parties. For it is precisely the lack of strings attached that allows us to claim that the infringed sovereign power's autonomy has been trumped temporarily for its own good; that is, in order for true sovereignty to be returned to the country. Hence, one of the main hurdles in justifying any covert operation is to be able to make a persuasive case that the country in which the operation takes place will have justice done to it through that operation. This is a high mark to set for covert operations, but justice demands it. Let us now turn to other cases to test the limits of justifiable covert operations.

REPLACING MOSSADEQ IN IRAN

The Eishenhower administration, fearing a Russian takeover of Iran, approved a plan originating from Britain's MI6 to overthrow the Soviet-influenced prime minister of Iran, Mohammad Mossadeq, and install the prime minister of the Shah's approval, Fazlollah Zahedi. Why the United States decided to enter into a joint operation with Great Britain requires some background information. In the months following World War II, the Soviet Union refused to comply with agreements made with the United States, Great Britain, and Iran to withdraw its troops from northern Iran. Moreover, the Soviet Union armed the communist Tudeh party and refused to allow the Shah to crack down on the party even after a failed revolt in 1945. Clearly, the Soviet Union was interfering with the sovereignty of Iran even at this early stage. Soviet troops finally left in 1946 but still gave full support to the Tudeh party and put in considerable time, effort, and money to rebuild it into a major influence on Iranian policy. The Tudeh party gave full support to Mossadeq as choice of a new prime minister in 1951 and, in the words of CIA operative Kermit Roosevelt, Jr., "provided him with a street army of well-trained thugs" (Roosevelt 1979, 90).

Mossadeq became prime minister in May 1951 and immediately nationalized the oil industry, thus causing great alarm to Great Britain, which was the majority owner of the Anglo-Iranian Oil Company. Mossadeq rejected an offered joint settlement proposal by US President Harry S. Truman and British Prime Minister Winston Churchill, and another offered by US President Eisenhower and Churchill. However, even before Eisenhower took power in 1952, the United States was beginning to become alarmed at the Soviet influence over Mossadeq. Truman had good reasons to believe that Mossadeq was allying himself with the Tudeh (Roosevelt 1979, 56, 79). By 1953, Mossadeq had formed an alliance with the Soviet Union in order to expel the Shah and take over as sole ruler himself. In February 1953, Mossadeq used Tudeh power to try to force the Shah to leave, but the action was unpopular with the people and he began to lose support. In recent months, the Tudeh had increased its influence in the Mossadeq government. Eisenhower was not persuaded by Mossadeq's pleas for more aid to keep out the communists precisely because he believed that Mossadeq was allowing the communists to grow stronger as means of keeping power himself. By this time, the Soviets were manipulating Mossadeq in so blatant a manner that they were, according to Roosevelt, "flaunting" their power in Iran in an attempt to intimidate the United States into simply letting the Soviets have their way (Roosevelt 1979, 119). In fact, one reason why the joint operation worked so well was because Mossadeq was viewed by the army and by much of the populace as someone receiving full backing by the Soviet-influenced Tudeh party.

Averell Harriman had been sent by former-president Truman to negotiate with Mossadeq and got nowhere. This diplomatic failure was taken by CIA head Allen Dulles as a clear sign that conflict was inevitable between the West-backed Shah and the Soviet-backed Mossadeq. After an October 1951 meeting with Truman and Dean Acheson, the latter came away from the meeting thinking Mossadeq a fanatic and more than a little unbalanced, especially when it came to the British (Acheson 1969, 504). Eisenhower's Secretary of State would share the same opinion and Ambassador Loy W. Henderson too considered Mossadeq a "madman." Roosevelt believed that the Soviet threat in Iran was "genuine, dangerous and imminent" and that Mossadeq was an "unwitting ally of the Soviets" (Roosevelt 1979, 11–12). The Eisenhower administration accepted Roosevelt's report and the plan (AJAX) proposed by MI6 chief director Sir John Sinclair. The CIA agreed to AJAX but wanted control over the operation since the United States was footing the bill.[5] Nevertheless, Eisenhower made it clear that if the operation were successful, the Shah would be under no obligation to the British on the petroleum issue.[6] The United States also insisted that the Shah should be able to choose Mossadeq's successor, even though they knew the likely choice was not going to be a popular one either to the British or to the United States. Thus, the motivating factor in moving against the Mossadeq government was one of combating communism and not a gain in oil concessions. True, Great Britain was hoping that the overthrow of Mossadeq would lead to a better deal for them over oil concessions, but that played little or no role in US plans. A glance at a map suggests why the joint powers were so concerned about a Soviet takeover of Iran: if the Soviets controlled Iran, they would control the Persian Gulf. Roosevelt reports a conversation he had with the Shah in which he made it clear that Zahedi was the Shah's choice and was by no means forced upon him. Roosevelt made it clear to the Shah and Zahedi that Iran was under no obligation to the United States or Britain for their actions. As far as the joint powers were concerned, the removal of Mossadeq and the Soviet threat was payment in full.

The operation was a relatively smooth affair. The CIA publicized the Shah's replacement of Mossadeq with Zahedi. A pro-Zahedi military group seized radio stations. Air Force General Hedayat Guilanshan led a column of tanks to a CIA safehouse to pick up Zahedi. They seized army headquarters and marched on Mossadeq's home. Three hundred people were killed.

Let's now summarize the main points that will help us critique the operation. The United States and Great Britain believed that Soviet control of Iran posed serious threats to the peace and wellbeing of the area and, thus, indirectly, to the security of the United States and Great Britain. The government of Mossadeq was aligned with and being manipulated by the Soviets. An alternative reading of the facts could lead us to conclude that the US simply doubted Mossadeq's ability to deal with an imminent Soviet-backed Tudeh coup.[7] In any event, what cannot be denied is that the United States was genuinely concerned about the Soviet threat. Negotiations with Mossadeq failed. General Zahedi was the Shah's choice for replacing Mossadeq, despite US and British worries about him. No obligations were placed on Iran for help. The Iranian people and army wanted the change in government.

Right authority was certainly met in this case. The heads of state in both the United States and Great Britain signed off on the operation. The intention was to bring to power an Iranian government that would keep out the Soviets. The cause was certainly just if the Soviets posed a genuine threat to the area; for, in that case, Iran would be getting its just due by preventing

Iran from being ruled by a Soviet-backed government. The evidence presented to the Eisenhower administration warranted genuine concern that the Soviets were already manipulating the Iranian government.[8] There was also reasonable prospect for success because the Iranian people and army did not desire Soviet influence and would back the Shah against Mossadeq. The question of the likelihood of the success of the mission is not easy to answer. In one sense, there was every likelihood of success, if success is measured by the goals of a counter-coup that would bring into power a government in Iran that would resist communist influence. However, the actions fostered a great deal of hatred, especially by the religious community, toward Great Britain and, in particular, the United States for interfering in the government of Iran. This hatred for the United States and the Shah who freely accepted US help went unabated throughout the United States' involvement in Iran, and contributed to the religious fanatics taking power in the late 1970s. However, we must keep in mind the consequences of refusing to act in Iran in the 1950s, which was a possible communist takeover. As troubling as the region has been since the 1950s, and especially since the overthrow of the Shah in Iran, the alternative of a Soviet puppet-state controlling the Persian Gulf is infinitely worse. Discrimination and proportion seem to have been met as well. There was no overkill in the sense of paramilitary aid or of targeting the innocent.

The law of noninterference was overridden for the sake of restoring Iran to a sovereignty not being manipulated by the Soviets. Iran under the Mossadeq government was not entirely self-determining, for the Soviets were manipulating his government, whether Mossadeq was fully aware of it or not. The communists in Iran were not in as strong a position to dictate to the government as they were in Italy at the time, but they were still in a position to move the government toward Soviet-friendly policies that would have, if left unchecked, inevitably led to Soviet domination in the area. There was a realistic prospect of achieving the goal of returning Iran to a sovereignty not manipulated by the Soviets, the United States, or Britain. There was no morally preferable action. Truman and Eisenhower attempted without success to negotiate with Mossadeq. The form of infringement was the least possible commensurate with achieving a Soviet-less Iran. We can see this by the very actions taken in the operation. After it was determined that Mossadeq was not able or not willing to deal with the Soviet influence in his government, the United States could have simply demanded a puppet in the government. The very fact that the United States allowed the Shah to choose General Zahedi over their own as well as British objections suggests that the joint powers were determined not to act in a heavy-handed manner in Iran. The negative effects of the infringement were minimized, partly due to the insistence not to use a heavy hand and demand a puppet, or at least more amenable prime minister. Also, the joint powers determined that the Iranian people wanted the very results desired by the joint powers.[9] There was no effort to impose on the Iranian people a kind of government or head of government that they did not desire themselves. Also, the joint powers did not carry out a military operation to impose its will on Iran. No overt force was used. Moreover, the force encouraged and supported by the joint powers was commensurate with getting the job done and no more.

The exploration of some counter arguments to the above would be useful in fleshing out the morality of the operation in Iran. One of the main arguments that could be brought to bear on the way I have summarized the operation centers on the character of Mossadeq. In an excellent synopsis of the events leading up to the events of the counter-coup, Gasiorowski maintains that Mossadeq was a liberal democrat and a nationalist. This picture is reinforced by Bill, who paints Mossadeq as a statesman squarely within the political middle. The party led by Mossadeq (the National Front) was a coalition of groups made up largely of urban middle-class and lower-class people. The main opposition group was the communist Tudeh party. This seems to counter the notion that Mossadeq's government could be overly influenced by the communist Tudeh party. Gasiorowski and Bill are not absolutely clear about this, but they seem to suggest that the British are responsible for planting the idea, first in the Truman administration and then in the Eisenhower administration, that the Mossadeq government was drifting toward communism. Moreover, Mossadeq was a popular leader with a stable government, which seems to belie the notion that the people and army would be ready to topple him.

Whether Mossadeq's party is more correctly described as liberal democrat or not is beside the point. Whatever description fits Mossadeq's party best, the United States and Great Britain believed that Mossadeq's government was being manipulated by the Soviets and at least partly through the Tudeh party. Roosevelt believed that Mossadeq was being duped, while Bill argues that the United States simply had no confidence that Mossadeq could resist a Soviet-backed takeover, but this is not important. Willing or unwilling, Mossadeq appeared to be heading a government that was on the path of being controlled by the Soviets. This is an important point; perhaps the most important to justifying the operation, and for two reasons. First, in order for the case to be made that justice was done to Iran by the operation, we must be able to show that Iran's government was not entirely autonomous but was, in fact, being manipulated by the USSR or at least in imminent danger of falling under Soviet control. For when it comes to assessing probability of success, scholars such as Gasiorowski and Bill argue that the overthrow of Mossadeq ended the slow progress of Iran toward a more democratic form of government. However, Gasiorowski's synopsis of the events, in particular, ignores the fact that that the Soviets were playing an effective role in getting their will imposed on the government and would have continued to do so at an ever-increasing rate. The Soviet Union was not going to leave Iran to govern itself. They had made this clear from the actions they took in the immediate aftermath of World War II and from all their subsequent actions in the region. As to just how popular Mossadeq was, intelligence predictions about the people and the army overwhelmingly backing the Shah against Mossadeq proved correct. The attempt to portray Mossadeq as a leader with the will of the people behind him simply will not suffice. In July 1953, Mossadeq had to stoop to rigging a referendum in order to stay in power. When in August 1953 the Shah replaced Mossadeq with Zahedi, Mossadeq refused to step down (which, by the way, makes the operation not a coup, for that occurred when Mossadeq was officially discharged but remained in power against the sovereign will of the Shah, but rather a counter-coup, and thus the appropriately titled book by Roosevelt) and became a rogue in power. The people clearly sided with the Shah and Zahedi.

Gasiorowski brings up another issue with US involvement that might call into question the need for the United States to overthrow the Mossadeq government (if not the need for no sort of operation in Iran). He argues that, while the United States had no significant economic interest in Iran before the 1950s, by 1950 two factors made Iran a place of consequence in US eyes: the growth of the communist Tudeh party and the growing unrest in the region caused by the nationalization of the oil industry by Mossadeq. Truman had determined by 1951 to keep Iran out of communist control and to stabilize the world oil market. However, according to Gasiorowski, "These goals did not call for undermining the Mossadeq government" (Gasiorowski 1987, 267). Under Truman, the CIA implemented a covert action plan—the BEDMAN program—in order to weaken the Soviet position in Iran. Truman also tried to influence Mossadeq on this issue through diplomacy. As we have seen, the diplomatic measures were a failure. The BEDMAN program employed propaganda and political action in order to turn popular opinion against the Soviets and the communist Tudeh party. The trouble with the program, as Gasiorowski sees it, is that it also weakened the National Front, even though that party was not communist. Gasiorowski can explain this apparent inconsistency of US policy only by conjecturing that the director of BEDMAN or other lower operatives were acting against the policy desires of Truman (Gasiorowski 1987, 83). However, there is not a shred of evidence to suggest that Truman and Acheson, who were usually on top of intelligence matters, were not kept in the know about the workings and results of BEDMAN. Even if reports of BEDMAN's workings were not forthcoming to Truman and Acheson, they could hardly fail to notice what was happening to Mossadeq's government as a result of BEDMAN if, indeed, it was a result of BEDMAN. There is a reason why the British felt so confident about US help in removing Mossadeq when they first sent chief MI6 officer Montague Woodhouse to Washington to seek that help in November 1952. The very effort suggests that the British had good reasons to think that the United States could be persuaded that it was time for Mossadeq to go for the best interest of everyone—including Iran.

The Iran case highlights is the necessity of popular support in the targeted country. Popular support is necessary both to show that the people are having justice done to them by this interference and for probability of success of the operation. The case also demonstrates how tricky it can be to establish whether or not, or how much, a country's sovereignty has been compromised by existing interference. One reason why the Iran operation is harder to justify than the one in Italy is that the Soviets were not so obviously influencing the Mossadeq government as they were backing and influencing communist candidates in Italy. We also notice the continuing importance of a "hands-off" policy with regard to the government that does come to power as a result of a covert operation. The joint operation in Iran is justifiable insofar as Roosevelt has been truthful about the lack of strings attached to the Shah and truthful about Zahedi being the Shah's true choice without coercion of any kind from the United States and Great Britain. Lastly, we begin to see that what counts as success in a covert operation is not always easily determined. Any realistic criticism of a covert operation must place a limit on how far in the future one must be able to see when one plans an operation. No one in the early 1950s could have foreseen what was to happen in the 1970s when the Shah was overthrown by religious factions. Neither could those who blamed the 1970s upheavals on the 1940s-50s operation foresee that, by the end of the century, the Iranian young people would become much more pro-West and pro-American and, therefore, presumably not much concerned with the events leading up to the removal of Mossadeq. Moreover, it is difficult to prove that the overthrow of Mossadeq led directly to the events of the 1970s. Even Bill admits that the United States had plenty of time and opportunity to change tactics in Iran after the counter-coup in order to influence change toward a more just government. In fact, it is with much less difficulty that we can believe that Iran would have become a Soviet puppet without the counter-coup. Such an effect was immediate, foreseen, and planned against, for that was the very purpose of the operation.

TRACKS I AND II IN CHILE

President John F. Kennedy initiated covert action in Chile in 1961 to back the center Chilean Christian Democratic Party. The Kennedy administration approved what is known as Track I, in which the CIA used propaganda and political influence much along the lines as the operation in Italy. The Kennedy administration argued that its actions were done to preserve Chilean constitutional order from the extremists on the left and right and to promote the growth of democratic institutions. Since the election battle came down to Salvador Allende and Eduardo Frei Montalua, it came down to preserving the constitutional order from extremists on the left with a center party candidate. The aid to Frei had to be covert so that he would not be discredited. The CIA rejected proposals to carry out a coup or use other means of overt force.

However, by 1970, the Christian Democratic Party had become more leftist and Frei could not serve again as president. Allende seemed likely to win the next election. US President Richard M. Nixon and Secretary of State Henry Kissinger wanted to prevent this, because they feared that "Chile would become a haven for communist operatives" and undermine other countries in the area (Barry 1992, 23). Allende won the popular vote and covert action, known as Track II, was begun in order to prevent him from taking office. Nixon ordered the CIA to assist in a military coup. CIA head Richard Helms thought that there was no more than one chance in ten of success but still approved of an operation in which the CIA encouraged Chilean military officers who opposed Allende to revolt.

On the face of it, the Track I operation seems more easily justifiable than does Track II. For both operations, there was right authority. The CIA did not act on its own initiative in either operation and was, in fact, a somewhat-reluctant participant in Track II. Just cause was certainly upheld in Track I, which was to prevent the spread of communism in a country already being interfered with by the Soviets and to facilitate the growth of democracy in a country whose present constitutional order was being threatened by a Soviet-backed party. Right intention also seems to have been met in Track I with the clearly stated objective of protecting Chile's constitutional order from extremist on both the left and right. True, as Krisian Gustafson has shown, the United States' primary aim was to keep the Marxist Allende out of power (Gustafson 2007, 1). Nevertheless, the United States backed a center party candidate (as it had done in Italy) and refused to use overt means of force. Probability of success was met, because Frei was popular with the people and could run a stable government. Discrimination and proportion are more problematic, even in Track I. Barry argues that there was no need for black propaganda if Allende truly was aligned with the Soviets. So there was no need to deceive and, as Bok has pointed out, deception requires justification, for it carries negative effects in itself. If Barry is right, then the black propaganda did not meet the criteria of proportion because the negative effects outweigh the good. Barry has a strong argument if Allende was not aligned at all with the USSR or was aligned with the USSR in so obvious a way that widespread publication of the truth would have worked just as well (as it would later work in Poland). The black propaganda could only have been justified if Allende was aligned with the USSR in such a way that publication of the truth would have received no real court of hearing among the people. The truth, in other words, would have been unconvincing because truth, as the cliché goes, can indeed be stranger than fiction. In such a case, black propaganda could be justified if it is keeping in line with the general truth of what is being alleged. So, for example, if Allende was aligned with the USSR and the black propaganda declares such an alliance in ways that are merely untrue in detail, then it could be justified.

Barry also argues the operation failed to meet the criterion of last resort. However, if we think of the criterion of last resort (a dubious criterion that is noticeably absent in the classical just war tradition) as one that calls for every reasonable means short of force to be tried if proportion is to be met, then we may say that the United States met this criterion, at least in Track I. We may conclude that, in the main, the United States attempted to do justice to Chile in the Track I operation. The United States succeeded in protecting Chile from losing its sovereignty to the Soviets and did not attempt to manipulate the governing structure in a way that gave the US a role in covertly governing the country.

The Track II operation is much less justifiable. Whether there was a just cause or not would depend on how we answer two questions. First, how likely was Chile to become a haven for communist operatives in the wake of an Allende victory? Second, how concerned was the United States with protecting Chilean constitutional order from extremists from both the left and right? Barry poses another just cause challenge by pointing out that the CIA had argued that no tangible economic loss would accrue to the United States if Allende took power, nor would a significant shift of the balance of world power take place between communism and democracy. However, the challenge does not address the original concerns of the Kennedy administration to get involved in the first place and that was to protect Chilean constitutional order and promote democratic institutions. Moreover, Barry admits that the CIA had also warned that an Allende victory would mean a considerable political and psychological blow (Barry 1992, 23–24). So, when we turn to the two main questions concerning just cause we may plausibly argue that, at best, the Nixon administration was right to be concerned about the results of an Allende victory but did not concern itself sufficiently with protecting Chilean constitutional order from extremists, as the results would show. In fact, the little concern for Chilean constitutional order also betrays a lack of right intention, which played out in a predictable fashion, with violations of discrimination and proportion. Lacking the intention to benefit the Chilean people for the good of the Chileans as well as the United States and the cause for democracy, the operation was conceived and carried out without counting the costs for the Chilean people and without concern for the kind of government that would take power. Perhaps most damning of all is the obvious lack of the probability of success. The head of the CIA gave the operation only one chance in ten of succeeding.

When we turn to the criteria that help us figure out if we are right to override moral norms about autonomy and international law concerning the inviolability of sovereignty, we again find Track I more justifiable than Track II. Were the operations initiated at least partly for the sake of preserving or creating a genuine Chilean sovereignty? We may answer in the affirmative for Track I but not for Track II. Did the moral objective of each operation have a realistic prospect of achievement? Again, we may answer in the affirmative for Track I but not for Track II. Were there any morally preferable alternatives? Oddly enough, we may answer in the negative for both operations, but we must remind ourselves that all the proposed actions surrounding the decision for Track II were bad. Hence, this should not be read as an approval of the operation. Was each operation the least possible form of infringement? This is more difficult to determine and much may depend on whether one agrees with Barry's assessment of Track I that black propaganda was not needed. There is no difficulty in determining that Track II does not pass the test. Were the negative effects minimized? We may answer in the affirmative for Track I, for the CIA backed a center party candidate, did not engage in overkill (questions about black propaganda aside), and employed the quickest and most effective path to the goal. Track II fails miserably on this front. There was little concern beyond keeping Allende out of power. True, as David Perry argues, the Chileans might not have objected to Allende being removed because he undertook unconstitutional actions and was a determined enemy of democratic structures (Perry 2009, 173), but there was no protection from the extremists from the far right.

We can glean from the operations in Chile that, as we move further away from a state of already compromised sovereignty, even more so here than what we saw in Iran, we make the operation that much harder to justify. We also begin to notice how a decided lack of moral virtue at the highest level can lead to questionable tactical decisions. In fact, the Track II operation can serve as a model of action decided on by those who, according to Aquinas, lack the moral virtues necessary to keep the unruly passions in check. The Nixon administration acted in anger and fear. Nixon did not heed his own head of CIA, the man in the best position to know about the likelihood of success of the operation. The administration did not try to do justice to Chile, as much as it tried to prevent the communists from taking power at any cost to the Chilean people.

LOOSENING THE SOVIET HOLD IN POLAND AND THE EASTERN BLOC

The Reagan administration continued the policy of the Carter administration with regard to its position on Poland. The United States threatened the Soviet Union with stern warnings and economic sanctions in the event of overt Soviet intervention in Poland. However, by October 1981, the Soviets had increased their covert influence throughout the Polish government and ruling communist party. The Soviets were trying to get the Polish government to institute martial law and crack down on the Solidarity movement. On December 12, 1981, while the Solidarity National Commission was meeting, the Polish government declared martial law and began making political arrests. The United States and NATO decided not to react with overt force. However, the United States used CIA-gathered information to make sure that everyone knew what was going on in Poland, particularly how ruthless the Soviets had acted in suppressing political opposition. The CIA had provided reliable information that exposed the Soviet regime as aggressive and oppressive. Robert Gates argues that the Soviet action in Poland actually served to bring NATO members closer together, which in itself probably hastened the decision to deploy INF (Intermediate Nuclear Forces) and, more importantly, started the Reagan administration thinking about how to employ covert operations in Eastern Europe for the first time in more than twenty years (Gates 1996, 236–37).

Reagan ordered the CIA to support the Solidarity movement as a way to weaken Soviet hold in Eastern Europe. The immediate goal was to sepa-rate the Poles from the Warsaw Pact and to encourage them not to fight in support of the Soviets. Reagan believed that if the Soviets lost Poland, they would eventually lose most of Eastern Europe and even their own hold in Russia itself. William Casey, Reagan's CIA director,[10] helped to form an alli-ance between the Reagan administration and Pope John Paul II, with the express purpose of turning back communism in Eastern Europe and Central America. Reagan and Casey realized that the pope was the one person to have access to all the various sides in Poland and was, therefore, in an excel-lent place to give and pass on crucial information.

The covert operation called for the CIA to provide Solidarity with "print-ing materials, communications equipment, and other supplies for waging underground political warfare" (Gates 1996, 237). The CIA also provided modest support to moderate members of Solidarity that would support the US policy to end martial law, release political prisoners, and, in its own words, "re-establish a social contract with the Polish people" (Gates 1996, 238). In March 1985, the CIA smuggled into Poland 40,000 postcards with a photograph of Father Jerzy Popieliusko, who had been murdered by the communist security services. In May 1985, the CIA arranged a pro-Solidarity demonstration at a soccer match and made sure that the televi-sion cameras got good views of the large pro-Solidarity banner. The CIA made available to Poles hundreds of copies of the map used by Hitler and Joachim von Ribbentrop and Soviet foreign minister Vyacheslav Molotov to divide up Poland between them, thus exposing Soviet intentions against Poland, even to the tune of doing a friendly deal with Nazi Germany. How-ever, the covert operations focused mainly on providing materials to publish underground papers and letters and taking out and distributing speeches and articles by underground leaders by paper or transmitting them over the radio. In violation of international law, the CIA sent coded messages over Radio Free Europe and Voice of America. The CIA also began what Gates calls a "worldwide propaganda effort" to expose all the human rights abuses in Eastern Europe and to trumpet the work of the resistance (Gates 1996, 450).

The covert operations in Poland appear to be a model of justifiable use of covert force. There is no question about right authority being met. The CIA acted on orders from the Reagan administration. The cause was certainly just in that the goal was to bring about the end of Soviet oppressive domina-tion in Eastern Europe and to promote democracy in Poland and the rest of

Eastern Europe. Right intention was met and evident in the actions taken by the CIA. Probability of success is more problematic. President Ronald Reagan, Casey, and the pope certainly thought the program could succeed, but it must be admitted that their beliefs flew in the face of accepted popular opinion on the issue. This brings us to the issue of who exactly gets to determine the probability of success for acts of force. In the end, the head of state must take the responsibility, based on the information available and advice from cabinet-level individuals. We saw that the Track II operation in Chile failed at this point because the one person in the best position to judge the likelihood of success, the head of the CIA, believed the operation had little chance of success. In the case of Poland, both the head of CIA and the pope—the one man who, in the words of Bernstein and Politi, "had access to all sides of the equation in Poland believed that the operations would succeed" (Bernstein and Politi 1996, 289). Finally, discrimination and proportion were observed throughout the operation.

The covert operations in Poland overrode the law of noninterference for the sake of creating a more-just form of government, not only for Poland but also for all of Eastern Europe. The communist government that ruled in Poland was excessively oppressive. The Reagan administration had good reasons to believe that their goals were shared by the Poles themselves. As Bernstein and Politi point out, Reagan did not envision overthrowing the communist government on behalf of the people, even if that could be done without initiating World War III, but by helping the Polish people do it themselves. So Reagan and the pope discussed how to keep Solidarity and other underground opposition forces going in the face of Soviet oppression and even avoid a successful Soviet crackdown. The basic idea was that "the natural political and economic forces" would create the Polish split from the Warsaw Pact and the Soviet Union (Bernstein and Politi 1996, 287). Reagan and Pope John Paul II both believed that the Soviet Union and its satellites were on the verge of collapse and all it would take is more pressure to bring about the inevitable fall. Poland was thought to be the best place to bring about this extra pressure, because of the popularity of Solidarity and other underground elements within Poland. There was no morally preferable alternative. In fact, there was no practical alternative at all, short of risking overt war with the Soviets. The form of infringement was the least possible in that there was no use of paramilitary forces and not even advice on how to govern Poland. Opposition forces already existing within Poland were merely aided and the Soviet actions and policies were exposed. The negative effects were minimized, in the sense that the covert operations enabled Solidarity to take its own course in changing Poland. Similar to the operation in Iran, though even easier to justify, the consequences sought by Solidarity itself were the benefits sought by the United States. The Reagan administration was certainly seeking a regime change in Poland and expected more good than evil to result if done by way of covertly aiding an existing and very popular opposition force and, so, avoiding goading the

Soviets to invade and occupy. Thus, the change made was sought without resort to a bloody revolution and allowed Polish citizens to take control of their own government.

The moral features of the operations in Poland hearken back to Allied operations in Nazi-occupied France during World War II. Poland was a Soviet satellite with little existing autonomy, much like the Vichy government in France after the German occupation. In both cases, the Allies decided to back existing underground elements. The great difference is that the United States was at pains to avoid using overt force in Poland, precisely because it wanted to achieve its goals without resorting to open warfare with the Soviet Union. Reagan was right about Poland. In the end, the decision is the head of state's to make and we must hope that the person elected to that highest office possesses enough moral virtue to know when the time has come to order a covert operation.

CONCLUSION

Allen Dulles once argued that covert operations were reasonable when faced with a great power that is openly antagonistic to the rest of the world and uses its power to bring down foreign governments (Dulles 1977, 221). In such cases, covert action would be acceptable if it was effective, appropriate, and if no other means were available that were as effective and appropriate (Hilsman 2000, 20). Former Secretary of State Cyrus Vance echoed this ideal when he argued that covert operations should be "absolutely essential to the national security" and when there is no other way to achieve that end (Goodman 2000, 34). In looking back at the four covert operations discussed in this chapter, we find that their justifiableness, in so far as they are justifiable, coheres with Dulles's argument. The operation in Poland is a perfect fit for Dulles's ideal; Track II in Chile does not fit at all; while the operations in Italy, Iran, and Track I in Chile fit more or less well, depending on how one interprets the facts of those cases.

Three of the most popular complaints against covert operations is that they somehow tarnish the image of the country that uses them (Hilsman 2000, 21); contradict the values of nations such as the United States that are supposed to function with more transparency (Goodman 2000, 27), presumably because they are democratic; and work at cross-purposes with the overt diplomatic tactics of the foreign services (White 2000, 45). Covert operations can certainly tarnish the image of those who employ them if those operations are unpopular, but it is hard to argue that all covert operations tarnish. The United State's image was certainly not tarnished by its operations in Poland, for example, and even if the cynic may reply that, by that time, there was little image left tarnishing, one could reply to the cynic that a similar operation carried out by any nation would hardly tarnish their image. The idea that covert operations contradict democratic values carries more weight, since such operations make it impossible for citizens to hold public officials accountable. However, the argument carries less weight if the covert operation is short lived and made public on its completion, so that citizens are not kept permanently in the dark and the results can be weighed by all. Carrying more weight still is the argument that covert operations hinder more peaceful and, some would argue, more effective tactics. Melvin Goodman argues that better intelligence in political and economic areas can be had through US ambassadors and embassy officers than through espionage activities. Thus, from his point of view, governments should shift resources from clandestine services to the State Department and other like agencies as the best cost-effective way to gain intelligence (Goodman 2000, 35). Similarly, Robert Keeley argues that the proliferation of spies abroad is a waste of resources, since most intelligence collection can be done by diplomats and others in the foreign service (Keeley 2000, 62–63). This may be so, but intelligence collectors cannot carry out covert operations when they are needed. Nevertheless, covert operations cannot pass the test of proportion if other means are available to solve the problem through peaceful diplomatic measures, and this means an adequate enough budget in those areas that can make those sorts of solutions more possible.

Covert operations may be justifiable in some circumstances, but never when more peaceful and effective means are available. However, even those who are in general agreement about the overuse of covert operations are also in general agreement about the necessity of keeping the option open and available. The most obvious areas of need would be against rogue states, for tracking down weapons of mass destruction, for combating international terrorism and other international criminal groups, and to rescue citizens trapped in hostile areas.[11] Thus, as long as there is conflict in the world, there will be the need for secret operations.

NOTES

1. There is no such dilemma when the operation occurs in enemy territory where the sovereign government terrorizes its own citizens as well as others. As Jeff McMahan argues, governments can lose their legitimacy through evil actions (McMahan 1987, 75–101). For a similar argument, see Perry 2009, 164–65.
2. Walzer, in a discussion on intervention in a rebellion, argues that once an insurgent power has attained enough territory and popular support to acquire belligerent rights equal with the established government, then outsiders should observe neutrality unless another outside power violates neutrality, which opens the door for other powers to do likewise (Walzer 1977, 90, 96–97).
3. Aquinas's discussion of the passions can be found in *Summa Theologica* I–II QQ.22–48.
4. I wish to meet one objection that has been levied at Colby, namely that by journalist Oriana Fallici (1976, 12–21), who asked Colby how he would respond to a foreigner who came to the United States in order to finance an American political party. Colby responded that he would turn her over to

the FBI, and, thus, Fallici was able to portray Colby as someone who holds a double standard: it is morally praiseworthy to interfere with Italian politics but not American. But the question is not a fair one. A fair sort of question to Mr. Colby would be what would he do about a British agent in the US for the purposes of backing a political party, if the USSR was already in the United States backing another candidate to the hilt? In other words, what if the United States was in the same vulnerable position as Italy in 1958? Colby might have given Fallici a different answer.

5. Wilber C. Eveland insists on the British brains behind the operation and even claims, "Roosevelt did little more than show up in Iran with CIA funds to encourage agents the British had organized and then released to American control" (Eveland 1980, 108–109).

6. Gasiorowski's assessment of the cause of the United States' actions appears to be correct: the concern was much more about communist influence in the area rather than oil concessions for the United States. As Gasiorowski points out, US oil companies were not interested in Iranian oil at the time. In fact, with the glut in the oil market, the US companies foresaw a cutback in their current operations in Saudi Arabia and Kuwait if they began operations in Iran, which would have created tensions with their Arab partners. US policymakers had to persuade US oil companies to get involved in Iran. See Gasiorowski 1987, 275.

7. This is the view held by Bill 1988, 83.

8. Gasiorowski argues that most of the middle level State Department and CIA officials did not believed a coup was necessary to prevent a communist takeover and that the original proponents seem to have been limited to the Dulles brothers, Wisner, and Roosevelt. See Gasiorowski 1987, 276 and nt.71, 285.

9. Gasiorowski's account of the coup suggest that it was the Eisenhower administration that decided to replace Mossadeq with Zahedi and that the Shah accepted Zahedi with some reluctance (Gasiorowski 1987, 277), but Roosevelt makes it clear that Zahedi was the Shah's choice and that neither the governments of Eisenhower or Churchill were enamored with Zahedi (Roosevelt 1979, 158).

10. Many considered him the clandestine minister of state and war as well. See, for example, Bernstein and Politi 1996, 286.

11. See Blum 2000, 90; Goodman 2000, 36; and Keeley 2000, 74.

BIBLIOGRAPHY

Acheson, Dean. (1969). *Present at the Creation: My Years at the State Department.* New York: W.W. Norton.

Aquinas, Thomas. (1948). *Summa Theologica.* 1256–1272. Translated by the Fathers of the English Dominican Provence. New York: Benziger Brothers.

Barry, James A. (1992). "Managing Covert Political Action: Guideposts From Just War Theory." In *The Ethics of Spying: A Reader for the Intelligence Professional,* edited by Jan Goldman, 248–65. Lanham, MD: Scarecrow Press.

Beauchamp, Tom L., and Childress, James F. (1994). *Principles of Biomedical Ethics.* 4th ed. New York: Oxford University Press.

Bernstein, Carl, and Politi, Marco. (1996). *His Holiness: John Paul II and the Hidden History of Our Time.* New York: Doubleday.

Bill, James A. (1988). *The Eagle and the Lion: The Tragedy of American-Iranian Relations.* New Haven: Yale University Press.

Blum, Jack A. (2000). "Covert Operations: The Blowback Problem." In *National Insecurity: US Intelligence After the Cold War*, edited by Craig Eisendrath, 76–91. Philadelphia, PA: Temple University Press.

Colby, William. (1978). *Honorable Men: My Life in the C.I.A.* New York: Simon and Schuster.

Daugherty, William J. (2004). *Executive Action and the Presidency.* Lexington, KY: University of Kentucky Press.

Dulles, Allen. (1977). *The Craft of Intelligence.* Westport, CT: Greenwood Press.

Eisendrath, Craig, ed. (2000). *National Insecurity: US Intelligence After the Cold War.* Philadelphia, PA: Temple University Press.

Eveland, Wilbur C. (1980). *Ropes of Sand: America's Failure in the Middle East.* New York: W.W. Norton.

Fallaci, Oriana. (1976). "The CIA's Mr. Colby." *New Republic* 174(11): 12–21.

Gasiorowski, Mark J. (1987). "The 1953 Coup D'Etat in Iran." *International Journal of Middle East Studies* 19(3): 261–86.

Gates, Robert M. (1996). *From the Shadows: The Ultimate Insider's Story of Five Presidents and How They Won the Cold War.* New York: Simon & Schuster.

Goldman, Jan, ed. (2006). *The Ethics of Spying: A Reader for the Intelligence Professional.* Lanham, MD: Scarecrow Press.

Goodman, Melvin A. (2000). "Espionage and Covert Action." In *National Insecurity: US Intelligence After the Cold War*, edited by Craig Eisendrath, 23–44. Philadelphia, PA: Temple University Press,

Gustafson, Kristian. (2007). *Hostile Intent: U.S. Covert Operations in Chile, 1964–1974.* Washington, DC: Potomac.

Hilsman, Roger. (2000). "After the Cold War: The Need for Intelligence." In *National Insecurity: US Intelligence After the Cold War*, edited by Craig Eisendrath, 8–22. Philadelphia, PA: Temple University Press.

Keeley, Robert V. (2000) "CIA-Foreign Service Relations." In *National Insecurity: US Intelligence After the Cold War*, edited by Craig Eisendrath, 61–75. Philadelphia, PA: Temple University Press.

Luther, Martin. (1967). "Whether Soldiers, Too, Can Be Saved." 1526. In *Luther's Works.* Vol. 46. Edited by Helmut Lehmann. Philadelphia, PA: Fortress Press.

McMahan, Jeff. (1987). "The Ethics of International Intervention," in *Political Realism and International Morality: Ethics in the Nuclear Age*, edited by Kenneth Kipnis and Diana Meyers, 75–101. Boulder, CO: Westview.

Perry, David L. (2009). *Partly Cloudy: Ethics in War, Espionage, Covert Action, and Interrogation.* Lanham, MD: Scarecrow Press.

Roosevelt, Kermit, Jr. (1979). *Countercoup: The Struggle for the Control of Iran.* New York: McGraw-Hill.

Ross, W. D. (1930). *The Right and the Good.* New York: Oxford University Press.

Walzer, Michael. (1977). *Just and Unjust Wars.* New York: Basic Books.

White, Robert E. (2000). "Too Many Spies, Too Little Intelligence." In *National Insecurity: US Intelligence After the Cold War*, edited by Craig Eisendrath, 45–60. Philadelphia, PA: Temple University Press.

5 Intelligence Collection and Coercive Interrogation

Intelligence agents sometimes resort to torture to get information. The United States, for example, was finally able to locate terrorist leader Osama Bin Laden only after a suspect was put through coercive interrogation, which is simply another way of saying some intelligence personnel tortured a terrorist in order to get the information they were seeking. Torture was generally accepted as a legitimate form of statecraft in pre-modern times. There is scarcely a word to be found against it in classical and medieval authors. Even Grotius, writing in the seventeenth century, demonstrates what to modern eyes can only seem as an alarming indifference to the treatment of captured enemies in war: "There is no suffering which may not be inflicted with impunity upon such slaves, no action which they may not be ordered, or forced by torture, to do, in any way whatsoever; even brutality on the part of masters toward persons of servile status is unpunishable except in so far as municipal law sets a limit and a penalty for brutality" (*The Laws of War and Peace* III.VII.III). We are often told that information crucial to the wellbeing of the common good can be had only by torture. Is such torture ever justifiable? A rough form of utilitarian reasoning might claim that torture could be justified if, for example, the information saved a great number of innocent lives.[1] Although there have been recent attempts to argue for the legalization of a limited form of torture,[2] post-Enlightenment thinking on the matter has been marked by sustained efforts to portray torture as an absolute evil that could never be a justifiable part of statecraft. These efforts have been successful insofar as international law has made all forms of torture illegal, but, as we have seen, legality does not exhaust morality.

My aim is to show the advantage of looking through the perspective of the just war tradition at the kind of coercive interrogation (or torture) intelligence agents may be tempted to engage in. I first argue that most arguments against torture as an absolute evil fail to compel anyone committed to the possibility of the just use of force. Because it is so difficult to argue that torture is an absolute evil, we may be tempted to employ it. Interrogation, whether it is soft or hard, is a tactic of warfare; that is to say, it is a form of force used against the enemy for the common good. The just war tradition teaches us that, even if a war is just, innocent civilians may not be intentionally targeted (noncombatant immunity) and all tactics must seek to do more good than harm (proportion). Proportion presupposes the idea of minimal force; that is to say, it is difficult to argue that an act of war causes more good than evil if the act of war uses more destructive force than is necessary to get the job done. Thus, I argue that if we consider torture as an act of force that must comply with just war criteria, we will gain four advantages. First, our efforts to abide by the criteria will force us to place strictures on torture so severe that the act will be very difficult to justify. Second, compliance with the criteria discourages the legalization of any form of torture. Third, knowing that any act of torture will have to comply with proportion and noncombatant immunity helps us to clarify when circumstances have occurred that might make torture justifiable to a clandestine agent. Fourth, we will see how only a person of exceptional character will be able to know when the criteria have been met.

DOES TORTURE CONTRADICT THE GOLDEN RULE?

Many argue that we may never torture for any reason, because torture always contradicts the Golden Rule, which enjoins us to treat others as we would be treated. Fleming Rutledge, for example, argues that we embody Christ (who taught the Golden Rule) by refusing to use our superior strength to take advantage of our enemies who are disarmed and in our power (Rutledge 2006, 385.). This is truly embodying Christ, truly following the Golden Rule, because we must love our enemies and realize that it is only by God's grace (or the lottery, if you like) that we are not in their shoes. Similarly, George Hunsinger argues that the Golden Rule requires you to put yourself in the other person's shoes (Hunsinger 2006, 377). The failure to apply the role-reversal test means that you are acting contradictorily to the humanity of others and yourself. Since we cannot will that we be placed in the tortured person's shoes, torture is always wrong. Unfortunately, Rutledge's argument fails to notice that we take advantage of superior strength all the time in war—*that* is typically how we win. Thus, Rutledge must mean "unfair advantage" or using advantage in an abusive, undeserved, way, like a bully does.[3] But this begs the question of whether or not torture is always unfair advantage like bullying, or simply a matter of making good use of superior force. Contra Rutledge, the question must be a matter of desert, and the assumption is that no one ever deserves to be tortured. But why is this the case? Can we not ask if some people deserve torturing in the same way that some people deserve to have other forms of force used against them? Can we not also will that we too should deserve torture in some circumstances in the same way we could will that we too deserve to have lethal force used against us in some circumstances? Once one accepts the premise that lethal force is a justifiable good, that some people deserve to have lethal force used against them, then one must conclude that we can conceive of the possibility that lethal force might be used against us if we act in such a way as to deserve it. A similar argument might be made for torture. This is why the role-reversal test does not necessarily rule out all acts of torture. Hunsinger cannot mean that we could never will that the use of force be used against ourselves, at least, not if he wishes to hold that the use of force is sometimes justifiable. In other words, the Golden Rule argument against torture does not work, because we could still will that it, like other forms of force, should be used against us in certain circumstances. We can, for instance, will how we think we ought to be treated if we ever became Nazi-like, committed war-like acts on innocents, and possessed information about a despicable and catastrophic attack on innocent civilians.

The Golden Rule position has many close relatives, including the argument that torture cannot meet the Kantian demand of universalizability. R. M. Hare's formulation of what counts as a right moral act is a good example: "When we are trying, in a concrete case, to decide what we ought to do, what we are looking for . . . is an action to which we can commit ourselves (prescriptivity) but which we are at the same time prepared to accept as exemplifying a principle of action to be prescribed for others in like circumstances (universalizability)" (Hare 1963, 89–90). For Hare, the proper question is, "What do you say (*in propria persona*) about a hypothetical case in which you are in your victim's position" (Hare 1963, 108). Similarly, Joseph Runzo argues that torture always violates what he calls "the moral point of view," which consists of two features: taking the good of everyone equally into account and accepting the universalizability of one's actions (Runzo 1996, 183).

Runzo's argument seems to be that, since we could never will harm for ourselves, we cannot will harm for others, at least not if we wish to adhere to the moral point of view. If so, then the moral point of view rules out all harmful acts of force against anyone. We could counter Runzo's argument by pointing out that some acts of torture could meet both features of the moral point of view. We can follow Aquinas, for example, and argue that, "what we ought to love in our neighbor is that he may be in God" (*Summa Theologica* II.II, Q. 25, A. 1). Thus, practically speaking, the only way to take the good of everyone equally into account is to desire everyone's eternal good (*Summa Theologica* II.II, Q. 26, A. 6), which does not preclude using force, even lethal force, against some people for the common good. For Aquinas, charity demands that we take the good of everyone into account, but there is an order of charity in which we ought to love God most of all (because he is the cause of all our happiness) and we love those nearer to us because we love them in more ways (*Summa Theologica* II.II, Q. 26, A. 2–7). Moreover, charity demands that, even though we love our enemies, in the sense that we desire their eternal good, we must come to the aid of our innocent neighbors who are being threatened by our unjust neighbors. So there is no necessary incompatibility between taking everyone's good into consideration and using force. Thus, by following Aquinas in what it means to take everyone's good into consideration, we can see how a particular act of torture by a clandestine agent or intelligence officer might meet Hare's requirement of universalizablity. We can hold that we desire torture always for certain people in certain circumstances. We may decide that there are concrete cases in which we may consider torture as the right thing to do and we would be prepared to prescribe this action for all those facing like concrete cases. Those circumstances may be very few and far in between, but they may exist. So, again, we could agree that, if we became Nazi-like in our intentions and capabilities, and if we had information about a catastrophic act by the enemy, then we ought to be tortured in order to gain the information necessary to stop the catastrophic act. We could universalize our act because we could will that we, and any other human being who became as dangerous as, say, a Heinrich Himmler henchman, should be tortured under similar circumstances.

DOES TORTURE CONTRADICT HUMAN DIGNITY?

Many opponents of torture simply declare that it should be absolutely forbidden because it is some sort of moral insult against human dignity and a violation of the *imago Dei* in human beings. A good example of this kind of argument can be found in official Roman Catholic teaching. In *Gaudiem et Spes*, under the title of "Reverence For Human Life," the document states that,

> Whatever is opposed to life itself, such as ay type of murder . . . willful self-destruction, whatever violates the integrity of the human person, such as mutilation, torments inflicted on body or mind, attempts to coerce the will itself . . . are infamies indeed. They poison human society, but they do more harm to those who practice them than those who suffer from the injury. Moreover, they are a supreme dishonor to the Creator. [Vatican Council of Catholic Bishops, 1966, par. 27]

Pope John Paul II uses this quote in his encyclical *Veritatis Splendor*, where he argues that certain acts are incapable of being ordered to God, "because they radically contradict the good of the person made in His image" (par. 80). Such acts "hostile to life itself" are intrinsically evil. However, both documents leave the main moral questions unanswered: Why is torture intrinsically evil? Why is torture always hostile to life? How is the interrogator's aim to coerce the will of the enemy morally different from the soldier's aim to kill the enemy outright? If mass killing does not necessarily "radically contradict the good of the person" made in God's image, then why does torture?

The failure to answer such questions may also be seen in Dietrich Bonhoeffer's argument that torture, like rape, is a serious violation "of the right which is given with the creation of man, and what is more, like all violations of natural life, they must sooner or later entail their own punishment" (Bonhoeffer 1955, 183). The argument that torture is a violation of a right given at creation is far from evident. One would need a great deal of careful theological argument (which Bonhoeffer does not provide) to get from a reading of the early chapters of Genesis to an absolute prohibition on torture. More important still is that such reasoning, if sound, would lead to the conclusion that all bodily harm is a violation. Perhaps this is what Bonhoeffer means and we must simply accept guilt for what must be described as the right thing to do. Larry Rasmussen has made a convincing case that Bonhoeffer's mature ethic was one of doing evil when necessary and accepting the guilt of the evil deed as a way not to whitewash the evil or to mislead others into thinking that what was once evil is now to be considered good (Rasmussen 1972, 48). However, even if Rasmussen is right about Bonhoeffer, it is still difficult to argue why torture should be absolutely prohibited, when killing and mutilating are sometimes allowed. In other words, Bonhoeffer, too, has failed to prove a moral distinction between torture and killing that would compel us to prohibit all acts of torture.

Nevertheless, Bonhoeffer's position merits closer attention. He argues that the human body "must never become a thing, any object, such as might fall under the unrestricted power of another man and be used by him solely as a means to his own ends" (Bonhoeffer 1955, 85). For Bonhoeffer, the body is the person; thus, to torture is to do direct harm to "the man himself." What exactly does Bonhoeffer mean by torture? He defines torture as

> the arbitrary and brutal infliction of physical pain while taking advantage of a relative superiority of strength, and in particular, the extortion by this means of some desired admission or statement. In such cases, the body is misused, and therefore dishonored, exclusively as a means to the achievement of another man's purpose, whether it be for the satisfaction of his lust for power or for the sake of acquiring some particular information. The innocent body's sensitiveness to pain is cruelly exploited. (Bonhoeffer 1955, 183)

There are serious problems with this definition. First, there is no reason to assume out of hand that all torture is arbitrary. As David Little has pointed out, the arbitrariness of most acts of torture is the very feature that makes them wrong and that when this feature is absent (in other words, when we present good reasons for torture), the wrong-doing is much less clear (Little 1993, 83). Second, the language of "brutality" and "superiority in strength" are not good arguments against the use of force against an unjust enemy. All killing in battle is brutal to some degree and, as we pointed out above, superiority of strength is generally how one wins a battle. Third, torture need not be used "solely" as a means to an individual's own ends, but the ends of the common good of relatively just state. Fourth, Bonhoeffer's use of the language of innocence in his definition of torture is very problematic. What if the captured person is not innocent? What if the state is not Nazi Germany or any thing like it? The fact that many anti-torture advocates use examples of innocent people being tortured by agents of blatantly evil regimes is something to ponder. When we consider, for example, Dianna Ortiz's very moving contribution to the literature (Ortiz 2006), written from the point of view of an innocent victim of brutal and unjust torture, we notice that one of the reasons the essay is so moving is precisely because we believe that she was wrongfully tortured. In other words, she presents the story of an innocent victim who did not deserve to be tortured. We would also be appalled at her plight if some soldier had simply shot her out of hand, but we would not conclude from that evil act that all soldiering should be prohibited, only that unjust soldiering should be subject to criminal prosecution.

Philip Quinn goes right to the heart of the *imago Dei* argument when he points out that the religious position against torture hinges on whether or not severely damaging things made in the image of God is always wrong (Quinn 1996, 157). Quinn provides an argument in five steps in which he seeks to prove that torture does indeed violate the *imago Dei*:

1. Torture severely damages human beings.
2. All human beings are things made in the image and likeness of God.
3. Hence, torture severely damages things make in the image and likeness of God.
4. Severely damaging things made in the image and likeness of God is always wrong.
5. Therefore, torture is always wrong.

There are two ways we can take issue with this argument. The first premise (and, therefore, the third) is not always true. Surely there are some mild forms of torture that do not always "severely" damage a human being. However, the more significant problem with the argument is found in the fourth premise. Quinn's concern is echoed in Jean Porter's argument that torture "subverts the will itself by assaulting undermining the delicate psychic forces that sustain the individual's integrity, sense of well-being and self-command" (Porter 2008, 343). However, it is hard to imagine how the same problem could fail to apply to any act of killing or mutilation in battle. The "delicate psychic forces" so important to personhood are eliminated in killing and can be assaulted in any form of brutal combat (again, we must remind ourselves of the difference between Hollywood and reality—most combat, even modern combat, is brutal and may issue in killings, severe burns, and mutilations). If it is true that to damage severely things make in the image and likeness of God is always wrong, then all acts of killing or mutilating in battle are acts that are always wrong. In short, all those who hold the fourth premise to be true are committed to strict pacifism, or to the position held by Bonhoeffer that we may do evil that good may come. Just war defenders have typically denied that a moral position such as Bonhoeffer's is to be recommended and are rather committed to the moral dictum that evil should never be done for some greater good (Ramsey 1988, 6).

DOES TORTURE HARM THE TORTURER?

Torture is not only thought to harm the one tortured, but many argue that it also harms the torturer in some special way that would lead us to conclude that it must be absolutely prohibited. According to this argument, to give clandestine agents and intelligence officers the power to torture is to give them access to acts that will leave them depraved. John Perry, arguing from the Roman Catholic Tradition, argues that the theological category under which war is placed makes all war and everything we do in it a sin. Thus, no matter how justified a war may be (and speaking as an adherent of official Roman Catholic teaching on war, Perry must admit that a particular war may be just), it "diminishes those involved, twists their moral perceptions and values, and leaves all involved spiritually less than they were before" (Perry 2005, 42). Those who have experienced war and lived to write about it do not always agree with Perry's conclusions. Nevertheless, Perry is simply echoing a popular refrain when he argues that war is dehumanizing, and it certainly is dehumanizing to some. In any event, he admits that a dehumanizing war may still be a just war. So why not one who uses torture? Killing is acceptable to Perry. So why not torture? Torture, according to Perry, should be absolutely forbidden because it is destructive in a way that is peculiar to it: it is destructive to the perpetrator as well as to the victim. This is so because the torturer intends "to diminish or even destroy the personhood of their victims. It is this subjective, interpersonally destructive aspect of torture that makes it different and morally worse than many other destructive aspects of war" (Perry 2005, 43).[4] David Sussman expresses a similar concern when he argues that torturers make their victims express the will of the torturer and, as such, the suffering is "not simply inflicted upon the self but as something the victim does to himself, a kind of self-betrayal worked through my body and feelings" (Sussman 2005, 21). In this sort of interpersonal violence, the torture victim brings about more suffering by resisting.

Perry makes much of the impersonal nature of just warfare as a way of mitigating the evil of what is done in war, and thus making it morally different from torture, and he believes that he is following the lead of Augustine. He agrees with the old adage that "war is hell," but adds that often the damage done in war is impersonal, in that soldiers do not actually see the face of their victims because they are dropping bombs or shooting at targets in a distance (Perry 2005, 30). Unfortunately, Perry has a confused idea about the "impersonal" in warfare and why it is valued by people such as Augustine (and Luther and Calvin, for that matter). When Augustine argues for the justice of acts of force at the impersonal level, he meant that the acts of force committed by a soldier would come from a sense of duty and love of neighbor and not out of a sense of hatred and revenge. In other words, Augustine argues that soldiering should always be the kind of job done with professional detachment toward the objects of force that would preclude the kind of intense emotional involvement that could lead to vicious acts (see, especially, the argument in *On Free Will* I.5). Augustine would not have been familiar with the sort of impersonal warfare that Perry so values. Fighting in Augustine's day was mainly hand-to-hand and quite brutal by modern standards. This may be a clue as to why there is so little to be said against torture in the ancient and medieval world: acts of torture were not so very empirically distinguishable from acts of war. When we think of the catalogue of tortures employed, for example, by the Gestapo—which include beatings with fists, with whips, with blunt instruments, kickings, burnings, electrocutions, and a form of dunking water torture not so different in effect from modern waterboarding—we should recall that, with the exception of the last two, these ordeals would likely be risked in most ordinary battles. In any event, when Augustine argued for the just war, he would have had in mind the very sort of violence decried by Perry and others as intrinsically immoral. Moreover, not all modern combat involves killing an unseen enemy. All battle is won by one side forcing its will on the other. More often than not, the side that forces its will on the other can do so only because of superior strength and does so, at some point, with interpersonal violence. Like victims of torture, those who surrender to superior force in combat rather than die fighting are often haunted by feelings of self-betrayal and the thought that they were bullied and frightened into giving up when they could have continued to resist. Like victims of torture, they reach a point in the battle where they realize that resistance will only mean further suffering. We must keep in mind that even modern soldiers must do a great deal of killing at fairly close range, and, so, engage in a great deal of interpersonal violence. In short, there is interpersonal violence in most forms of combat. There may be a difference of degree in the intensity of the interpersonal in torture when compared to most forms of combat (but not all), but this is a difference in degree and not in kind. Killing intends to destroy personhood, even more so than torture. Killing may provide a "cleaner" way to destroy personhood if done at long range but torture cannot be meaningfully distinguished from killing by positing an "interpersonal" characteristic to the former that does not exist in the latter.

DOES TORTURE HARM THE SOCIETY THAT PRACTICES IT?

Torture need not erode the character of the agent who employs it, but there still remains the worry, expressed by David Gushee, that the systematic use of torture erodes the character of the nation that practices it (Gushee 2006,

359). The argument is echoed by Perry, who adds that any society that practices torture will begin a moral slide until it "cannot distinguish between good and evil" (Perry 2005, 36–37). McCoy, too, argues that once torture begins, its users become debased and overconfident of its effectiveness. This overconfidence leads to a lack of control—a lack of limitations on what you do and to whom you do it—which further debases the practitioners (McCoy 2006, 13). Thus, according to McCoy, states that allow torture eventually end up allowing it to spread beyond a few targets to countless suspects. As Luban puts it, "escalation is the rule, not the aberration" (Luban 2005, 48). We could point to many such instances: the escalation of torture by the French in Algeria, the period when the CIA became involved with torture from 1950 to 1962 through a psychological warfare program—a "veritable Manhattan Project of the mind" is how McCoy describes it (McCoy 2006, 7)—or even more recently in the War on Terror where prisoners such as Abu Zubaydah are tortured despite the fact that the interrogators do not believe them to possess any useful information.

Scholars have shown how torture gets out of hand even for relatively just nations such as France and the United States, but no one has shown that torture necessarily degrades society. Richard Posner has pointed out that France, the UK, and Israel all used torture without sinking into barbarism (Posner 2004, 294–95). The examples of debased societies that employ torture are countries with thoroughly evil and corrupt regimes (two popular examples in the anti-torture literature are Nazi Germany under Hitler and Chile under General Augusto Pinochet).[5] These governments routinely tortured innocent people and did so because the governments were already corrupt. In other words, the torture practiced in those societies may more convincingly be read as a symptom of prior corruption rather than as a cause. Nevertheless, the overconfidence that can come to agents who routinely torture does lead to the overuse of the tactic, which does, indeed, necessarily imply that the just war criteria of proportionality has been violated, and probably noncombatant immunity as well. Any attempt to give torture a legal backing, and thus establish its use as protected by law, must reckon with this problem.

THE ARGUMENT FROM INTUITION

Most people find torture repugnant, and some argue that this repugnance reflects something morally important about torture; namely that there is something deeply wrong about it even if we cannot articulate reasons why. Perry, for example, argues that most people shrink back from torture because this repugnance rests "upon a collective moral intuition" (Perry 2005, 38). He uses the example of former Israeli Defense Force Colonel Yehuda Meir, who admitted that it was harder to give soldiers the order to beat than to give them orders to kill: "You don't learn how to torture in army school. You are taught how to use a gun and shoot someone far from you." We are also reminded by Pere Guy Gilbert, a former French soldier in Algeria where French forces routinely tortured, that some soldiers who tortured in the line of duty suffered mental health troubles as a result (Peters 1985, 158–59). We could counter that ordinary combat soldiers who never tortured also suffer similar troubles, and yet we do not conclude from this that we ought to prohibit soldiering. Nevertheless, torture is repugnant to most human beings. The question, however, is whether or not repugnance is a good enough reason to prohibit all torture. Would our moral intuitions be different if we knew all the sickening details about the results of the successful terrorist's plans? We must also consider that most people find many health sustaining acts such as surgery very repugnant viewing, but we don't prohibit surgery. The analogy to surgery is particularly apt because, as Luther once observed, in cases of both surgery and soldiering, we do terrible harm (not evil) in order to achieve good (Luther 1967, 95).

There are similar arguments in medical ethics concerning cloning and the mistreatment of dead bodies that serve as a helpful comparison. Leon Kass argues, for example, that ordinarily the feeling of revulsion concerning X is not an argument against X. Our society used to feel repugnance for many things that are now accepted. However, there are "crucial cases" where "repugnance is the emotional expression of deep wisdom, beyond reason's power to fully articulate it" (Kass 1997, 20). Incest, bestiality, raping, and murdering are examples of activities that repel us and yet we often struggle to give full rational justification for why we feel the way we do about them. Kass's arguments against human cloning are instructive. He argues that human cloning is an activity for which we should feel revulsion. A feeling of repugnance for human cloning is a revolt "against the excesses of human willfulness, warning us not to transgress what is unspeakably profound," namely, human reproduction (Kass 1997, 21). The description of the activity in question is crucial, for as Kass reminds us, "The way we evaluate cloning ethically will in fact be shaped by how we characterize it descriptively, by the context into which we place it, and by the perspective from which we view it. The first task for ethics is proper description." The failure to describe properly human cloning is what Kass attacks.

Kass is surely right about the importance of proper description of an action. Is the intelligence officer using physical coercion to extract a piece of information that will save lives, or is the officer punishing or being merely sadistic? We find that the proper description of an act of surgery or an act of torture could be read in similar ways: inflicting pain for the sake of cruelty or for the common good. Also, the context within which we describe the acts makes all the difference: we may simply be torturing or trying to save innocent lives. We could view the acts from the perspective of those who order the torture, those who actually torture, or those who are tortured. When it comes to viewing torture from the perspective of the victim, all the difference in the world will be in who the tortured person is, what he has done, and what he plans to do. The argument from repugnance is an argument based on feelings, and feelings can fluctuate depending on the details of the story we tell. The same description of the acts of torture—the beatings, the kickings, the electrocutions, or the dunks in cold water—could be used of three different scenarios that would produce three distinct sets of feelings. If we were to witness the Gestapo using these tactics on an innocent person for the sake of showing mastery and cruelty, our repugnance and sense of outrage will be at a maximum. If we were to witness the Gestapo using these tactics on French resistance hero Jean Moulin, our repugnance and outrage, while significant, would probably not have the same intensity as it did with the innocent bystander because Moulin "played the game," knowing this fate awaited him if he was ever caught. If we were to witness the same techniques used on Himmler in order to get the names of Nazi undercover agents in the field, and thus save thousands of innocent lives, it may be difficult to muster much feeling at all. Recall the rhetorically persuasive language of innocence used by some who have suffered so cruelly at the hands of the unjust. We will invariably place more moral weight on the repugnance felt at the thought of an innocent person being tortured for reasons of sheer cruelty than, for instance, the thought of a Gestapo agent, with his own history of cruelty and barbarity, being tortured in order to find out information about a mass attack on Jews.

Joel Feinberg, however, has argued that a feeling of repugnance toward a practice should not be allowed to outweigh the good that accrues to human-kind from that practice. Feinberg is thinking primarily of the use of human cadavers for research purposes at the Department of Transportation and the harvesting of organs for transplantation. Cadavers were used as crash test dummies in order to improve safety conditions on automobiles. Some had protested in language identical to what we find in the anti-torture literature, that the practice violated the "fundamental notions of morality and human dignity" (Feinberg 1985, 31). Feinberg argues that an erroneous use of symbols is at the heart of the matter: "The error consists of attaching a value to a symbol, and then absorbing oneself in the sentiments evoked by the symbol at the expense of real interests, including the very interests the symbol represents" (Feinberg 1985, 32). The sincerity of the sentiments expressed is not decisively important, for "profoundly worthwhile sentiments can fail as decisive reasons for legislative actions when the restrictions they support invade legitimate interests of others." The point is that repugnance by itself cannot always outweigh humanitarian benefits.

Feinberg objects to arguments made by his opponents that rely on a type of abstract reasoning that proceeds in a vacuum that has no connection with the practical world. There are real people who are suffering and dying, and these people could be helped by practices that many find repugnant. "It simply will not bear rational scrutiny to claim that there is a right not to be horrified, or not to have one's capacity to be horrified weakened, of the same order as the right not to be killed" (Feinberg 1985, 35). Feinberg agrees that persons sometimes do need to learn how to shudder, "but it is even more commonly the case that people have to learn how *not* to shudder." He uses the profession and practice of the pathologist and surgeon to make his point: they often must examine dead bodies and in so doing "skin them open like game, cutting, slicing, and mutilating them" (Feinberg 1985, 35). (The words could be taken right from Luther's surgery analogy to defend just soldiering). If most people have failed how to learn how not to shudder at such practices, few would wish to see those practices prohibited simply because they cause most people to shudder.

The conclusion is that we have to analyze exactly what we find repugnant about a practice and figure out if our repugnance is enough to justify prohibiting the practice. Most people find killing repugnant but allow that acts of killing are justifiable in some circumstances. The mere presence of repugnance, the mere presence of a collective moral intuition, is not enough to prohibit absolutely a practice that may save thousands of lives, such as soldiering or intelligence officers using torture. As Feinberg suggests, the erroneous use of symbols may be at the heart of the problem. The body is thought to be sacrosanct—it is the visible representation of personhood and autonomy. The problem is that we become so absorbed in the sentimentality of personhood and autonomy that we wish to forbid absolutely a tactic that might conceivably save those very interests. There may be a circumstance in which an act of torture may save many real people from suffering and dying. The desire not to be horrified should not necessarily override the desire to save innocent lives.

JUSTIFIABLE TORTURE AND LEGALIZATION

The arguments that attempt to prove that torture is an intrinsically evil act are not persuasive, because the reasoning behind them tends to condemn equally all forms of force harmful to those targeted. This suggests that torture, at least theoretically, may sometimes be justifiable when it is necessary to save innocent lives and to preserve justice and order. Coercive interrogation, if it is ever justifiable, should be considered as a tactic of a just war and, so, subject to the just war criteria, as are all acts of state-sponsored force. Assuming that the war in question has met the criteria for establishing the justice of going to war, we must still subject any act of torture to the criteria of noncombatant immunity and proportion. Combatants in this instance would refer not to regular uniformed soldiers, but to terrorists, or to certain state agents of political regimes so corrupt that they are terroristic in conception, such as Gestapo agents for Nazi Germany (I take it that if any uniformed state agents could be proper objects of torture, it would be Gestapo agents). Moreover, only those combatants that we have good reasons to believe may provide us with timely and critical information may be subject to torture. These reasons must be specific to an alleged attack and specific to the person being interrogated. In other words, we must already possess good information about a particular plan of attack and we must possess good information that this particular person under interrogation has knowledge about this attack. Such strictures are necessary to insure that torture does not become disproportionate. We must keep in mind that proportion in such circumstances would mean that the severity of any act of torture must be proportionate to the expected good. "Expected" here means being aware of how certain we are that the desired information is to be had by this particular prisoner. "Good" here means being aware of what we hope to achieve by gaining the information. The more severe the torture, the more proportion demands that we are reasonably certain that the information can be discovered and that we will gain knowledge that will save innocent lives. None of this is to argue that legal protection should be afforded to the interrogator who turns to torture in the exceptional circumstance.

Past experience suggests that states cannot be trusted with the power of legalized torture. As we have seen, states that legalize torture typically overuse the tactic, which is a violation of the just war criteria of proportion (and probably noncombatant immunity). This is true, not only of states that are essentially corrupt in nature and whose recourse to torture may be read as a further symptom of their abhorrent nature, but also of relatively just states such as the United States, France, and Israel. When, for example, the CIA thought it had legal protection for some of its harsh interrogation methods against terrorists such as waterboarding, the rules it had laid down for the tactic were not always observed and that the tactic was overused. Also, the negative consequences of legality—namely the failure of torture to get useful information—are too great to risk. Of course, one may counter that all acts of force can fail to achieve their purpose, but that is no reason to prohibit those acts. Moreover, if we can trust the government with weapons that could wipe out most of the life on the planet, why can we not trust the government with the task of legal torture? At first glance, this looks like a strong argument, for we do indeed believe that states can be trusted to kill for defense of the commonwealth and trusted to possess enough nuclear weapons to make the earth uninhabitable. The problem is that acts of war are typically more public than acts of torture. When combat troops behave in a particularly vicious manner, there are usually plenty of witnesses, not only within the military but sometimes without, as well. Interrogation, like most acts by clandestine agents and intelligence officers, is by its very nature a less-public act than soldierly combat. Moreover, a state that legalizes torture may become a state that slips into systematic injustices against the legitimate rights of others. We have good reasons to believe that states that legalize torture tend to overuse the tactic. They become enticed by the comparatively easy methods of interrogation that do not require the more hard-earned skills of the physically noncoercive interrogator. Torture can become the easy solution to the agent who lacks patience and physically noncoercive skills. We must keep in mind that the typical interrogation will not be one of the "ticking bomb" variety, but rather one in which it is believed (with good reasons) that the prisoner has some knowledge about the plans of a terrorist group. What sort of plans, when they are to take place, how far developed they are, and who exactly is involved—these will usually be unknown variables. Unless we already have more specific ideas in mind and reasons for believing that this particular terrorist can illuminate them, torture cannot be allowed as a proportionate tactic. Thus, legalized torture is not likely to meet the demands of a just war.

Posner argues that legal creations such as the torture warrants favored by some may actually whitewash questionable practices. Thus, he argues that it is better to leave the legal prohibitions in place but with the understanding that they will not be enforced in extreme circumstances (Posner 2004, 296). Similarly, David Gushee argues that if a ticking bomb situation should arise, it should be handled without legalization and one on an individual basis, "knowing fully that he would have to answer for his action before God, law, and neighbor" (Gushee 2006, 362). Oren Gross has argued that public officials in this position exemplify a "truly exceptional case" in that they may have a moral obligation to disobey the law with "preventive interrogational torture" but still expect legal ramifications for their disobedience (Gross 2004, 231–32). Legal rigidity in cases like this could undermine the very rule of law that laws against torture are supposed to protect.

The argument is that going outside of the law to do what is morally appropriate preserves the law, while bending the law ends up undermining the law. Society determines the consequences for individuals who break the law—it decides reward or punishment.[6] Public officials will have to acknowledge their acts and attempt to justify them. Gross quotes Justice Robert Jackson that the chief restraint on those who have the duty to use force is their "responsibility to the political judgments of their contemporaries and the moral judgments of history."[7] The separation of the issue of the act of interrogation and public ratification will make the interrogator think before acting. A moral calculus will have to be made. There is no need for a moral calculus if the law can be bent, for you can always claim necessity, as did French General Jacques Massu, who authorized torture on a wide scale in Algeria. Here is where concerns for legality and just war morality coincide. The very likely threat of legalized torture getting out of hand, and thus undermining the very laws that torture is supposed to protect, also leads to the violation of the just war criteria of proportion (and probably noncombatant immunity as well), thus undermining the very criteria that make acts of force justifiable.

KNOWING WHEN TO BREAK THE LAW

We now come to the point where we can ask what sort of person is likely to know when and how to break the law in order to preserve the rule of law and all that laws are formulated to protect. Dietrich Bonhoeffer's own life and thought provide helpful ethical tools in helping us see what kind of person this will be. As Bonhoeffer became increasingly convinced that Hitler's regime had to be undermined from within Germany, he came to argue that illegal acts may be morally good acts. This line of reasoning led him to agree to be a participant in a plot to assassinate Hitler. For Bonhoeffer, we mature as human beings as we learn to accept responsible action for our neighbors (Bonhoeffer 1963, 33). Those who are responsible are the true followers of Jesus Christ, who supports all who suffer in a just cause (Bonhoeffer 1955, 60). The character of Bonhoeffer's responsible person is ably summarized by Rasmussen as one of "sobriety, realism, and pragmatism" (Rasmussen 1972, 42). Responsible people are responsible because they are willing to reject ideology that spells out absolute ethical rules and accept the reality of circumstances in the world, which offer us choices between the relatively worse and the relatively better (Bonhoeffer 1955, 233–34 and 1972, 150–51). Being responsible may mean being willing to violate civil law and even divine law. However, these violations cannot be normative (Bonhoeffer 1955, 239–40 and 1972, 10–11). For Bonhoeffer, such acts are an *ultima ratio*, which he holds to be an irrational act but a responsible one because it is aiding the neighbor. The test for justice in resorting to the *ulitma ratio* and breaking the law is whether or not we will restore the rule of law by breaking it.

As we saw in the first chapter, Rasmussen argues that Bonhoeffer fails to spell out the criteria that would let us know what to do when we are presented with what appears to be an exceptional circumstance. He argues that Bonhoeffer provides us with no way to test the exceptional command to be sure that it is in fact the exceptional command we are supposed to obey (Rasmussen 1972, 153). Bonhoeffer, however, does argue for a kind of self-proving in which God grants perception of the "essential nature of things" (Bonhoeffer 1955, 69). As I argued in the first chapter, this self-proving can be had by the person of virtue, can be had by a person who has what John McDowell characterized as a "perceptual capacity" to know what counts as right action in a given circumstance. McDowell's argument is that you cannot have one virtue without all the virtues since sensitivity—"the ability to recognize requirements which situations impose on one's behavior"—is virtue in general (McDowell 1979, 333). Following this line of thought, just acts in war—including the ability of agents to know when and how to interrogate—are actually "manifestations" of a single sensitivity.

A further comparison with a similar argument by Bernard Williams is helpful in elucidating this point. Williams is concerned with the kind of moral incapacity, "that is in question when we say of someone, usually in condemnation of him, that he could not act or was not capable of acting in certain ways" (Williams 1995, 46). What enables or disables one from acting in certain ways is related to questions about the kind of person we are talking about, that is, it is related to issues of character. For our purposes, this also means that moral incapacity can be used descriptively of someone in a positive way, such as when someone says, "I do not have the capacity to kill or torture innocent people intentionally." Knowledge is key here, for a moral incapacity means that someone is incapable of doing something knowingly. To have a moral incapacity means that I will never try to do so-and-so for appropriate kinds of reason. In such cases, a deliberative conclusion not to do something is just the conclusion that I cannot do it. This is contrasted with other facts about a situation that are mere "inputs into the decision." Of course, a moral incapacity can function in "inputs into the decision," but this means that there is a further incapacity "upstream" from the "input" process. Thus, for example, my moral incapacity to torture someone may play a part in the decision-making process about whether I should, for instance, torture (and I mean beat, kick, electrocute, or dunk in cold water) a Gestapo agent who I am reasonably sure has knowledge about where a certain imminent raid on Jews is about to take place. I hesitate to torture because I have a moral incapacity against harming others, but "upstream" from this is a moral incapacity to allow unjust Nazis to exterminate innocent people. The over-arching incapacity here is what is operative; that is to say, I will torture the Gestapo agent because I "just" cannot stand by idly while a group of innocent people are exterminated. The issue of character then comes to the forefront, for as Williams says, "the incapacity to do this thing is an expression of those dispositions as applied to this situation through this very deliberation" (Williams 1995, 52). So I would not be able to act in such-a-such-a-way without the dispositions that were in some sense already there before I had to act. We also notice that the just war criteria of noncombatant immunity and proportion are not violated. Such criteria can never be overridden, because they are the very criteria that make any use of force justifiable in the first place. They serve as a useful fence around what may count as morally acceptable act of physical interrogation. In short, one cannot be said to have acted in accordance with virtue if one violates the criteria. This means that one could never torture a noncombatant (which rules out torturing or threatening to torture a combatant's loved ones if they are noncombatants) and could never torture more than is necessary to get the information or torture in ways that are otherwise inherently evil, such as rape.[8]

We are now on very different moral ground than, for example, Walzer's heroic torturer who forces himself to do evil in the face of a supreme emergency for the common good (Walzer 1973, 160–80). For, our virtuous interrogator would follow Nagel in holding that it is incoherent to claim that one could sacrifice one's moral integrity justifiably in the service of a higher goal. For, "if one were justified in making such a sacrifice (or even morally required to make it), then one would not be sacrificing one's moral integrity by adopting that course: one would be preserving it" (Nagel 1972, 132–33). So, in a so-called supreme emergency, to go against what you previously prohibited should evidence a preserving of the value found in the original prohibition. Thus, we value a certain way of life, a certain kind of society, that holds certain views about the integrity of the human being (which gave us legislation such as outlawing torture), and it may be that the only way to preserve this way of life, this society, is to torture on a particular, isolated occasion and without legal protection. Thus, we do not do evil in this sort of act, we do not incur moral guilt, but rather merely go against what we normally prohibit. The prohibited act would have to be of the intrinsically evil type in order for the act to be described as evil, and, as we have seen, it is very difficult to show how torture is an intrinsic evil. In any event, it will require an interrogator of exceptional character to know when the time has come to torture.

CHARACTER AND INTERROGATION

The character of the virtuous interrogator needs to be fleshed out in further detail. Former CIA operative William Johnson argues, "Interrogation is such a dirty business that it should be done only by people of the cleanest character" (Johnson 1986, 104). The issue of character is important because the person who interrogates is the person with an opportunity to torture. Torture should not be left to any clandestine agent or intelligence officer. The circumstances that may indicate the moral justification for torture are likely to be circumstances of emergency and, as Hare warns, "it is extremely difficult to think clearly and consider all sides of the case" when you are faced with an emergency (Hare 1963, 44). Too, we must not fool ourselves that the military and intelligence bureaus recruit only people of good will. For a great deal of the world's soldiery, the warning by Puritan divine and chaplain to Oliver Cromwell's army still holds true: "It must be a very extraordinary army that is not constituted by wolves and tigers" (Baxter 1830, 124). Choosing the virtuous from among the wolves and tigers is a moral necessity for those who wish to give moral approval to any form of interrogation that goes beyond simple questioning. The temptation to torture will be great for an interrogator, and the greater the consequences of not finding out the information we think we can get from a prisoner, the greater the temptation to torture. In order to avoid torture, the interrogator, ideally, will be the kind of person who possesses the sort of character that makes them immune to the temptation to torture unnecessarily, and at the minimum this means persons who have proven that they can think clearly and act well under pressure, persons who can see into the essential nature of the circumstance that is tempting of torture.

Many experienced interrogators hold that noncoercive interrogation gets better results than does torture. McCoy points out that FBI interrogators, in the face of pressure to torture in the War on Terror, stand by their practices of noncoercive questioning as the best way to get information out of a detainee.[9] Lt. Col. Anthony Shaffer, an experienced interrogator in Afghanistan, maintains that coercive questioning is not likely to yield good results. Nevertheless, his helpfully detailed description of a successful interrogation of a suspected terrorist revealed that Shaffer did threaten to send the prisoner to Guantanamo, which amounted to a threat of torture (Shaffer 2010, 94–116). Similarly, Christopher Andrew reports that MI5 agents in World War II were not disposed to using torture, being "quite convinced that these Gestapo methods do not work in the long run" (Andrew 2010, 252).[10] Nevertheless, they did regularly employ psychological pressure "to isolate the prisoner, intimidate him and demonstrate his powerlessness." McCoy is helpful in alerting us to well-established alternatives to torture, such as those practiced by Marine interrogator Major Sherwood F. Moran, who was very successful in employing long conversations seasoned with empathy for the detainee (McCoy 2006, 202–203). Moran is quoted in Stephen Budiansky's essay on the famous interrogator as holding that the successful interrogators have one thing in common: they are nice to their subjects. Thus, successful interrogators need not use brutal methods on their subjects, but might actually get better results when they "know their language, know their culture, and treat the captured enemy as a human being" (Budiansky 2005, 32). They have the patience to get to know their prisoners and to seek a more reliable form of information.

The virtue of patience is a must but so also is the ability to know when something more than noncoercive questioning is required. We do well to remember what Christopher Andrew surmised about Jim Skardon, a master MI5 interrogator known for his noncoercive techniques and an uncanny ability "to gain the confidence of some of those he questioned," namely that this ability was also his greatest weakness (Andrew 2010, 429). One of the reasons it took MI5 so long to root out the "Magnificent Five" of Soviet agents working as moles within Britain's secret services is that Skardon lacked that capacity to see into the essential nature of things. He lacked the wisdom to realize when he was being had and when the time had come to do more than gain the confidence of suspects. Thus, the most important characteristic of a successful interrogator is "his own temperament" and "his own character" (Budiansky 2005, 35).[11] Ironically, despite Skardon's notorious failure, the person who knows how to extract information without torture that may be the most trustworthy with the task of knowing when to torture. For, only a person who possesses the excellence of noncoercive interrogation will have the necessary experience to know when the time has come to resort to more physically coercive methods if circumstances demand it.

Deliberation about when to torture requires moral knowledge and this sort of moral knowledge does not come easily, especially to those who may have become used to an easy road to torture that the "legal necessity" argument offers. The Israeli experience in this field is telling. In 1987, the Israeli Landau Commission held that moderate force in interrogating terrorists is permissible by virtue of the law of necessity. In 1999, the Israeli Supreme Court ruled that coercive activities are illegal.[12] However, the court left open the "necessity" defense for individuals. As Miriam Gur-Ayre has pointed out, this position could allow for force to be used against innocents (Gur-Ayre 2004, 191), a direct violation of noncombatant immunity. Even though terrorists are not innocent, not every terrorist is a proper target for physically coercive interrogation. What kind of interrogation they can be subjected to is a matter that must be decided on by someone with sufficient moral knowledge and practical experience, and this knowledge and experience is not likely to be found among those who are used to pleading necessity for the legal protection of their acts of torture.

The experience needed for the virtuous interrogator is also not likely to be found in military personnel trained to torture. Lieutenant Colonel David Grossman has shown how, in order to train soldiers to be more efficient killers, current military training encourages the habit of unreflective obedience rather than moral reflection (Grossman 1995). This habit of discouraging moral reflection is expanded in the training of elite units, including those that are tortured as part of their training process and taught, in turn, how to torture. Jessica Wolfendale rightly argues that, in order for soldiers to be virtuous members of their profession, they must be "guided by professional ideals and a concept of integrity that will lead them to act ethically; to obey the laws of war and to carry out their duties effectively" (Wolfendale 2007, 184). Soldiers who have their moral sensibilities deadened by their training will not be virtuous soldiers; they are likely to lack integrity and will certainly not be the sort of people who are likely to be trusted with knowing when the time has come to break the law. More encouraging is what we have seen in Britain where in the wake of media reports that British Secret Services were condoning the use of torture, Dame Eliza Manningham-Buller, Director General of the Security Service, wrote a circular in 2006 entitled "Ethics and the Security Service," in which she stressed, "The Service goes to some length to recruit people with a keen sense of conscience who will raise questions if they are uncomfortable" (Andrew 2010, 825).

CONCLUSION

Reinhold Niebuhr once argued that the pacifist is not a responsible citizen because the pacifist refuses to do what God has ordained for human good: use force to protect the innocent (Neibuhr 1957, 29–40). Just war adherents disagree with Niebuhr that the responsible citizen is the citizen who does evil for a good cause. The just war tradition holds that killing in a just war is permissible—even morally praiseworthy—when those killed are enemies who pose a direct threat. What makes those acts just is their compliance with just war criteria, particularly proportion and noncombatant immunity. If torture is ever justified, then, like all acts of force in war, it would have to be proportionate and never visited intentionally on an innocent person. If it is indeed true that physically noncoercive means of interrogation are likely to be more successful than torture, then proportion would demand Moran's preferred method. Proportion restrains us from using more force than is necessary to get the job done. If torture is not required, then torture is excluded.

Torturing a prisoner is, in the apt words of Henry Shue, "an assault on the defenseless" (Shue 2004, 48). Nevertheless, torture is not an absolute evil. Arguments that try to prove otherwise tend to prove too much; namely that any act of force harmful to the enemy is an evil that should be forbidden. I have argued that torture, insofar as we are describing an act of interrogation initiated with the sole purpose of gaining information crucial to the lives of many innocent people, must be regulated by the same moral criteria that oversee all acts of force for a just purpose: the just war criteria of proportion and noncombatant immunity. Those criteria are not likely to be met by countries that legalize torture. Thus, if torture is ever a justifiable act, it will be so without the benefit of legal protection. I wish to emphasize that nothing in this chapter should be read as a disapproval of an absolute legal band on torture for any reason. On the contrary, I hope I have shown how anything less than an absolute ban would lead to violations of the just war criteria. We do not need to prove that torture is an inherently evil act in order to urge that it should be illegal in all circumstances. Nevertheless, legality does not exhaust morality. Not every illegal act is evil, even if it is in the best interest of a society to punish an illegal act that may be morally praiseworthy. I have argued that it will take a person of extraordinary character to be able to know when the time comes to torture. At a minimum, they will be skilled and experienced practitioners of noncoercive interrogation. When would it be absolutely necessary to torture a captured combatant? When we are reasonably certain that the prisoner possesses information about an imminent attack that would threaten the lives of many civilians, and we are equally certain that noncoercive methods are not likely to yield the crucial information in time to save the innocent. This may be a very rare occurrence but it is not impossible to imagine. The prohibition on torture, however, should not serve as a prohibition against all forms of interrogation. How to distinguish interrogation from torture can be a problem,[13] but this should not dissuade us from legitimate forms of interrogation.[14]

NOTES

1. Jeremy Bentham gives the classic utilitarian argument for torture when he argues that torture is possibly justifiable as the lesser of two evils. In other words, more utility may be had by torture than by another action. See Bentham 1962, 211a-b.
2. For examples of the pro-torture warrants position, see Dershowitz, 2004, 257–80; Krauthammer 2005, 12; and McCarthy 2004, 17–24.
3. In fact, Rutledge uses the example of a bully (Rutledge 2006, 382).
4. Perry 43. Those persuaded by this sort of argument may be led to believe that what distinguishes torture from other forms of force, such as killing and mutilation, is that victims of the latter can die a noble or dignified death but torture makes such a death impossible. While it is true that some acts of torture aim at denying the victim any kind of nobility, this aim is not always met. Victims of torture can die nobly, as we know from the stories of intelligence agents who died under torture. Anthony Cave Brown, for example,

recounts the story of British agents caught and tortured by the Gestapo. They did not talk and died under torture "in the best tradition of the service" (Brown 1975,190). In short, it was, and can be, a matter of professional and/ or national pride to withstand torture, even to the point of death.

5. A good example of this kind of literature is Cavanaugh 1998, in which he argues, "Torture is one instance of a larger confrontation of power over bodies, not just individual bodies but social bodies as well" (1–2). Cavanaugh is especially interested in the social body of the Church and how an ecclesial body can respond to repressive political regimes. However, the study focuses on the experience of Chile and the Roman Catholic Church under Augusto Pinochet, where torture was used mainly for punishment and deterrence when not purely sadistic. Moreover, even when torturing for information, the Pinochet regime was a corrupt regime that rendered all its acts of force morally suspect. Unsurprisingly, Cavanaugh does not provide arguments that would clarify why Pinochet's acts of torture were any more morally abhorrent than his acts of killing. Thus, Cavanaugh's attempt to display "how torture was used as a social discipline to atomize and scatter all social bodies which stand between the individual and the state" (15) has limited application: namely to torture used by regimes such as Pinochet's.

6. Gross suggests that the argument here is similar to that made by Walzer concerning Bomber Harris (see Gross 2004, 241–42; and Walzer 1992, 323–25). There is a similarity, but the difference is crucial; namely that Walzer wishes to defend an individual who targeted innocent people, while Gross wishes to defend individuals who target captured terrorists.

7. Gross 2004, 244, quoting from Jackson's dissenting opinion in *Korematsu v. United States*, 323 US 214, 248 (1944).

8. This may lead us to test the limits of torture techniques and wonder if any are inherently disproportionate, even if not inherently evil, like rape. I take it that some forms of extreme physical coercion, such as electrocutions and waterboarding, would be almost impossible to justify in terms of proportion outside of a clear-cut circumstance, such as one described above concerning the captured Gestapo agent. I also take it that what used to be known as "the third degree" (beatings and sleep deprivation techniques) would be easier to justify in terms of proportion.

9. McCoy dismisses CIA director Porter Goss's claim that tough interrogation techniques have been successful because the CIA refuses to document their successes. McCoy makes much of the fact that the CIA does not have one documented "ticking bomb" case to show for all their tough interrogation techniques. He argues that this is "the usual Catch-22 logic that surrounds such CIA claims" (McCoy 2006, 197). However, this reasoning may ignore the obvious: even if the CIA had been successful, its success is of the very sort that the CIA would not wish to reveal. History shows that the best intelligence coups are the ones that are kept secret. In making this point, I am not arguing for the justice of any act of torture committed by the CIA, but only that failure to make public the details of intelligence coups, however obtained, follows standard procedure for most intelligence services.

10. Andrew is quoting the diary of agent Guy Liddell.

11. Moran's advice is supported by another famously successful interrogator for the German Luftwaffe, Hans Joachim Scharff. See Budiansky 2005, 32.

12. The ruling is in *H.C. 5100/94 Public Committee Against Torture In Israel and Others v. The State of Israel, the General Security Services and Other*, 53 (4) PD817 (1999).

13. Richard A. Posner (2004, 291–92) argues that torture lacks a stable definition, because what counts as torture for one may not count as torture for

another (291–92). This may be true but, as Dr. Johnson says somewhere, the fact of twilight does not mean you cannot tell day from night. The fact that there are certain acts of interrogation that border on torture do not prevent us from recognizing some acts as torture, pure and simple. Nevertheless, Heather MacDonald is surely right to argue that interrogators should be allowed to use stress techniques against unlawful combatants on a regular basis without the threat of legal action (MacDonald 2006, 95). Such techniques are not what most people would describe as torture.

14. This chapter is a revision of an essay that first appeared in Cole 2012.

BIBLIOGRAPHY

Abbot, Walter M. (ed.). (1966). *The Documents of Vatican II*. Translation directed by Joseph Gallagher. New York: Herder and Herder.

Andrew, Christopher. (2010). *Defend the Realm: The Authorized History of MI5*. New York: Vintage Books.

Aquinas, Thomas. (1948). *Summa Theologica*. 1256–72. Translated by the Fathers of the English Dominican Province. New York: Benziger Brothers.

Baxter, Richard. (1830). *A Christian Directory*. 1654. In *The Practical Works of Richard Baxter*, vol. 6. London: James Duncan.

Bentham, Jeremy. (1962). *Panopticon versus New South Wales*. 1812. In *Works of Jeremy Bentham*. Edited by John Bowling, vol. 4. New York: Russell and Russell, Inc.

Bonhoeffer, Dietrich. (1955). *Ethics*. 1949. New York: Simon & Schuster.

———. (1963). *The Communion of Saints*. New York: Harper and Row.

———. (1972). *Letters and Papers from Prison*. Edited by Eberhard Bethge. New York: MacMillan Publishing Company.

Brown, Anthony Cave. (1975). *Bodyguard of Lies*. New York: Harper & Row.

Budiansky, Stephen. (2005). "Intelligence: Truth Extraction." *The Atlantic Monthly* 295(3): 32–35.

Cavanaugh, William T. (1998). *Torture and Eucharist: Theology, Politics, and the Body of Christ*. Oxford: Basil Blackwell Publishing.

Cole, Darrell. (2012). "Torture and Just War." *Journal of Religious Ethics* 40(1): 26–51.

Danner, Mark. (2004). *Torture and Truth: America, Abu Ghraib, and the War on Terror*. New York: New York Review Books.

Dershowitz, Alan. (2004). "Tortured Reasoning." In Levinson 2004, 257–80.

Feinberg, Joel. (1985). "The Mistreatment of Dead Bodies." *The Hastings Center Report* 15(1): 31–37.

Greenberg, Karen J. (2006). *The Torture Debate in America*. Cambridge, MA: Cambridge University Press.

Gross, Oren. (2004). "The Prohibition on Torture and the Limits of Law." In Levinson 2004, 229–53.

Grossman, David. (1995). *On Killing: The Psychological Cost of Learning to Kill in War and Society*. Boston, MA: Little, Brown & Co.

Grotius, Hugo. (1925). *The Laws of War and Peace*. 1646. Translated by Francis W. Kelsey. Oxford: Clarendon Press.

Gur-Ayre, Miriam. (2004). "Can the War Against Terror Justify the Use of Force in Interrogation? Reflection in Light of the Israeli Experience." In *Torture: A Collection*, edited by Sanford Levinson, 183–98. New York: Oxford University Press.

Gushee, David P. (2006). "Against Torture: An Evangelical Perspective." *Theology Today* 63(3): 349–64.

Hare, R. M. (1963). *Freedom and Reason*. Oxford: Oxford University Press.

Hunsinger, George. (2006). "Torture, Common Morality, and the Golden Rule: A Conversation with Michael Perry." *Theology Today* 63(3): 375–79.

Johnson, William R. (1986). "Tricks of the Trade: Counterintelligence Interrogation." *International Journal of Intelligence and Counterintelligence* 1(2):103–113.

Kass, Leon R. (1997). "The Wisdom of Repugnance." *The New Republic* 216(3): 17–26.

Krauthammer, Charles. (2005). "The Truth About Torture." *The Weekly Standard* 118(1):12.

Levison, Sanford, ed. (2004). *Torture: A Collection*. New York: Oxford University Press.

Little, David. (1993). "The Nature and Basis of Human Rights." In *Prospects for a Common Morality*, edited by Gene Outka and John P. Reeder, Jr., 73–92. Princeton, NJ: Princeton University Press.

Luban, David. (2006). "Liberalism, Torture, and the Ticking Bomb." In *The Torture Debate in America*, edited by Karen J. Greenberg, 35–83. Cambridge, MA: Cambridge University.

Luther, Martin. (1967). "Whether Soldiers, Too, Can Be Saved." 1526. In *Luther's Works*, vol. 46, edited by Helmut Lehmann, 87–137. Philadelphia, PA: Fortress Press.

MacDonald, Heather. (2006). "How To Interrogate Terrorists." In *The Torture Debate in America*, edited by Karen J. Greenberg, 84–97. Cambridge, MA: Cambridge University.

McCarthy, Andrew C. (2004). "Torture: Thinking About the Unthinkable." *Commentary* 11(12): 17–24.

McCoy, Alfred W. (2006). *A Question of Torture: CIA Interrogation, from the Cold War to the War on Terror*. New York: Henry Hold and Company.

McDowell, John. (1979). "Virtue and Reason." *The Monist* 62(3): 331–50.

Nagel, Thomas. (1972). "War and Massacre." *Philosophy and Public Affairs* 15(6): 132–33.

Niebuhr, Reinhold. (1957). "The Ethic of Jesus and the Social Problem." In *Love and Justice: Selections from the Shorter Writings of Reinhold Neibuhr*, edited by D.B. Robertson, 29–40. Louisville, KY: Westminster/John Knox Press.

Ortiz, Dianna. (2006). "Theology, International Law, and Torture." *Theology Today* 63(3): 344–48.

Parry, John T. (2004). "Escalation and Necessity: Defining Torture at Home and Abroad." In *Torture: A Collection*, edited by Sanford Levinson, 145–64. New York: Oxford University Press.

Paul, John II. (1994). *Veritatis Splendor*. In John Wilkins, *Considering Veritatis Splendor*. Cleveland, OH: The Pilgrim Press.

Perry, John. (2005). *Torture: Religious Ethics and National Security*. Maryknoll, NY: Orbis Books.

Peters, Edward. (1985). *Torture*. New York: Basil Blackwell.

Phillips, D. Z. (1996). *Religion and Morality*. New York: St. Martin's Press.

Porter, Jean. (2008). "Torture and the Christian Conscience: A Response to Jeremy Waldron." *Scottish Journal of Theology*. 61(3): 340–58.

Posner, Richard A. (2004). "Torture, Terrorism, and Interrogation." In *Torture: A Collection*, edited by Sanford Levinson, 291–98. New York: Oxford University Press.

Quinn, Philip L. (1996). "Relativism About Torture: Religious and Secular Responses." In *Religion and* Mortality, edited by D. Z. Phillips, 151–70. New York: St. Martin's Press.

Ramsey, Paul. (1988). *Speak Up For Just War or Pacifism*. University Park, PA: The Pennsylvania State University Press.

Rasmussen, Larry. (1972). Dietrich Bonhoeffer: Reality and Resistance. Nashville, TN: Abingdon Press.

Runzo, Joseph. (1996). "Reply: Ethical Universality and Ethical Relativism." In *Religion and* Mortality, edited by D. Z. Phillips, 171–87. New York: St. Martin's Press.

Rutledge, Fleming. (2006). "My Enemy, Myself." *Theology Today 63*(3): 380–85.

Scarry, Elaine. (2004). "Five Errors in the Reasoning of Alan Dershowitz." In *Torture: A Collection*, edited by Sanford Levinson, 281–90. New York: Oxford University Press.

Shaffer, Anthony. (2010). *Operation Dark Heart: Spycraft and Special Ops on the Frontlines of Afghanistan and the Path to Victory*. New York: St. Martin's Press.

Shue, Henry. (2004). "Torture." In *Torture: A Collection*, edited by Sanford Levinson, 47–60. New York: Oxford University Press.

Sussman, David. (2005). "What's Wrong with Torture?" *Philosophy and Public Affairs. 33*(1): 1–33.

Vatican Council of Catholic Bishops. (1966). *Gaudiem et Spes*. In *The Documents of Vatican II*, edited by Walter Abbott, 199–308. New York: Herder & Herder Association Press.

Waldron, Jeremy. (2006). "What Can Christian Teaching Add to the Debate about Torture." *Theology Today 63*(3): 330–43.

Walzer, Michael. (1973). "Political Action: The Problem of Dirty Hands." *Philosophy and Public Affairs 2*(2): 160–80.

——. (1992). *Just and Unjust Wars: A Moral Argument with Historical Illustrations*. 2nd ed. New York: Basic Books.

——. (2004). *Arguing About War*. New Haven, CT: Yale University Press.

Williams, Bernard. (1995). *Making Sense of Humanity and Other Philosophical Papers*. Cambridge, MA: Cambridge University Press.

Wolfendale, Jessica. (2007). *Torture and the Military Profession*. New York: Palgrave MacMillan.

6 Assassination

Governments have a long history of using assassination as a way to deal with enemies on an individual basis without resort to more overt and full-scale military operations. They have also resorted to assassination in war as a way to eliminate the political leaders of enemy nations. The United States during World War II, for example, put Boston industrialist Stanley Lovell to work on various plans to assassinate Hitler (Marks 1979, 15–19). Assassination is usually associated with the various jobs carried out by a "clandestine service." Some members of the spying profession have sought to disassociate their service from the job of assassination. Former MI6 agent J. C. Lawson argued, for example, that a secret agent's

> personal predilections in favour of keeping the ten commandments may be such that no act of his is likely to stain his country's good repute; but then an intransigent attitude towards moral standards in war-time will also impair his efficiency as an agent. "Thou shall not kill" does not veto extermination of the enemy. What then is my conclusion? Roughly this, that the ethics of secret service in war-time do not permit the furtherance of schemes whose object is homicide, but neither do they prohibit enterprises from which the risk of incidental homicide cannot be excluded. (Lawson 1920, 29)

Lawson, in an unusual show of chivalry for a spy, shows a notable distaste for assassination even in time of war, though he is not against operations that may lead to killing the enemy, as long as the intention of the operation is not simple killing. Lawson served in MI6 during World War I. If his view on assassination was a popular one, the view had certainly become quaint by World War II. The OSS was very successful in using partisan groups in France and Yugoslavia for assassination. US intelligence services continued the practice during the Cold War by encouraging and supporting anti-communist partisan groups to assassinate leaders of the Soviet Ministry of Internal Affairs (MVD) and Ministry of State Security (MGB). British MI6 reportedly followed the same practice.

Assassination is usually defined as a political killing (Zellner 1974, 2; and Lackey 1974, 57). According to this definition, if the individuals targeted have a purely military function, say low-ranking generals and anyone else below them on the military hierarchy, then we do not think of them as being assassinated, but merely killed in action, even if they were singled out by the enemy. The point of the definition is that, in order to qualify for an assassination, the target must have some policy-making clout. Such targets may not be politicians in the sense of holding an elected office, or even members of a political cabinet, but they must play a role in creating the policy of the government for which they serve. Thus, we could add to the list any military official of high rank who is singled out for killing. While it is true that targeted killings of this kind are best described as acts of assassination, the definition should not be restricted to targeted killings of policy-making agents. Eisenhower was a target for assassination while he served as Supreme Allied Commander in the European theater of war. Had German paratroopers been successful in killing him during the Battle of the Bulge, we would have called that act an assassination just as well as if the target had been Churchill. Also, when partisan groups target the officers of occupying forces, as the French Maque often did during World War II, those are assassinations. When Israeli agents target Iranian nuclear scientists, that too is assassination. The targeting of members of criminal gangs, including terrorist gangs, and the peacetime targeting of individuals in the secret services of enemy nations also count as acts of assassination. Thus, for our purposes, an assassination is the targeted killing of specific individuals deemed dangerous to the common good.

Acts of assassination must be distinguished from acts of terrorism. The distinction is an important one, because terrorists so frequently employ assassination as a tactic that one can too easily fall into the trap of treating assassination as something that only terrorists do. Walter Laqueur, for example, treats assassination as the work of an individual or group in a position of relative weakness to the political powers they wish to overthrow or influence. The weak resort to assassination since they do not have the political or military power to make the changes they wish. Thus, for Laqueur, assassination ends up being synonymous with terrorism (Laqueur 1977, 3–20). Indiscriminate killing is certainly terroristic but not all terrorist acts are indiscriminate. Any discriminate targeting of specific individuals is an act of assassination, whether those targeting have a just cause or not. However, one does not need to be in a position of weakness in order to assassinate. The strong may choose to do so, for many reasons.

The introduction to the Church Committee Interim Report states that assassination may be morally distinguished from killing in war or in covert operations because it is a "cold blooded, targeted, intentional killing of an individual foreign leader" (U.S. Congress 1975, 6). Unfortunately, the committee does little to tell us how or why a "cold blooded, targeted, intentional killing" is morally different from killing in war or in covert operations. Not all killing in war or in covert operations is "hot blooded." Are the "cold-blooded" killings in war and covert operations unjust or somehow more morally blameworthy because they are more under the control of reason and not so "hot blooded?" This seems a counter-intuitive claim and certainly far away from the Augustinian argument that what makes killing possibly justifiable is precisely the cold-blooded nature of the office-holder who does not use violence for personal reasons. Perhaps the committee was thinking more about the person targeted—political leaders like those who serve on the Church Committee. In any event, the committee is certainly right to point out a salient feature of assassination: it is reasoned, cold-blooded, specific targeting. However, the moral problems of assassination can differ, depending on the target.

Every assassination must deal with legal questions, which always impinge on morality even if morality may trump legal concerns in some cases. That is to say, since assassination is illegal in many countries, and probably under international law as well, then, like covert operations, we must be very careful of our justifications for overriding a legal prohibition in the name of "doing the right thing." Also, any attempt to justify the assassination of a political leader must concern itself with questions about the likely consequences. If you kill a military or political leader, the reprisals against innocent people could be horrific. If you kill the leader of a nation, then that nation is without a leader until someone takes his or her place, which can invite civil war. Thus, for our limited purposes, we may concentrate on broaching two potential moral problems with assassination: is assassination a tactic morally similar to covert actions: illegal but sometimes justifiable? Can assassination meet the demands of the just war criteria? The criteria of noncombatant immunity and proportion will be discussed in detail, for both are a matter of some controversy when applied to assassination. Who counts as a legitimate target for assassination can be very tricky. Trickier still is trying to figure out if more good than evil will result, especially in cases where rebellion or regime change is a likely outcome.

ASSASSINATION, MORALITY, AND LAW: A BRIEF OVERVIEW

Assassination was the typical way of dealing with tyrants in the ancient world. Such an act was considered noble. Assassination is not something that seems to concern early and medieval Christian philosophers. Cassian (*Conferences* 6.10.1), Jerome (*Homilies on the Psalms* 20 and 90), Origen (*Homilies on Judges* 4.1), and Augustine (*City of God* 17.13) do not feel compelled to defend, for example, the act of assassination recorded in Judges 3:12–31, where Ehud delivers Israel from oppression by assassinating Eglon, the king of Moab, in the way they feel compelled to defend lying and atrocious acts of violence. Jerome, in particular, says, "The man, Ehud, who is written of in the book of Judges, is said to have two right hands because he was a just man and killed that fat stupid king" (*Homilies on the Psalms* 20). Aquinas argued that a tyrant could be killed and uses the example of Ehud and Eglon as an example, but warns that assassination should not be carried out by a private individual but by someone with public authority (see *On Kingship* I.6 and *Summa Theologica* II–II Q.42, A.2). John of Salisbury also defended the assassination of a tyrant, appealing to the biblical stories of Ehud killing Eglon, Jael killing Sisara, and Judith killing Holofernes as proof that no blame is "attached to any of those by whose valor a penitent and humble people was thus set free, but their memory is preserved by affection in posterity as servants of the Lord" (*Policraticus* VIII.20).

Grotius, who considers assassination part of the job description of a spy, argues that killing a political leader with poison should be outlawed in order that the dangers of war "might not be too widely extended" (*Laws* III.IV.XV). Grotius does not appear to be worried about trying to meet the requirements of proportion but that political leaders should be protected from treachery. Nevertheless, when Grotius wryly observes that the agreement against poisoning originated with kings—those most likely targeted for poisoning—one cannot help but think that he was not satisfied with the reasoning behind the prohibition. One also thinks of the remark attributed to US President Kennedy when asked about whether or not he wished to assassinate a particularly dangerous enemy: "We can't get into that kind of thing or we would all be targets" (quoted in U.S. Congress 1975, 287). Grotius is more adamant in his defense of assassination by someone who has not violated "an express or tacit obligation of good faith, as subjects resorting to violence against a king, vassals against a lord, soldiers against him whom they serve, those also who have been received as suppliants or strangers or deserters, against those who have received them" (*Laws* III. IV.XVIII.1). For an enemy agent to penetrate into a political leader's realm and manage to kill him is an act entirely consonant with just war fighting. However, it is equally just for the potential victim of the spy to treat the captured spy more harshly than a regular soldier. For Grotius, there is no violation of the law of nations when spies are employed to assassinate but neither is there a violation when captured spies are not given the same rights as regular prisoners of war.[1]

Grotius's arguments are still reflected in contemporary international law that does not protect captured spies to the same degree that it protects prisoners of war, which is not to say that international law affords captured spies no protection. We see this particularly in 1907 Hague Convention IV, Annex, Section II, Article 30, which states, "A spy taken in the acts shall not be punished without previous trial" (Roberts and Guelff 2005, 79). This stricture was an attempt to put an end to the common practice of spies being shot out of hand (when not tortured first). Nevertheless, belligerents are not required to treat spies as prisoners of war: they may be tried and punished. In fact, the 1949 Geneva Convention IV Relative to the Protection of

Civilian Persons in Time of War, Part I, Article 5 states that captured spies have forfeited the rights given to captured soldiers but "shall nevertheless be treated with humanity, and in the case of trial, shall not be deprived of the rights of fair and regular trial prescribed by the present Convention" (Roberts and Guelff 2005, 79). The 1977 Geneva Protocol I, Part III, Section I, Article 37 prohibits perfidy but Article 39.3 states that the prohibition does not apply to the "existing generally recognized rules of international law applicable to espionage." Further, Article 46.1 states that those who engage in espionage "shall not have the right to the status of prisoner of war and may be treated as a spy" (Roberts and Guelff 2005, 443, 446). Thus, spies are not forbidden certain tactics that are forbidden to regular soldiers but, if captured, they are not given the same protection that is given to regular soldiers. When governments formulate policies that argue for the legality of assassination ("targeted killings") of terrorist leaders in wartime, they are understandable only within the logic first articulated by Grotius: in wartime, spies can do things ordinary soldiers cannot. Naturally, if those who carry out "targeted killings" are not regular soldiers, or are regular soldiers out of uniform (in other words, if they are spies), and they are caught by the enemy, then those who employ them cannot cry foul if the enemy does not treat them as legitimate prisoners of war. That, too, is following the logic of Grotius.

Assassination is probably illegal under international law. The 1907 Hague Convention IV, Annex, Section II, Article 23 (b), which states that it is "forbidden to kill or wound treacherously individuals belonging to the hostile nation or army," and the 1977 Geneva Protocol I Additional to the Geneva Convention of 1949, and Relating to the Protection of Victims of Non-International Armed Conflicts, Part III, Section I, Article 37, which prohibits attacks that rely upon "perfidy," have been read by some scholars as prohibitions on assassination.[2] Nevertheless, the articles need not be read as touching on assassination. Thus, when rumors began to swirl that the CIA had been practicing a policy of assassination for years, certain US presidents created a policy on assassination in what should probably be read as an attempt to pacify the growing negative public opinion about the tactics of the CIA. Perhaps, too, the newly created policy should be read as an effort at preemptive reciprocity, but lingering doubts about the CIA's public denials of the tactic, particularly with regard to operations in Nicaragua in the 1980s and the George W. Bush administration's pro-assassination policy toward terrorist leaders, leads one to doubt that preemptive reciprocity played a leading role in the decision. In any event, official US policy has forbidden assassination since 1976, when President Gerald Ford signed Executive Order 11905, which states, "No employee of the United States Government shall engage in, or conspire to engage in, political Assassination." Presidents Jimmy Carter and Ronald Reagan affirmed the prohibition in Executive Orders 12036 and 12333, respectively. Government lawyers working for President George W. Bush have argued that the Executive

Orders on assassination do not apply in wartime, and so paved the way for current US policy about taking out "high-value targets" by capture or kill methods in the War on Terror. Nevertheless, assassination is illegal under US law (except, perhaps, when US Congress declares war, something it has not been given much of a chance to do in the recent past), but so are covert operations that interfere with a sovereign government, and we have seen how some covert actions may be justifiable. The key to justifying assassinations that may be illegal can be found in trying to figure out if the proposed act can meet the demands of the just war criteria.

ASSASSINATION AND THE *JUS AD BELLUM*

The first criteria that must be established if we wish to justify an act of assassination are those that establish the justice of the conflict itself: right authority, just cause, right intention, and reasonable hope for success. For our purposes, right authority would mean that the established head of state would have to authorize the particular act of assassination. What would count as a just cause for an assassination? In cases of military figures with little political clout, the just cause of the assassination would be identical with the just cause of the war itself. In cases of political assassination, Ramon Lemos has argued that the existing government's practices and policies must be "seriously incompatible" with the promotion of the common good (Lemos 1974, 80). Lemos adds that no act of assassination in a rebellion could be justified when the target is in office in a republican or democratic form of government, for such a person would represent the will of the people, and so the conspirators would be setting themselves against the majority and determining for everyone else what the laws and policies should be. This is a problematic restriction, for it assumes that the majority sentiment is always right or at least morally and legally inviolable to acts of force, which would lead us to some strange conclusions, such as it would have been wrong to assassinate the president of the Confederacy, Jefferson Davis, during the US Civil War because he represented the will of the people, or even stranger, that Neville Chamberlain would have been wrong to order the assassination of Adolph Hitler for the simple reason that Hitler was elected by the German people. Thus, we should hold that there is just cause for a political assassination when that politician plays a key role in formulating or carrying out policies that are seriously incompatible with the common good.

We turn now to the criterion of right intention. Douglas Lackey has argued that we must show that good results are intended and show how the assassination will bring about these results. The key question one must ask is, "What precisely would be the state of the world, if things work out as you intend?" (Lackey 1974, 6). We must be able to show that the intention is good. We can do this in two ways. First, we can we show that the means are efficient, necessary, and can produce more good than evil. Second, we should be able to show that the assassination was planned and carried out with due attention to the consequences.

When we turn to the criterion of reasonable hope for success, we notice that the stricture is meant to make sure that our acts in war are likely to succeed in accomplishing what we intend for them to accomplish. If we are targeting, say, a politician, we must ask if the assassination is likely to contribute significantly to the promotion of the common good. We would do well to keep in mind the dangers: The target could be replaced with a like-minded figure. There may not be sufficient sentiment within the community for any change in policy or direction. There could be an increase in retaliatory violence that would make success very costly, perhaps too costly.

Some have included a kind of last-resort criterion for assassination. Haig Khatchadourian, for example, has argued that political assassination is morally unjustified because the victim's right to life is abrogated without his consent, without due process of law, and it is, therefore, a case of enemies taking the law into their own hands. Also, it is never the last resort. Even the attempt to assassinate Hitler was unjust, because the same objective could have been attained by kidnapping and setting up a provisional government (Khatchadourian 1974, 51–52). The first part of the argument works only if the target is not legitimate. If it is true that all political leaders are protected by international law from being targets of assassination, then we have to ask if the act of assassination is worth the price of overriding the law. However, "last resort" in this argument is meaningless; that is to say, it is a criterion with no practical purpose other than prohibiting the very act the criterion is supposed to be able to justify in some circumstances. If last resort is not met in the case of Hitler, then it can never be met, which is, I believe, the point of Khatchadourian's argument, but the point is mistaken. The criterion of last resort must have some practical use; it must mean an exhaustion of all reasonable alternatives and not mean exhaustion of all possible means. We see the reasoning of the former on display in Lemos's argument that an assassination is justified only if it is extremely probable if not certain that (1) the changes sought cannot be made through a lesser evil within a reasonable amount of time, and (2) the assassination contributes more significantly to the change that promotes a greater good than any other act in a reasonable amount of time (Lemos 1974, 80). These strictures have the advantage of not turning "last resort" into a rational exercise for eliminating all acts of force on the dubious conclusion that we have not exhausted every possibility. We should always seek peaceful alternatives when circumstances allow us to do so. We should also realize that assassination can achieve the same goal as some wars: elimination of a particularly evil head of state. The real question is not one of last resort, but whether or not the proposed assassination is the only or best way to achieve our goals.

ASSASSINATION AND DISCRIMINATION:
WHO MAY BE TARGETED?

The just war criterion of noncombatant immunity means that we must discriminate in choosing our targets and we may never intentionally target those who do not deserve to be targeted. There is no difficulty in this when the target is a military or intelligence figure, but what about political leaders or even lower-ranking politicians and cabinet members who may play a role in formulating war plans and preparations, or scientists who work on military projects? Rachels has argued that politicians responsible for the injustices and sufferings that lead them to be targeted may have their right not to be killed trumped by their unjust behavior. Such politicians forfeit their rights by not respecting the rights of others (Rachels 1974, 16–17). In international law, those who qualify as targets in wartime are those who are direct participants in the conflict. This includes those who fire weapons, practice sabotage, deliver ammunitions to combatants, or gather intelligence. Mere contributions to the general war effort do not count and this includes working in a weapons factory. This argument is supported by David, who argues that since all citizens contribute to the general war effort to some extent, to target such people is to render the concept of noncombatancy meaningless (David 2002, 249). However, contra David, we must distinguish general and particular war efforts. Making clothes is general, but making ammunition and weapons is particular. All workers in, say, an airplane factory, would be legitimate targets in a bombing campaign. Any creator or key person in the manufacturing process of armaments—conventional or nuclear—could be a just target of assassination if the outcome is significant.

What must we look for when we say that someone is a legitimate target for assassination? Khatchadourian makes a good point when he argues that we cannot simply think that our target deserves killing. Instead, our motives "must be grounded on actual facts as far as ascertainable in the circumstances, not on mere assumption or presumption of guilt, a downright error, or prejudice" (Khatchadourian 1974, 44). We must have good reasons for assassination, and those reasons must be founded on objective facts. Let's turn to the infamous case of the British Secret Service's involvement in the torture and murder of Grigori Rasputin in late Czarist Russia during World War I. Rasputin was using his considerable influence in the court to persuade the tsar to make a separate peace with Germany, which would prove harmful to Britain. British agents with Russian help tortured Rasputin in order to get at the truth of the matter and then killed him. Rasputin certainly had no combat status but served a role roughly analogous to a cabinet member. If we assume that Rasputin was acting in good faith; that is to say, if he was advising the tsar to do what he honestly thought was best for the country and not acting as a paid agent of Germany or some other interest opposed to Russia and not acting out of malice toward Britain, then Rasputin was not giving advice for the purpose of harming Britain, and, therefore, was not a proper target for assassination.

Members of the military who also serve as political leaders can pose a special problem. Let's take as an example the case of Reinhard Heydrich, who was targeted by British Intelligence and Czech underground fighters. In the case of Heydrich, it is hard to define his combat status. He was both a member of the military and a head of state. This brings us to Walzer's worry about assassins: they generally target nonmilitary persons (especially government officials and heads of state) who are not normally considered as legitimate objects of attack in a just war. If Heydrich was a legitimate target, then so are the Prime Minister of Britain and the President of the United States (Commander-in-Chief of the Armed Forces), even if they do not wear a uniform, as Heydrich did. In fact, many leaders of nation-states are the titular (and sometimes actual) leaders of the armed forces. If you play an active role in the planning of military strategy, then you are a combatant. Titular heads of the armed forces may or may not play such a role in forming military strategy. Heads of state certainly play a role in establishing military policy, and this would make them legitimate targets in the eyes of classical just war theory (although, as we will see below, the criterion of proportion would still have to be met). Nevertheless, as Walzer suggests, this "only partially represents our common moral judgments, for we judge the assassin by his victim, and when the victim is Hitler-like in character, we are likely to praise the assassin's work, though we still do not call him a soldier (Walzer 1977, 199–200).[3] Heydrich was, arguably, more Hitler-like than Hitler. He did not allow the cold reasons of war-time expediency to stand in the way of his ruthless treatment of Jews. However, we are even more likely to praise the assassin's work if proportion and noncombatant immunity are preserved both in the act itself and the aftermath. The aftermath of the Heydrich assassination was excessive Nazi reprisals that may have outweighed any good achieved by the assassination.

There has long been an unwritten law that enemy agents are proper targets for assassination. Testimony to the Church Committee on Alleged Assassination Plots confirmed that the law was upheld in the CIA: "In the international clandestine operations business, it was part of the code that the one and only remedy for the unfrocked double agent was to kill him and all double agents knew that. That was part of the occupational hazard of the job" (quoted in U.S. Congress 1975, 121). The United States supported the assassination of Soviet intelligence rings in the US zone of Germany and Czechoslovakia. One may counter, as did former CIA paramilitary expert Franklin Lindsay, that such killings should not be referred to as assassinations but as simple killings of enemy soldiers (Simpson 1988, 151–52). But agents are not soldiers and one would not formulate intricate plans to knock off a dozen or so soldiers in the way one works out plans to eliminate a group of enemy agents.

The question of who could be a legitimate target for assassination in a terrorist organization is difficult to answer. For our purposes, terrorism names the use of violence, unusually indiscriminate, in order to undermine the morale of some enemy. Terrorist tactics can be more or less just, depending on their conformity to the moral criteria of discrimination and proportion. Terrorist organizations may or may not have a high degree of organization but they are usually not organized governments like Nazi Germany or the Soviet Union. The typical range of opinions on treating members of terrorist groups as proper targets can be found in Ben-Naftali and Michael, Casses, and Ruys on how to consider Palestinian terrorists. Ben-Naftali and Michaeli argue that members of terrorist organizations, such as Tanzim and Hamas, should at all times be considered combatants, not simply when in the act of terrorizing (Ben-Naftali and Michaeli 2003, 271–72). Thus, they should be distinguished from ordinary citizens even though they are not members of the military of some recognized government, such as Nazi Germany. In sharp distinction, Cassese argues that Palestinian terrorists should be treated as citizens, because if they are treated otherwise, then we would be authorizing the Israeli military to shoot any civilian (Cassese 2003, 7–10). Ruys also argues that Ben-Naftali and Michaeli are wrong because their approach treats all members of terrorist organizations equally when, in fact, they are not "equally intensely engaged in hostilities against Israeli civilians and military personnel" (Ruys 2005, 26). This would contravene the customary rule about doubtful cases of civilian status.

Ben-Naftali and Michaeli get the better of the argument. To give terrorists the status as noncombatants does not reflect reality. Also, it is likely to result in an increase in civilian casualties. To be a member of a terrorist organization is equivalent to being a member of the enemy military. In fact, being a member of a terrorist organization is barely distinguishable, morally speaking, from being a member of Hitler's SS. The comparison is apt. Members of both groups work to undermine the liberties protected by the rule of law. Nevertheless, not every member of the Nazi military, including the SS, was equally intensely engaged in hostilities, but they were all legitimate targets by virtue of their being members of the enemy military. Terrorists should get no special protection from international law simply because they lack the dark uniforms and swastika emblems. There is no risk of contravening the customary rule about doubtful civilian status. A member of a terrorist organization gives up ordinary civilian status. Of course, proportion must be upheld when targets are chosen. Assassinating an SS army cook would not be proportionate even though military cooks are all official members of the military and do not count as illegitimate targets in larger military strikes against enemy forces. In like manner, if a terrorist group is organized to such a degree that it includes members who do not actually participate in violent operations or in intelligence gathering (a very doubtful proposition), then it would not be proportionate to target such members. Nevertheless, we can recognize leadership status even within loosely bound criminal gangs.

Although all members of terrorist groups are legitimate targets for large military strikes, any terrorist targeted for assassination must be someone of importance within the organization, or a known participator in violent actions, or an intelligence gatherer. In summary, all members of terrorist groups are proper targets in large-scale attacks but only high-value terrorists should be targeted for assassination.

ASSASSINATION AND PROPORTION

Former CIA head Richard Helms testified that he was opposed to assassination for three moral and practical reasons: (1) it is very hard to keep it a secret, so it will do political damage and hurt the country's reputation; (2) it is very difficult to tell if you are better off or not after the assassination; and (3) it invites reciprocal action (U.S. Congress 1975, 281–82). Each of these concerns reflect a concern for proportion, a just war criterion that demands that more good than evil come of our proposed acts in war. Proportion leads us to ask if a proposed act achieves the best overall balance of maximizing goodness and minimizing evil. We must also ask if a proposed act is the only way of getting the job done or if there are less objectionable means; that is to say, is there a means that does not carry the same risks for bad consequences? Consider, for instance, the assassination of IRA commander John Francis Green in January 1975. A British intelligence team was sent to Ireland in 1974 commanded by Captain John Ball, who had set up the Army's first covert observation post in Republican Belfast, and with Lieutenant Robert Nairac as his second-in-command. Ball and Nairac contacted intelligence officers in Armagh, told them they were under orders from MI6, and asked them for suitable targets. The name of Green was given and Ball and Nairac ran him down and killed him. Ball and Nairac were probably not under orders from MI6, which meant the assassination lacked proper authority.[4] In any event, the consequences were disastrous. The IRA ended its truce, blaming British SAS for the assassination (Ball and Nairac had both been members), and thus was able to regain political momentum to keep their movement alive. The renewed violence also cut short covert talks between the IRA and moderate Protestant clergy.

Consider also the alleged Israeli (and possibly the United States) attempt to thwart Iranian nuclear capabilities through a series of assassinations of key scientists. The assassination of Mustafa Ahmadi Roshan, a department supervisor at the Natanz uranium enrichment plant, in January 2012 is a good example. The assassination was carried out by a motorcyclist who attached a magnetic bomb to Roshan's car. The bomb, a low-yield type designed to kill only one or two people, exploded soon after the motorcyclist sped away and both Roshan and his driver were killed. The concerns about discrimination are largely met if, indeed, Roshan was a key figure in the development of nuclear armaments capabilities for a regime openly hostile to Israel. Collateral damage concerns appear to be met by the method of assassination—a low-yield bomb placed specifically on the vehicle in which the target is a passenger. Drivers of state officials, particularly military or key civilian personnel of those who work on military capabilities—such as nuclear scientists—may not be proper targets of assassination, in the sense that they should not be specifically targeted, but neither can they be counted as innocent civilians. Much like military drivers, they inhabit a profession in which they make themselves morally legitimate collateral damage. The main concern of such assassinations is proportion. The good of the assassination is that it can discourage Iran's desire to possess nuclear weapons, or at least slow the development of such weaponry, and do so in a way that does not provoke the same reactions as overt air strikes on nuclear facilities. Too, the tactic gives Iran's regime a face-saving out if it decides to forgo the pursuit of nuclear weapons capability. The negatives include concerns about undercutting peaceful negotiations and possibly hardening Iranian resolve for nuclear weapons capability.

We should also keep in mind the ramifications that come from where we choose to assassinate. We could violate the sovereignty of a nation if we choose to assassinate within its borders without express permission. Neil C. Livingstone has rightly argued that, as a matter of proportion, we should try to assassinate legitimate targets when not on their national soil in order to avoid giving the state a reason to retaliate or to wish to break off any advantageous political relationship (Livingston 1982, 175). In order to balance these concerns when considering the demands of proportion, one would have to make a decision, probably based in large part on intelligence reports, on how important Roshan was to the nuclear program. (I take it that the establishment of such a program as fact would be necessary to justify the assassination as a discriminate act.) Would his death likely cause a significant delay in the program? Is there any good evidence either way that the previous assassinations (there have been a total of five as of January 2012) have discouraged or incited Iran's resolve to possess nuclear weapons? These questions could be answered in such a way as to justify the assassination. (Remember, I am merely trying to show how such actions might be justifiable. I am not trying to justify any particular act of assassination.)

PROPORTION AND COLLATERAL DAMAGE

Planned assassinations must take into consideration the probable collateral damage when the choice of weaponry is not the proverbial assassin's dagger or bullet. New cyber warfare capabilities give us unprecedented opportunities to assassinate discriminately. Agents may be able, for example, to gain access to unencrypted wireless signals used to control a combination defibrillator and pacemaker. The same agents who may be able to cause a pacemaker to malfunction, thus killing someone who deserves to be killed, may also be able to degrade medical system data in order to change the results of medical tests. While the target in question may be adversely affected by the change, another result may be that medical professionals begin to distrust their computer screens, and this would most certainly mean less effective health care for innocent patients. Nevertheless, in the contemporary assassin's arena, missiles and bombs are just as likely as bullets or cyber weapons to be used. We see this concern reflected in Lt. Col. Anthony Shaffer's description of a typical operation against enablers of the Taliban in Afghanistan. Information led the operations team to believe that only members and enablers (those supplying arms and money) and members of the Taliban would be present. Nevertheless, the team used smart bomb technology to cut down on any possibility of disproportionate collateral damage (Shaffer 2010, 64–65). In order to explore the topic in more depth, let us take a look at three cases in which Israeli defense forces carried out assassinations on terrorist leaders. In the first case, an Israeli Defense Forces (IDF) helicopter fired three missiles at terrorist leader Hussein Abayat, who was driving his car through a crowded street. Abayat was killed, but so were two innocent civilians, and other bystanders were wounded. In the second case, the IDF fired a one-ton warhead missile into a building in Gaza in order to kill Salah Shehada, the head of a military wing of the Hamas. Sixteen bystanders were killed (including nine children), eighty people were injured, and four residential buildings destroyed, thus displacing all the residents. In the third case, the Mivtah Elohim (Wrath of God), an Israeli special anti-terror squad, raided Beirut in April 1973 in order to kill Palestinian terrorist leaders. They succeeded in killing three leaders but more than a dozen others were killed.

The Israeli justification in each case was prevention of a terrorist attack on civilians. In order to decide proportion in the first case, we would have to know if there was any other way to bring Abayat to justice, or any other way to kill him when he was more isolated. These questions could be answered in such a way as to lead us to conclude that the assassination was proportionate. However, we would have a hard time justifying the second case in which the "overkill" seems obvious. In the third case, we would have to know whether or not the terrorist leaders have played an active role and intend to continue playing an active role in attacking Israel, and if there was any other way of laying hands on the terrorist leaders or eliminating them. The targets must constitute a present threat. Assassination cannot be used as a form of punishment. Too, the reaction from Lebanon must be weighed. Are they likely to retaliate because the assassination took place on Lebanese soil? Again, as in the first case, these questions could be answered in such a way as to make the act proportionate.

The description of the targets in the above examples as "leaders" is key. Just as we are hard pressed to justify an attack on three ordinary enemy soldiers in which a dozen innocent people are killed, so too we would be hard pressed to justify such an attack on members of terrorists groups who do not serve in a leadership capacity. Even leading IRA strategist Michael Collins argued for the assassination only of those thought to be more irreplaceable than regular soldiers, namely intelligence officers and high-level public officials. His concern was mainly for proportion. He considered regular soldiers too easily replaceable, so it did not warrant the risk to civilians to target them (Wilkinson 1974, 87). Similarly, the official Israeli underground group, the Hagana, used assassination as a tactic but it did not resort to attacks on Arab civilians (Bauer 1970, 11–15). The concern was not merely for discrimination (Arab civilians do not deserve to be attacked) but for proportion, since the danger was harsh reprisals by the British and, perhaps, a lack of worldwide political support (especially from the United States) for the ongoing project of creating a new state of Israel. Other Israeli underground groups were not so discriminate. The Israeili Irgun Zvai Leum founded in 1936, which modeled itself on the IRA, used more indiscriminate forms of assassination, such as planting bombs on buses. The Irgun blew up the British Headquarters at the King David Hotel, killing and wounding well over 200 people. Of course, one could argue that since the British saw fit to headquarter in a civilian hotel, even if it was a separate part, then they are responsible for the collateral damage. Here we should remind ourselves of Paul Ramsey's argument concerning the Vietcong's tactic of using innocent people as shields because they knew how loath US troops were to fire on civilians. Ramsey held that the responsibility for civilian casualties in such circumstances falls on those who place the innocent in harm's way.[5] Thus, even if one were to consider the British cause in Palestine just, they could hold a share in the blame of the harm done to civilians. Nevertheless, in order to justify the Irgun attack, one must show that no other means to get the job done were available and that the expected deaths of so many innocent people did not outweigh the good they expected to achieve. True, the British were quartered away from civilians as much as possible, and the Irgun gave warning of the attack. But the likelihood of civilian casualties is so high in such attacks that it is nearly impossible to justify.

The Israeli Stern Group, which broke away from the Irgun, employed even more disproportionate acts of assassination, because it considered all British as proper targets. This breakdown of the usual distinction between soldier and civilian can lead to vastly disproportionate acts of violence.[6] The National Liberation Front (FLN) in Algeria, which used bombs in crowded areas, went even further in their erasure of the traditional lines of discrimination and proportion. They were given a moral defense by Frantz Fanon and Jean-Paul Sartre, who argued that not merely every white European in Algeria was a proper target, which would roughly mirror the Stern Group's attitude toward non-Jews in Palestine, but also that every existing white European was a proper target (Fanon 1968). The basic idea is that personhood can be recreated through the violent act toward oppressors. Unfortunately, the reprisals against the FLN were typically horrific, for the French SAS simply responded with murder raids that targeted FLN members and villages suspected of hiding them.

Assassins who wish to be more discriminate typically need to get rather close to their targets. In order to do so, they must not be conspicuous as enemy agents. Thus, spies who take on the job of assassination usually must disguise themselves as citizens or even as members of one of the enemy's military units. This blurring of the lines between combatants and noncombatants, which increases of the likelihood of collateral damage, has led the entire business of assassination to be questioned in more recent times as a tactic that can meet the demands of proportion. Walzer, for example, argues that secret agents of legitimate governments are not protected by the laws of war, even if their cause is just, because they do not wear identifiable uniforms that make them distinguishable from ordinary citizens (Walzer 1977, 183). The concern here is that if military units cannot distinguish combatants from noncombatants, then the killing of noncombatants will increase substantially. US military tactics in Vietnam give weight to the concern, as does the necessity of targeting children in the War on Terror. Lt. Col. Anthony Shaffer reports that the use of children by terrorists means that children have to be covered (aimed at with intent to kill) in areas where terrorist operate (Shaffer 2010, 44–45). International law, however, has not been too strictly enforced in this matter, nor, again, is it clear that justice is always served by following the law. Let's take three famous examples: the alleged attempt to assassinate General Eisenhower, the real (and unsuccessful) attempt to assassinate General Erwin Rommel, and the real (and successful) attempt to assassinate S.S. General Heydrich, who was serving as Reich protector of Bohemia and Moravia. German commando troops led by Otto Skorzeny wore Allied uniforms both in order to misdirect Allied troops during the Battle of the Bulge and, possibly, to infiltrate General Eisenhower's headquarters, with the purpose of killing as many officers as possible, including, and especially, Eisenhower.[7] Skorzeny ordered his troops to wear their German uniforms underneath the Allied uniforms and, when it came time to use firearms, to take off the Allied uniforms before actually firing a weapon. Skorzeny claimed that he had received legal advice from a colonel who interpreted the 1907 Hague Convention IV, Annex, Section II, Article 23 (f) prohibition on wearing the enemy's uniform as merely prohibiting the use of arms while in the enemy's uniform. Apparently, the legal advice Skorzeny received was correct because he was acquitted in his war crimes trial. The point is that Skorzeny, who certainly lacked just cause and right intention, was nevertheless concerned enough with the lawful restrictions of a tactic meant to prevent civilian casualties that he took care to follow the law, even though it hampered his mission. On the other hand, the British espionage unit sent to North Africa to assassinate General Rommel did not wear official insignias to identify them as enemies.[8] Here we find an espionage group with right authority, just cause, and right intention, but a lack of concern for a tactic that might encourage the enemy to be freer in choosing their targets. In short, the British commando raid on Rommel's headquarters actually served to increase the likelihood of German troops opening fire on civilians. More troubling still is the assassination of Heydrich at the hands of partisan Czech nationals (supported by British MI6) who never donned a uniform at any time before, during, or after the assassination. As Kelly suggests, "This episode fulfills all the requirements of the war crime of assassination. The treachery lay not in the selection but rather in the fact that the attackers hid their intent under the cloak of civilian innocence" (Kelly 1965, 104).

The concern for proportion is what gives rise to contemporary worries that "targeted killings" sanctioned by the United States against high level terrorists are not justified. In this case, the good sought, namely the death of high-ranking members of Al Qaeda, does not outweigh the evil, namely the loss of a moral high ground (claims that terrorists assassinate but the United States does not lose their credibility), the loss of political esteem which loses the United States its potential allies, and, perhaps most troubling, the escalation of reprisal assassinations. The tit-for-tat reprisal assassinations experienced by Israel and its enemies in the past decades gives pause to anyone considering assassination as an effective and proportionate political tool. Nevertheless, the temptation to use the tactic can be great, especially when there does not seem to be another way to deal with terrorists short of a large-scale invasion. Thus, the Obama administration was not too squeamish about increasing the number of targeted killings in Afghanistan during the last year of the war.

The United States has also increased its use of drone attacks for directed killings in Pakistan. Even Pakistani officials willing to aid in the war against terrorism argue that the over-use of drones is alienating the local people and, so, making the tactic harder to justify as proportionate. This alerts us to the simple fact that drone attacks can go wrong, despite their cyber sophistication. On June 23, 2009, an attack in South Waziristan killed eighty noncombatants. Attacks like these create outright enemies, as well as increased sympathy for the enemy. We should also keep in mind that drones are weapons and not thinking robots. Thus, drones do not kill but the people controlling them are the true assassins. There is a real concern that, when assassins carry out their operations thousands of miles from the scene of the attack, the assassination could be treated as a mere video game, with less concern about the loss of innocent life in the eagerness to "win the game." Such concerns are intensified if the arguments from many mid-level intelligence officers are to be believed, namely that most of the terrorists killed in Pakistan during these missions are not high-level commanders but low-level fighters, who, though certainly legitimate targets, are hard to justify as worth the cost in collateral damage to innocent civilians.

PROPORTION AND REGIME CHANGE

Excessive reprisals for assassination are not the only moral concern: assassination can lead to a bloody regime change. There lies the problem, for the consequences of assassination are hard to calculate and, therefore, hard to hurdle when trying to justify the act. When we consider the traditional just war conditions—right authority, right intention, just cause, reasonable hope for success, proportion, and noncombatant immunity—the conditions that pose a special problem for rebellion or regime change are right authority, proportion, and reasonable hope for success. Augustine, for example, rules out rebellion because of the disorder and chaos that follow the initiation of a civil war (*City of God* 11.22). Aquinas attempts to come to terms with the problem of a justifiable rebellion when he argues that a tyrannical government is not just, because it is not directed to the common good. Therefore, those who rebel against a tyrant do not commit the sin of sedition,

> unless indeed the tyrant's rule be disturbed so inordinately that, his subjects suffer greater harm from the consequent disturbance than from the tyrant's government. Indeed it is the tyrant that is guilty of sedition, since he encourages discord and sedition among his subjects, that he may lord over them more securely; for this is tyranny, being conducive to the private good of the ruler, and to the injury of the multitude. (*Summa Theologica* II–II Q.42, A.2)

We notice that the problem of proportion is addressed first. The confusion of neighbor against neighbor can lead to an inordinate amount of bloodshed, and, even if the rebellion succeeds, the greatest resentment between neighbors. Similarly, we find Luther condemning all wars of rebellion against temporal government because "the mob neither has any inclination nor even know what moderation is. And every person in it has more than five tyrants hiding in him" (Luther 1967a, 106). Luther, like Augustine, was concerned about the breakdown in civil government that occurs during a rebellion. A government cannot govern if it is under attack from within. Luther was horrified by the peasants who rebelled in Germany, and urged the princes that, "There is no place for patience or mercy. This is the time of the sword, not the day of grace" (Luther 1967b, 53). Nevertheless, as Luther recognized, rebellion is justifiable if proportion can be maintained. How might it be maintained? A minimum condition would be that the rebel forces have recognized leaders who can command obedience among the fighters. Discipline in civil war can get out of hand in a hurry. There must be a clear chain of command and soldiers willing to obey those commands, if combat is to be discriminatory and proportionate. The concern for troop discipline and the likelihood of an effective post-civil war government is what led Calvin to suggest that the common people should not revolt against a tyrant unless led by magistrates or other government officials who have been appointed to restrain the will of the tyrant (Calvin 1960, 1518–1519).

Assassination, therefore, cannot be ruled out if the likely consequences that lead to a desirable regime change are consonant with justice.[9] We may be able to find such a scenario in which prudence dictated that assassinating a nation's leader is a morally praiseworthy act, whether legal or not. For example, imagine the position of German theologian and underground spy

Dietrich Bonhoeffer when, in November 1942, he is invited for an evening to the home of a friend. Among the other guests is Werner von Haeften, staff lieutenant in the Army High Command and a member of the Kreisau Circle, which took part in the various plots to assassinate Hitler. Von Haeften tells Bonhoeffer that he (von Haeften) is able to approach Hitler armed with a pistol. He then asks Bonhoeffer: "Shall I shoot? May I shoot?" (Rasmussen 1974, 140). Bonhoeffer's opinion was important to von Haeften and to the entire Kreisau Circle, because the common denominator in the circle was a belief in Christian ethics. As two historians of the German Resistance put it: they saw "Christianity as the basis of society" (Hoffman 1977, 192), and, "In Christianity they found the answer to the desperate need for ethical values which could guide men in such catastrophic times" (Dulles 2000, 92). A majority of the group had originally opposed assassination, because they thought it might do more harm than good. Only when they reasoned that the failure to eliminate Hitler meant the certain destruction of Germany did they begin to change their way of thinking. Bonhoeffer points out that the future of Germany is the main moral issue in the decision to assassinate Hitler. If the Nazis remain in power, the situation could become even worse. For Hitler was known to restrain some of the worst elements in his party for reasons of sheer war-time expediency, a tendency that Bonhoeffer fears will not be matched by Hitler's henchmen. Thus, the only person who could tell von Haeften whether or not to assassinate Hitler is someone who can foresee the consequences, presumably someone else in the High Command.

The problem for Bonhoeffer is not whether or not assassination could be a morally good act (it certainly could be), but whether or not someone could be in a position to wrest control of the government from the Nazis. That group must also be able to command the allegiance of the German people. First, let us consider right authority in this rebellion. The group planning the rebellion included notable and recognizable political and military leaders. If successful, the leaders of the rebellion would likely have commanded the obedience of many citizens as well as much of the military. Assassinating Hitler would no doubt cause bloodshed between the military forces still loyal to the dictator (much of the SS, which include some of the best fighting troops) and the resistance fighters supported by the German regular army (the Wehrmacht). However, as long as right authority is in place there is no reason to assume out of court that proportion cannot be met. In short, once right authority is established in a rebellion, the question of proportion must be calculated as it would be between two enemy nation-states. The only remaining condition that poses an innate problem is likelihood of success. Thus, it is reported that Bonhoeffer believed that, "There must be reasonable assurance that tyrannicide can be successfully executed. The important corollary is that the act of assassination must be coordinated with the plans of a group capable of quickly occupying, or remaining in, the key organs of the totalitarian dictatorship" (Rasmussen 1972, 145). Like proportion, it can be settled only on a case-by-case basis. The more recent attempts to effect regime change in Syria with Bashar al Assad, son of Hafez al Assad, is a case in point. The change does no good if the new regime is the same or worse. In any event, the point is that, once just war conditions are met, there is no reason why assassination and regime change cannot be morally praiseworthy.

The problem is more difficult to solve when the regime is a terrorist organization. The United States spent untold sums in trying to track down and eliminate Osama Bin Laden by means of kill or capture. Cyber capabilities helped with the operation. Agents intercepted phone messages that eventually led them to Abu Ahmed al-Kuwait, a courier for bin Laden. CIA officials kept the knowledge from Pakistan's intelligence service to prevent leaks from Pakistani agents sympathetic to Al Qaeda. There has been increased friction between the two services ever since the operation was completed, even to the point where the United States began accusing Pakistan's spy agency of playing a direct role in supporting insurgent attacks against the American Embassy in Kabul in September 2011. Thus, we must ask, was the operation against bin Laden worth the friction, which surely hinders the capture of other terrorists? No doubt it would be if bin Laden were in the same political position as a Hitler. But bin Laden was not the leader of a country. To kill him is surely a good, but it comes with costs, and that is where proportion must be satisfied.

CONCLUSION

Assassination has been a part of the *modus operandi* of clandestine groups since their conception. The skills required to get close enough to people to find out their plans are the same skills required to get close enough to kill. Assassination at first glance may appear to be a "cleaner" method of dealing with an enemy and certainly preferable than outright war with its terrible costs economic, environmental, and human. A second glance, however, reveals reasons why we have moral qualms about the tactic. Even when we can make a good case for right authority, just cause, and right intention, we must be able to show that the planned assassination is the only or best way to achieve our goals. This is not easy to do. Moreover, when the target is a head of state, we have to show that we have carefully considered all the consequences for the people of the state whose political head we plan to eliminate. Do the citizens of that state have justice done for them when we assassinate their head of state? We must also consider the consequences of escalation. Will enemies simply begin a game of *quid pro quo* killing in which it may be hard to stop? While it is not impossible to answer these concerns in a way that may justify some assassinations, the justification is hard to achieve, especially in cases of political leaders where the consequences are difficult to fully imagine. Nevertheless, we should not follow Neil C. Livingston in defining assassination as "systematic murder" when used as a morally legitimate instrument of national policy. Livingstone argues that when nations are faced with terrorism, they face the dilemma of "behaving like terrorists or submitting to them" (Livingston 1982, 175). When just, assassination is not murder, which always names an unjust killing. To target specific individuals who deserve to be targeted is not necessarily unjust. Livingstone goes on to argue that targeting terrorists should not be a crime, because they threaten us in the same way as enemy soldiers threaten us. Exactly. Targeting terrorists who play an active role in attacking us is morally equivalent to targeting enemy soldiers who do the same.

However, just as we held a strong distinction between legality and morality in the chapters on covert operations and on coercive interrogation, so too do we now remind ourselves of the moral usefulness of this distinction. Ben-Naftali and Michael argue that individual targeted killings ought to be legal, but not as a state policy. This is roughly like the idea that torture should never be legalized as a state policy, but some individual acts of torture should be legal. The same problems that plague the torture legalization argument plague assassination: the likelihood of abuse because of the possibility of legal protection, the too easily white-washed cases, the easy slide into laziness. For why go to the trouble of bringing dangerous enemies to justice when you can simply kill them?

The Church Committee opined that assassination "violates the moral precepts fundamental to our way of life" because it undermines the American people's faith and support of their government and foreign policy. The committee was, of course, thinking mainly of the alleged assassination plots associated with the United States during the Cold War, plots hatched as a way of dealing with troublesome leaders in peacetime. However, it is hard to figure out exactly what moral precept could be violated by the assassination of certain notorious figures such as Heydrich or Hitler, or leading members of criminal and terrorist gangs, unless that moral precept is found in the just war criteria. The supplemental view to the Church Committee report by Senator Charles McC. Mathians, Jr., which, perhaps, falls into that dubious category of political showboating and should not be taken seriously, nevertheless shows how difficult it is to categorize assassination as an absolute evil (U.S. Congress 1975, 345–46). Accusations about violating the sacredness of human life, barbarism, and no place for assassination "in a world striving toward civilization" are morally trite when faced with dangerous enemies who cannot be dealt with by other means or by means short of full-scale war. The opposing supplemental view by Senator Barry Goldwater, which, perhaps, too may be categorized as simple political cant, does in this context appear to be more well thought out, for Senator Goldwater points to a reality faced by many political leaders: "Should a President of the United States have the right to aid the destruction of either a Josef Stalin or Adolph Hitler in peacetime?" One would certainly hope so.

NOTES

1. In more recent times, Joseph Kelly, who differentiates spy qua gatherer of information and spy qua assassin, nevertheless argues that there is a similarity in how both do jobs that are recognized as legal under the laws of war (if the assassins are in uniform when they kill) and that both, if captured, can lawfully be treated more harshly than regular soldiers (Kelly 1965, 106).
2. See, for examples, Kelly 1965 and Eichensehr 2003.
3. The legality of assassinating figures such as Heydrich is vigorously debated in international law literature. See, for example, the arguments of Green 1993, 144–45; and Dinstein 2004, 95. Questions of legality aside, if the law forbids absolutely the assassination of figures such as Heydrich and Hitler, then that law ought to be ignored when advantageous circumstances permit.
4. Attempts to determine the facts of British operations in Ireland during this period are hard work indeed. I have relied on the story as told by Geraghty 2002, 228–29.
5. See the argument of Ramsey (1968, 427–64) on how conduct just counter-insurgency tactics.
6. The Stern Group did not always attack indiscriminately. They often targeted specific British officials, such as High Commissioner Harold MacMichael and Walter Guinness, Lord Moyne.
7. Skorzeny's own account of the incident can be found in Skorzeny 1995, 329–57.
8. Rommel was reported to be particularly angry about the lack of identifying insignias. Nevertheless, he ordered a Christian burial for the enemy dead. See Brown 1975, 94–96.
9. Gabriel Palmer-Fernandez, whose essay is mainly concerned with assassination during peacetime, nevertheless argues that adequate concern must be given for a just rebellion. When the criteria for a "just revolution" are met, then political assassination is justified when (1) the political effects produce significant change, (2) less suffering and injustice is the likely consequence, and (3) discrimination is observed. Discrimination here means anyone in the chain of command of political oppression. Thus, Palmer-Fernandez's criteria of a just assassination closely mirror the just war criteria of likelihood of success, proportion, and noncombatant immunity. See Palmer-Fernandez 2000, 160–76.

BIBLIOGRAPHY

Aquinas, Thomas. (1948). *Summa Theologica*. Translated by the Fathers of the English Dominican Province. New York: Benziger Brothers.
——. (1949). *On Kingship*. Translated by Gerald B. Phelan. Toronto: Pontifical Institute of Mediaeval Studies.
Augustine. (1984). *City of God*. Translated by Henry Bettensen, London: Penguin Books.
Bauer, Yehuda. (1970). *From Diplomacy to Resistance: A History of Jewish Palestine 1939–1945*. Philadelphia, PA: Jewish Publication Society of America.
Ben-Naftali, Orna, and Michaeli, Karen R. (2003). "We Must Not Make a Scarecrow of the Law: A Legal Analysis of the Israeli Policy of Targeted Killings," *Cornell International Law Journal* 36: 234–92.
Brown, Anthony Cave. (1975). *Bodyguard of Lies*. New York: Harper & Row Publishers.

Calvin, John. (1960). *Institutes of the Christian Religion*. 1559. Translated by Ford Lewis Battles. Philadelphia, PA: The Westminster Press.

Cassese, A. (2003). "Expert Opinion on Whether Israel's Targeted Killings of Palestinian Terrorists is Consonant with International Humanitarian Law," available at http://www.stoptorture.org.il/, 7–10.

Cassian, John. (1997). *The Conferences*. Translated by Boniface Ramsey. New York: Paulist Press.

David, E. (2002). *Principes de droit des conflicts armes*. Brussels: Bruylant.

Dinstein, Yoram. (2004). *The Conduct of Hostilities Under the Law of International Armed Conflict*. Cambridge, MA: Cambridge University Press.

Dulles, Allen. (2000). *Germany's Underground: The Anti-Nazi Resistance*. 1947. New York: Da Capo Press.

Eichensehr, Kristen. (2003). "On the Offensive: Assassination Policy Under International Law," *Harvard International Review* 25(3).

Fanon, Frantz. (1968). *The Wretched Earth*. Preface by Jean-Paul Sartre. New York: Grove Press.

Geraghty, Tony. (2002). *Who Dares Wins: The Special Air Service—1950 to the Gulf War*. London: TimeWarner.

Green, L. C. (1993). *The Contemporary Law of Armed Conflict*. Manchester, UK: Manchester University Press.

Grotius, Hugo. (1925). *The Laws of War and Peace*. 1646. Translated by Francis W. Kelsey. Oxford: Clarendon Press.

Hoffmann, Peter. (1977). *The History of the German Resistance 1933–1945*. Translated by Richard Barry. Cambridge, MA: MIT Press.

Jerome. (1996). *Homilies*. Translated by Marie Ligueri Ewald. Washington, D.C.: Catholic University of America Press.

John of Salisbury. (1963). *Policratiicus*. Translated by John Dickinson. New York: Russell & Russell Publishers.

Khatchadourian, Haig. (1974). "Is Political Assassination Ever Morally Justified?" In *Assassination*, edited by Harold Zellner, 41–56. Cambridge, MA: Schenkeman Publishing Company.

Kelly, Joseph B. (1965). "Assassination in War Time." *Military Law Review* 30:101–111.

Lackey, Douglas. (1974). "Assassination, Responsibility, and Retribution." In *Assassination*, edited by Harold Zellner, 57–68. Cambridge, MA: Schenkeman Publishing Company.

Laqueur, Walter. (1977). *Terrorism*. Boston, MA: Little, Brown and Company.

Lawson, J. C. (1920). *Tales of Aegean Intrigue*. London: Chatto & Windus.

Lemos, Ramon. (1974). "Assassination and Political Obligation." In *Assassination*, edited by Harold Zellner, 69–84. Cambridge, MA: Schenkeman Publishing Company.

Livingstone, Neil C. (1982). *The War Against Terrorism*. Lexington, MA: Lexington Books.

Luther, Martin. (1967a). "Against the Robbing and Murdering Hordes of Peasants." 1525. In *Luther's Works*. Vol. 46. Edited by Helmut Lehmann. Philadelphia, PA: Fortress Press.

———. (1967b). "Whether Soldiers, Too, Can Be Saved." 1526. In *Luther's Works*, vol. 46, edited by Helmut Lehmann, 87–137. Philadelphia, PA: Fortress Press.

Marks, John. (1979). *The Search for the "Manchurian Candidate": The CIA and Mind Control*. New York: New York Times Books.

Origen. (2010). *Homilies on Judges*. Translated by Elizabeth Ann Dively Lauro. Washington, D.C.: Catholic University of America Press.

Palmer-Fernandez, Gabriel. (2000). "Justifying Political Assassination: Michael Collins and the Cairo Gang." *Journal of Social Philosophy*. 31(2): 160–76.

Rachels, James. (1974). "Political Assassination." In *Assassination*, edited by Harold Zellner, 9–22. Cambridge, MA: Schenkeman Publishing Company.

Ramsey, Paul. (1968). *The Just War: Force and Political Responsibility*. New York: Charles Scribner's Sons.

Rasmussen, Larry. (1972). *Dietrich Bonhoeffer: Reality and Resistance*. Nashville, TN: Abingdon Press.

Roberts, Adam, and Guelff, Richard. (2005). *Documents on the Laws of War*, 3rd ed. New York: Oxford University Press.

Ruys, Tom. (2005). "License to Kill? State-sponsored assassination under international law," *Institute for International Law*, Working Paper No. 76 (May): 1–32.

Skorzeny, Otto. (1995). *My Commando Operations: The Memoirs of Hitler's Most Daring Commando*. Atglen, PA: Schiffer Publishing.

Shaffer, Anthony. (2010). *Operation Dark Heart: Spycraft and Special Ops on the Frontlines of Afghanistan and the Path to Victory*. New York: St. Martin's Press.

Simpson, Christopher. (1988). *Blowback: American Recruitment of Nazis and Its Effect on the Cold War*. New York: Weidenfield & Nicolson.

U.S. Congress. Senate. Select Committee (Church Committee) to Study Governmental Operations with Respect to Intelligence Activities. Ninety-Fourth Congress. (1975). *Alleged Assassination Plots Involving Foreign Leaders: An Interim Report*. Washington, DC, Government Printing Office.

Walzer, Michael. (1977). *Just and Unjust Wars*. New York: Basic Books.

Wilkinson, Paul. (1974). *Political Terrorism*. New York: John Wiley & Sons.

Zellner, Harold, ed. (1974). *Assassination*. Cambridge, MA: Schenkeman Publishing Company.

Afterword

In a world where governments must work hard to protect their citizens from harm from neighbors near and distant, the secret services provide crucial help. Spies gather information that may be important to the wellbeing of the common good. Sometimes, that information is obtained by using illegal coercive methods. Spies may also be usefully employed to act as saboteurs, to organize and run covert operations, and to assassinate enemies when necessary. These jobs are not the traditional jobs of the warrior and, in fact, those attached to a Western medieval chivalric tradition of warfare would disdain such acts as unworthy of the honorable warrior, for spies do not "play fair." But we must keep in mind that the Greek and Byzantine tradition did not disdain the job of the clandestine services and even championed them in the epic *Digenes Akritas*. This should alert us to the partly relative and cultural nature of what counts as an honorable defense of the common good. We must also keep in mind that fairness is a way of talking about justice, and justice can be achieved by the jobs carried out by spies. I have argued that we can know what counts as justice in the jobs spies do by looking at them through the perspective of the traditional just war criteria. I have also argued that, although we may do well to move away from an outmoded ideal about what counts as right conduct in a battle, we do not adopt a no-rules approach. What counts as "fair play" may change over time, but there is still a category of "fair play"—of justice in war—that does not change, and that category is specified in the just war criteria. No act a soldier or a spy carries out can be called just if it is disproportionate or indiscriminate.

The jobs specific to the clandestine services carry temptations for horrible abuse. Too often, extreme circumstances can become the norm, at least for a short period of time. Professional ideals and just war principles are necessary for discerning what proposed acts are just acts, but the professional spy who lacks character cannot be trusted to do the job well and justly. Only people of character are likely to adhere to professional ideals and moral principles. Yet even people of strong character can be tested to the limit when faced with extreme circumstances, especially if those circumstances are endured for any length of time. Thus, moral principles become a way to check the passions that tempt us to the merely expedient. The virtues of prudence and self-control are uppermost for the spy. A good spy must have the wisdom to discern when the extreme circumstance has been entered into, when it has passed, and what to do within the acceptable boundaries of proportion and discrimination. The just spy can never do evil that good might come, can never appeal to necessity in the extreme circumstance to justify an evil act.

Kidnapping civilians, killing captured enemy, killing members of one's own group, making deals with the unjust, remaining in jobs that inevitably issue in harm done to the innocent for the sake of subversion, telling and living lies, running covert operations in friendly or neutral countries, using coercive interrogation on prisoners, assassinating enemies—all are potentially justifiable and, so, good acts. When are they good? When they cohere with the just war criteria. For the just war criteria enable us to see when such acts could be justified, but we need wisdom to recognize it, courage to seek it, and self-control to act in concert with the good, even when tempted to do otherwise.

The moral principles specified in the just war tradition provide those helpful checks against our passions that can blind us to what is the right thing to do in a given circumstance. Desire for revenge can move us to kill those who do not deserve or need to be killed. Desire for our personal safety and relatively quiet way of life may move us to stay in jobs that require us to harm the innocent, so long as we seek in some way to get some of the innocent "off the hook." That same desire for safety may move us to leave jobs where we could serve as effective saboteurs. Desire for political gain and prestige may move us to act against friendly or neutral countries with secret operations. Desire to be done with a seemingly intractable enemy may move us to assassinate. Even what looks like a very understandable desire to save many innocent lives may move us to torture an innocent person or to torture when the likelihood of achieving crucial information is a long shot at best. The moral principles that would aid us in resisting such temptations are most effective when held by people of strong character. Thus, virtue and moral principles are complementary to one another, and necessarily so. Spies that are good as spies and good as citizens must be people of moral virtue with a strong and useful set of professional ideals and moral principles. Professional ideals and moral principles will do little good for people who lack good character, and good character is benefited by a cognized set of ideals and principles that remind professionals of the good they seek to do, why they seek to do it, and how it may be sought.

The moral position argued for here is vastly different from a kind of moral realism which says that one must do evil, get one's hands dirty, if one wishes to be a responsible person, a person who is useful in protecting the common good. Moral realism says that evil acts are necessary for the protection of the common good. The problem with such a position is that there are no checks on what may be done to protect the common good besides necessity. For the moral realist, necessity is the only criterion that must be met by those whose job it is to use force for the protection of the common good.

The just war position also incorporates the principle of necessity; it can be found in the criterion of proportion, which tends to limit acts of force to what is necessary to get the job done. To use more force than necessary is useless overkill. Besides, the *jus ad bellum* helps us establish if we have just reasons to fight, and these reasons limit us to necessary wars. But the just war position incorporates more than necessity in limiting the use of force. Just war principles are absolute, in the sense that they are foundational for the justification for using any force. Thus, to violate a just war principle is to undermine the very moral foundation for using force to begin with. Just war principles must be adhered to not only to check our desire for acquiring more and more but also in order to prevent a slide into placing our own safety, or that of our citizenry, above what is just.

The difference between moral realism and just war morality has important practical consequences. Let's take coercive interrogation as an example. Moral realist interrogators have but one restriction, and that from the principle of necessity, which dictates that we do not torture unless it is the only way to achieve the protection of the common good. Just war interrogators must consider the principle of necessity and also whether or not this particular act of torture is proportionate and discriminate. Moral realists are not so constrained and may torture anyone in any way, provided the criterion of necessity is met. Just warriors may be faced with a circumstance in which the act of torture is necessary, absolutely necessary, but still may not torture because the act would be indiscriminate or not proportionate. Say, for example, the wife of a terrorist leader is captured. She has admitted to interrogators that she is aware of a "ticking bomb" plot that will kill thousands of innocent civilians but she refuses to say more. The moral realist may—must—torture the woman. The just warrior cannot. She is not a proper target.

Just war morality agrees with moral realism's claim that we live in the kind of world where one must use force if one wishes to protect the common good. In contrast to moral realism, just war morality denies that using force to protect the common good is always a matter of doing evil that good may come. The just war criteria draw the boundary markers around what may count as just acts of force for the common good. When proposed acts of force fail to meet any one of the criteria, those acts are evil and may not be carried out by the agent who desires to be just.

Spies may not be moral philosophers measuring everything they do by the word of God, to recall the language used by Le Carré's burned-out spy, but they need to be people of moral virtue if they wish to be good and useful citizens. They must also internalize moral principles that serve as useful check in extreme circumstances. The just war criteria serve that purpose and, therefore, ought to be foundational for the moral formation for any spy.

Index

Made in the USA
Middletown, DE
20 January 2025

69842673R00093